AF506170

Let's bake the future

Editors:

Katalin Herzog,
Ton Mars,
Linda Nijenhof,
Peter de Ruiter,
Margo Slomp

2007

Frank Mohr Instituut:

MFA *Interactive Media and Environments,*
MFA *Painting,*
MFA *Scenography*

Hanzehogeschool Groningen,
Groningen, The Netherlands

Content

Foreword

With its advanced courses, MFA Painting, MFA Interactive Media and Environments (IME) and MFA Scenography, the Frank Mohr Institute has a special place, both in the Hanzehogeschool Groningen and in the city of Groningen. The cooperation between the city of Groningen and the Frank Mohr Institute has borne fruit in recent years. In the Netherlands it provides a very special combination of artistic talent, scientific knowledge and theoretical reflection. New forms of artistic practice and academic study have been and continue to be developed in this relationship. In the advanced courses of the Frank Mohr Institute this has taken a form which produces graduate artists who are nationally and internationally recognised.
There is a long tradition of training in the arts in Groningen, particularly in painting. The Minerva Academy was founded in 1798; in addition to navigation and architecture, it was possible to study art there. In the academy the 'arts' focused on the spiritual development of the people, while the other two courses served Hanseatic navigation and trade. Almost two hundred and ten years after the Minerva Academy was founded, the courses in the arts are more present than ever in the city. This is reflected in the expansion in the past ten years with three advanced courses institutionalised in the Frank Mohr Institute. There is a relatively larger number of visual artists living in Groningen than in other places in the Netherlands; this is also indicative of the influence of the art courses on the city. Therefore the search for promoting Groningen as a more creative city also looks at whether it is possible to concentrate and improve the accommodation of all the art courses in the Hanzehogeschool in the centre of the city. This is a sign of the recognition of the influence which is undeniably present, both in the atmosphere and in the economic prosperity of the city. Just as art cannot flourish without interacting with society, this society, as embodied in the city, cannot do without art.
In 2000 the present director of the Groninger Museum, Kees van Twist, expressed the hope that some sort of 'Groningen School' would develop. In my opinion, cooperation between the University of Groningen, the Groninger Museum and the Hanzehogeschool could certainly be an opportunity for this, with the active support of the city of Groningen.
Once again, artists have graduated from the Frank Mohr Institute this year. As ambassadors of the three advanced courses in Groningen, there is a great future awaiting them in every respect. I wish them every success in this.

Marian van Os,
Vice Chairman of the Executive Board,
Hanzehogeschool Groningen

Introduction
Let's bake the future

A programme, in which the artistic and scientific disciplines are central in art education, links the associative and the logical.

Art is created on the basis of fascinations.
Artists who want to investigate this, will slow down their activity by thinking.
Artists who want to think, can intensify this by studying.
Artists who study, discover ideologies and systems.

A programme, in which the artistic and scientific disciplines are central, links fascination and insight.

Art is created on the basis of frictions.
Artists who experience this, ask questions and start to experiment.
Artists who experiment, wish to transcend indolence.
Artists who avoid indolence, encounter new questions.
Artists who ask new questions, work critically.

A programme, in which the artistic and scientific disciplines are central, links friction and criticism.

Art is created on the basis of choices.
Artists who recognize this, start to compare.
Artists who compare, come across radicalism.
Artists who radicalize, encounter resistance and conflict.
Artists who resist, go their own way.

A programme, in which the artistic and scientific disciplines are central, links choice and radicalism.

Art is created on the basis of methods.
Artists who consider this critically, design visual problems.
Artists who develop new methods, tone down accepted meanings.
Artists who tone down meanings, make new connections.
Artists who make new connections, continue to fascinate.

This book presents the work of ten young artists who graduated
from the Frank Mohr Institute in June 2006: Rachel van Balen, Siebe
de Boer, Sibylle Eimermacher, Marloes van der Hoek, Wikke van Houwelingen, Karl Klomp, Saskia Koops, Marieke Küttschreutter, Xinjian
Lu and Alex Winters.
Each representation of the MFA courses of the Frank Mohr Institute
in this book is preceded by an essay about its relevant field of study,
with a focus on the interpretation of 'research' in the visual arts.
Margo Slomp, core tutor theory of the MFA Painting course, gives her
view on how and what kind of artistic research is carried out by the
students for the purpose of making art. Linda Nijenhof, core tutor
theory of the MFA Scenography course, describes different types of
artistic research which are current within the field of theatre. Arie
Altena, core tutor theory of Interactive Media & Environments course,
gives a view on 'how to do strange things with technology' to under-
mine the debate about 'research' in an elegant way.
In December 2006 and January 2007 the art historians, and alumni
from the Faculty of Arts (K&A and KCM) of the University of Groningen: Natalja Oosterbaan, Josien Beltman, Jacob van Stolk and Gitta
Snijders, conducted interviews with each of the artists. The outcome
of these interviews can be read in this book.
In the section 'The Institute' the important facts about the training
and the institute can be found, during the period that the artists were
studying there (September 2004 -June 2006).
I would like to thank all those who made this book possible. Special
thanks go to the artists because they give face to the Frank Mohr
Institute. This book is commemorating an important moment in their
development towards an enduring artistic career.

Ton Mars,
Head of the Frank Mohr Institute,
School of Fine Arts and Design,
Hanzehogeschool Groningen

MFA Interactive Media & Environments

Alumni Siebe De Boer
Karl Klomp
Xinjian Lu

Doing strange things with technology
Arie Altena

"People doing strange things with technology", runs the 'tagline' of
Dorkbot which is a loose network of small organisations spread across
the whole world.[1] They organise evenings at which artists, musicians,
designers, scientists and technicians show what they make with the
aid of technology: robots, software, art objects, musical instruments,
interactive objects, games and 'circuit bending' appliances. Who the
technicians are and who the artists are is not always easy to tell, but
within the universe of *Dorkbot* this is not important. It is a question of
what you can do with technology.
An artist is someone who makes something and then shows it. It can
be an object, a performance or merely the description of a concept.
In order to make something, something has to be done and the one
who makes something uses material. A writer works with language,
whether narrative or conceptual, and uses a laptop, for example, with
word processing software. A painter works visually and uses paint for
this. The photographer also works visually and uses chemical-opti-
cal or digital means in order to record a scene. The 'dorkbot people'
work visually and/or conceptually and use computers and software.
Their material is the technological structure of contemporary reality. They use electronic circuits, micro-controllers, Arduino boards,
mobile telephones, electronic toys, resistors, video cameras, copper
wire, hard drives, RFID, and so on. The list can be endlessly added
to with the names of old and new technologies and items from the
Conrad catalogue, for example, the mail order company for all sorts
of (technical) components. Nothing of what I am mentioning here is
exclusively technological; they are all elements and building blocks
of today's social world and are directly or indirectly connected with
everything that happens there and that we wish for. Whoever makes
art with such material, produces something that concerns our world.
I do not see this as exceptional; there is nothing in our world more
natural than making art of this kind.
Dorkbot is the domain par excellence of 'do-it-yourself' artists, rang-
ing from individuals and collectives with their hands in the material,
'circuit-benders' who screw open equipment in order to create new,
strange and unexpected circuits and to exploit technological 'faults',
to scientists who spend their days in technological laboratories. *Dorkbot* generates enthusiasm since there you can knowledgeably 'mess
around' and experiment. The result may look rather less 'slick' and
'finished' than the products of innovative, technological design or of
well presented (interactive) installation art, but this is to point to the
most essential difference. What the example of *Dorkbot* makes clear,
and this is why I begin my essay with it, is that knowledge of the
material and of the technologies employed is the best path to making art. The reason I mention art here is that an artist does not just
need a superficial knowledge of the technique that he uses and about
which he wants to say something. He has to know how it works. The
'black box' of technology has to be opened in order for 'something'
to be done with the material, for insight to be gained into it and for
something meaningful to be created.

[1] *www.dorkbot.net*

In the development of technology, the functioning of things is hidden further and further away, translated and encapsulated into other technologies and ways in which we deal with the world. There is nothing wrong with this, since it means we can make use of extremely complex matters without understanding their full process. It would be extremely difficult, for example, to be able to communicate with computers only in machine language. We do not have to know how a mobile phone works in order to be able to call up someone and send text-messages. Nor do we need to know how the Internet functions in order to send each other e-mails or to purchase a book online. We have turned such technological processes into 'black boxes' that we are able to work with, without knowing what is going on in the 'box'.

The artist who chooses such a technology as his material will turn it to his advantage by opening the 'box' in order to see what processes take place within it. If only to understand which choices - and these are both technical as well as political and cultural choices - have been made and laid down in the design of the software, for example. Anyone not doing that, runs the risk of making only superficial choices and uninteresting art. What exactly someone needs to know depends on the questions that one poses as an artist and on the vision or experience that one wants to convey. Sometimes digging a bit deeper than the 'consumer surface' is already enough when someone is making work about the cultural and social use of technology. Sometimes an artist has to go much deeper, certainly if he wants to carry out an idea of his own. One needs to know things and have insight into, because they touch on the concept, and there are skills for executing the work, either as a prototype or as a final work of art. There are no rules determining how many 'layers' have to be peeled off or the extent to which the 'box' has to be demolished in order to be reassembled in a different way. Technology always has to be 'unpacked', sometimes only minimally, and this does not have to be complicated. The 'unpacking', however, should always stem from the artist's curiosity and the desire to make something new. It is a self-evident part of the creative process.

The most important competences of an artist who works with technology are a basic knowledge of electronics and programming in order to be able to make a prototype.[2] Some knowledge of electronics is necessary in order to execute the work, to 'do something' with equipment that has been taken apart and to be able to experiment. Knowledge of programming is necessary for understanding the process of technology. It is not necessary, and even undesirable, for an artist to become a professional programmer, but a world opens when an artist can do a bit of programming. One then knows the way of thinking that lies at the basis of how computers function and thus of the major part of the technology that surrounds us. Knowledge of programming is also necessary for the insight involved in building one's own work and to be constantly able to experiment. It means too, that the artist can explain what he wants to programmers who are helping to build the work, and that he can understand what is or is not possible, what is simple or what is extremely complicated.

[2] *These skills were also formulated, in about the same terms, by Anne Nigten (V2_), together with Kristina Andersen (STEIM, from whom I have borrowed the term 'unpacking technology') during a closed meeting at the Willem de Kooning Academy in Rotterdam.*

Artists inevitably run into problems with programming while making their work. In order to make it easier, various software programmes have been developed that enable artists to programme without learning a programming language. Musicians work with *MAX/MSP, Pure Data* and *Super Collider* and *'script'* their own 'patches' themselves: a part of their artistic skill lies in this. Visual artists are increasingly making use of *Processing,* originally developed as a didactic instrument for teaching artists how to programme. Artists making installations work with 'microcontrollers' that process data input. Coupling hardware and software to each other is one of the most normal operations for artists in this field. The more complex the project, the more important it is to be able to make prototypes. One cannot afford to work for two years on a complicated installation, only to come to the conclusion after a year and a half that it might well have sounded good on paper, but does not work at all in practice.

In an ideal world, students beginning a masters course should have command of a certain basic knowledge and basic competencies. All students beginning at the MFA Interactive Media and Environments course should have a basic knowledge of electronics, and be able to do a bit of programming and making prototypes. In addition it goes without saying that they are already profoundly interested in the contemporary world and its technological structure, and are making, or want to make, art with the aid of these technologies. If this knowledge and these skills and attitudes are present, then the student can enter the depths. In reality, however, the situation is different. There is hardly any undergraduate course, and in any case no art academy, where students can graduate with this stock-in-trade. If they already possess it then it is either because they have followed a different educational route or because they have taught it themselves. The students do, however, enter the masters course with the desire to familiarise themselves with these things.

The remarkable thing that happens, at least for those who believe in an ideal world, is that the masters course also has to provide training in these basics, in addition to the other things that are relevant. It is certainly the case that students following the course make progress in terms of knowledge and skills, and also broaden their insight into their own ideas, precisely through being involved with the basics, either via a workshop given by a guest tutor or in a workplace. As long as undergraduate courses do not provide the basis, this situation will continue.

But this has also given rise to something positive. It means that it is possible to work with electronics, hardware and software at the masters level and to combine this with a broadening of insight into the role of technology in today's culture. That is one of the aims of the theoretical part of the MFA Interactive Media and Environments course of the Frank Mohr Institute. Among the questions discussed are: *What is technology? Can one see technology as separate from society or is it inextricably interwoven with reality? What is the role of technological processes in our culture?* Such questions can be posed in general, but one can also bring in the philosophy of technology, science and technology studies and the sociology of technology. Many examples can be cited from the history of art and technology, with a lot of fascina-

ting case studies about the development of technology, stranded and unrealised possibilities, paths not taken and late successes of written off technologies. Such case studies illustrate, for example, that technologies are always embedded in social processes, that they are connected with culture, including politics, economy, law and art. This knowledge sharpens the view of today's culture and all (so-called) new technologies and the effect they have on social intercourse. The practical way that technology is dealt with in the masters course is focussed on 'unpacking' it, and this is also the case within the theory-education that has to do with technology. In its turn, theory clarifies matters that recur in practice. In the words of *Dorkbot,* it is a question of 'doing strange things with technology'.
This results in questions and experiences; political or personal questions, strange and absurd questions, impressive experiences of beauty, incomprehensible experiences and ones that make you realise or understand something. This is what I always hope for with art and it is also what I hope that students on a course like that of MFA Interactive Media and Environments in Groningen will realise.

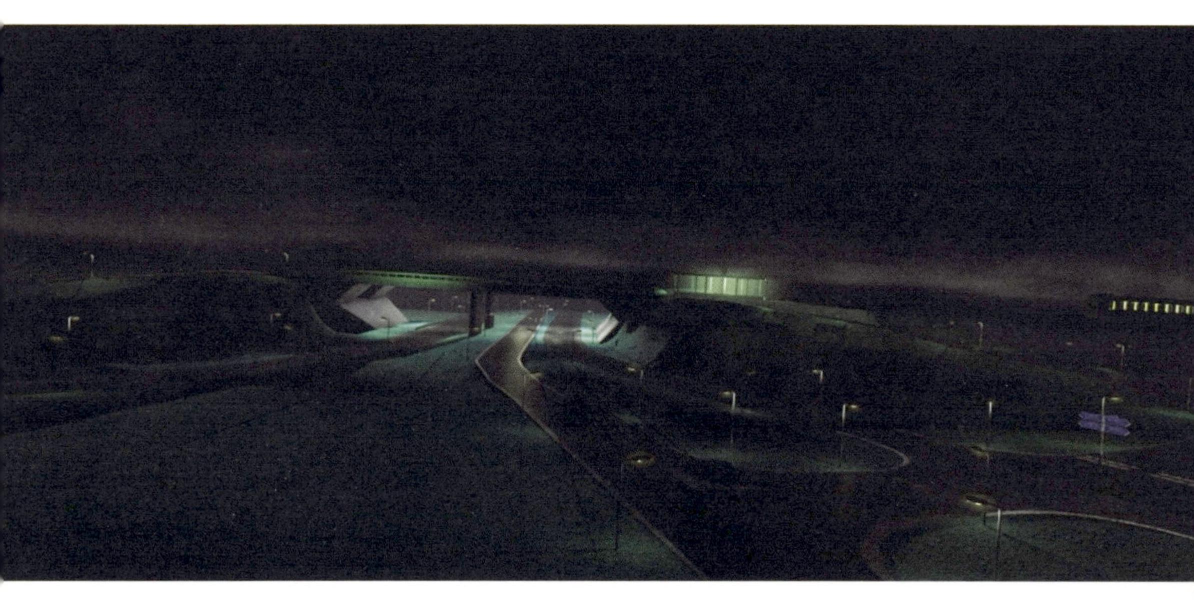

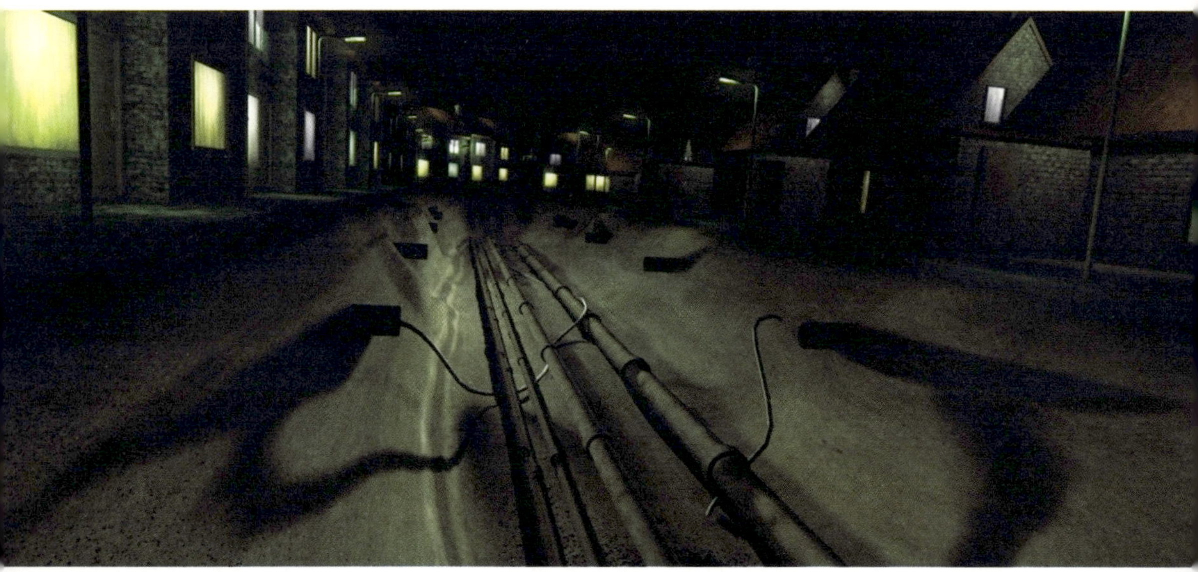

Siebe de Boer

Night has long fallen as I aimlessly wander through the empty streets of the city. The sporadically illuminated windows and empty office buildings around me form the basis for an encounter with the sublime; the ambivalent experience of a city at night. As I walk I analyse my surroundings in geometric shapes, so that later I can model my encounter with this nighttime landscape in polygons, pixels and pencil drawings.

The landscape is very important for me. During my walks I leave my misery and memories behind in exchange for wondrous impressions and images. Like music and smells, streets can be containers full of emotions and thoughts, which suddenly become alive when I walk through them. In this way the landscape is a carrier for my world of ideas. Environments which make a big impression on me because of their beauty, grandeur, or conversely, because of their alienating emptiness, slowly are populated with stories, ideas and feelings blend with the magic of the electrical urban landscape.

Wandering through this landscape is often accompanied by a sense of alienation, astonishment and nostalgia. It is constantly changing. Developments follow each other at an increasing rate, like the tides. Memories become unrecognizable; streets change, images change. I change. A romantic desire for a place which is ultimately still affected by this alienation, which I am trying to shake off, and the feeling of inability and melancholy that accompany this, provides an undertone for the soul of my world.

I am impressed by places where technology plays a role, which both attract and repel me. This contradiction is part of the experience of the 'sublime landscape'. A landscape can serve as a mirror for the culture which creates and organizes it. In the urban landscape both the acquisitions of the human spirit and its shortcomings are revealed in a theatrical show; we are capable of achieving great heights, but in doing so we become increasingly distanced from ourselves.

The landscapes I create are a reflection of me. I try to follow the footsteps of my walks through the nighttime world on the basis of my memories and experiences. My past, present, future, emotions, thoughts and ideas are threaded together as though in a dream, linked by a journey through this sublime world of contradictions. A romantic self-portrait in polygons, pixels and pencil drawings.

All images:
Siebe de Boer,
Bright Light,
Black Out
2006
Stills from 3D
animation with
pencil drawing,
DVD, 5,10"

A nighttime ride through an artificial world *An interview with Siebe de Boer by Gitta Snijders*

Did he chose his house and the neighbourhood he lives in because of their appearance? Behind the asphalted roads of the Damsterdiep in Groningen is a narrow industrial street, flanked by functional, red brick apartment buildings, five floors high with long rows of windows. This long, monotonous street at night could be the subject of a 'still' in one of his films.

Siebe de Boer explains why his cities exist only at night: "The sensation of alienation is strongest at night, when natural light gives up on us and we abandon ourselves completely to artificial light." This is a logical consequence of the essence of his work: the substitution of the natural by the technological. No more daylight, but the light of street lamps instead. No more trees, just towering walls of buildings. The artist sees his computer animated cities as recreations of nature, a world transformed by its inhabitants where natural organisms are distorted, curbed and improved. His cities show the technical traces left by man. Paradoxically enough, the very same man is conspicuous by his absence.

These cities exist only in the artists short, computer animated films; in his digital world. His cities are desolate and dark, illuminated only by rows of windows and street lamps. Nothing lives, nothing breathes, nothing moves, except for passing trains. All organic traces have disappeared, down to the very last blade of grass. According to the artist, all that remains is an "artificial cyborg landscape". The cities are made up of rectangular blocks, light from street lamps, streets and train tracks, everything plunged into an eternal night. They are fairy tale-like, almost magical places, appearing to the viewer silently

and strangely. The artist takes his viewers with him on a journey as through a
dream, from which once sucked in by the
motion it is difficult to extricate oneself.

Siebe de Boer has made a striking
development. In six years he has
transformed himself from an impatient
artist, someone who would fill sheet
after sheet of paper with scribbles, into
a computer artists who now sometimes
spends day after day just waiting. The
last few months he roamed alone at
night the corridors of the Frank Mohr
Institute, waiting for the computers to
finish calculating. "A friend gave me a
miniature golf set, so I would at least
have something to do. Actually it is a
rotten job. I do it for my own purposes; I
would not be able to do this for anybody
else." Accordingly his short films are
about a very personal experience that
may well have definitively changed
his view about his surroundings. It is
the experience of the sublime, more
precisely the experience of the 'technological sublime'.

**In your thesis: 'Het sublieme: de eeu-
wige afwisseling tussen enthousiasme
en ironie', (The sublime: the perennial
alternation between enthusiasm and
irony), you describe the history of the
sublime and the 'technological sublime'
as they emerged through the centuries.
What does the 'technological sublime'
mean to you?** *"The sublime is originally
one of the characteristics of the Romantic
period when experiencing the landscape was
still an important theme. In this time nature
and progress were at odds with each other.
The great thinkers of the Enlightenment and
the Romantic period, like Kant and Schiller
had ideas about the sublime. The sublime
is characterised as a mental state where
emotions stand in opposition to the intellect
when confronted by a great power which is
beyond one's imagination. During such an
experience there is room for both admiration
and fear. Loneliness, melancholy, silence and
alienation enhance the experience of the
sublime and make it into something very
intense. In our contemporary world where
cities and technology are slowly displacing
nature, the experience of the sublime is still
possible; think of the skyline of New York.
The 'technological sublime' transforms the
relationship between man and nature into
a relationship between man and the man
made. Just as it was with the sublime, the
'technological sublime' is the experience of
being confronted with something that is
more grandiose than you are. The amazing
thing about the 'technological sublime' is
that its landscape is made by man himself.
That which we have created makes us now*

insignificant; we no longer have any control over it. Besides being overwhelming it is also frightening, and this is precisely is the experience of the 'technological sublime'.

With my cities I want to convey my personal experience of the 'technological sublime'. I felt this myself while walking at night through the meadows of Friesland. The road was dimly lit and the surrounding was barely discernible. In the distance behind me I saw the lights of the train, the last one that night.

Parallel to the train tracks stood a row of electricity poles that seemed to stretch into infinity. In this artificial world nature seemed to have the worst of it. Technology was so much more present; in Friesland of all places! It was a scene of pure magic that confused me and still does.

I often walk alone at night through the city; this is an unreal experience. If, bathed in the light of countless street lamps around me, I try to get a grip on what I am looking at, I am left utterly groping in the dark. This inconceivability is what for me constitutes the magic and wonder of the city. By constructing this world anew in my work, I try to convey these experiences and to grasp them a bit more, to capture the magic. But it is also a very ambivalent sort of magic."

Why is this magic of the 'technological sublime' so ambivalent? *"The artificial world that we have created for ourselves is also frightening. We have become dependent on it, to the point where we have not only replaced nature with technology, but are also replacing ourselves. The confrontation with the technological traces in a lifeless landscape reminds us of this. Our technological progress enables us to make bigger steps than our mind is capable of grasping. Although we welcome these new means with open arms, there are only a few people who understand how they work. We use technology as a solution, but at the same time we do not understand it."*

You combine in your work pencil and charcoal drawings with computer images, as a reflection of the contrast between the organic and the techno-logical aspects in your cities. Why do you combine old and new technics with each other? *"The pencil and charcoal draw-ings give structure to the smooth computer-generated surfaces. They give the world a 'handwriting' of its own and a tangibility that the computer lacks. Working with the computer creates an estrangement from the work, whereas drawing with pencil is more direct and tangible. But drawing on its own is too crude. I was always fascinated by the atmosphere of urbanised landscapes. But the idea of a journey through the landscape, and the experience of it could not be captured in a drawing. I began to reconstruct these places,*

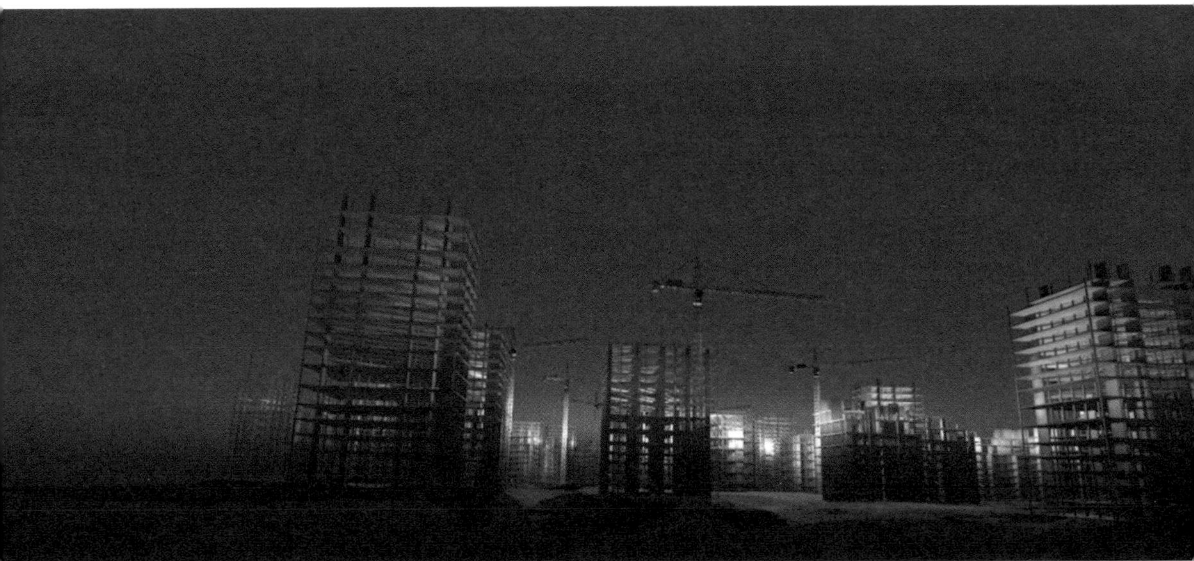

using a sort of peep-show box lined with my drawings. Cutting up the drawings made it very messy. As an experiment I started to use the computer to make a digital maquette, so I could also experiment more easily with light and form. This digital peep-show turned out to be much more interesting than its predecessor.

I saw the possibility to make a film out of this, something I wanted to do for a while. This was my graduation project at the Minerva Academy. During my first year at the Frank Mohr Istitute, it was sometimes difficult to find my way around the programme offered by the Interactive Media and Environments course, since my work was somewhat inbetween. It is still difficult to place my work. It is media art, but is it closer to paintings or rather to computer presentations? Media art seems so new, yet according to some it is not. It should be about technology and then again, according to some, it should not. In any case I had to learn to think very clearly about what it was that I wanted to do. I simply had to do something with my fascination for technology in landscapes.

I really must have the need to do it because the films I make are so laborious. In five minutes I can use up to thirty paintings. The last two months I have been busy with this work day and night. I find it wonderful, but draining. The computer needs to calculate everything: where the shadows fall, how the angles run. Sometimes a fragment of a few seconds might take three or four days to produce, and when you actually see the result it may be that a frame is disjointed or that a beam of light is falling the wrong way. Then you have to start all over again."

Despite the man made environment, people are absent in your work. In your first film there are some human shades appearing now and then, but in your latest film every living thing has disappeared. What was the reason for this? *"In my first film you could indeed still see people, but that did not work well. They did not fit in the world I wanted to create. Because you do not see a living soul anywhere, the surroundings become the main protagonist. By placing a person in it,*

a human scale reappeares and man has the main role. So, I have purposely removed all living 'material'. I still had some pastures in my first film. It was not recognisable grass, just a straight, green surface. But even this reference to something as organic as grass I found uninteresting. In a sense my cities exist in a vacuum, they are digital, they have never existed.

During a series of lectures about new media theory I came in contact with the theories of Baudrillard who distinguishes simulation as the fourth and last phase of the image: objects and worlds that only exist in a digital reality. I have not yet gone very far into this, but in the future I certainly will because it is remarkable how applicable it is to my work. My work is wondrously immaterial; it exists only in binary codes. Such three dimensional blocks simply do not exist. They never lived; there is not a molecule of oxigen around them. They are sterile, there has never been a speck of dust on them. In this world rain has never fallen; it is pure."

In your films you take the viewer on a journey through your city, designed completely according to your plan, moving according to your laws. There is no possibility to escape from these images, no other choice then to follow and to experience. Why didn't you choose an interactive environment? *"The camera movements refer to an architectural fly-through, like the ones used to present new building projects. In addition, the unbroken camera movement means that the viewer cannot avert his gaze from what he is experiencing, so it is easier for him to associate himself with the camera. He is lifted up and, as though in a dream, different experiences are threaded together into a nighttime ride through an artificial world in which technology plays the main role. For me this was a logical step. In my drawings I was busy with these kind of images. I knew what I wanted, but never reached the effect. Through the motion in my films you really get the feeling that you are roaming the city in the dark. It is different from a static image in a drawing because now you can really go into it. Such a virtual camera gives you the possibility to go across it, into it, and* *inbetween it. But only according to my plan. If I were to walk through the city with a camera and use those images, then chance would play a role. Precisely because I build the city from scratch in the way I want it to be, and because it is such arduous work to build it, that is why it is so real. It is my world, so I decide how you are going to look at it. At this moment I do not want to make a virtual reality where people can walk around according to their own route. I am the travel guide who determines when and what*

is seen. It would be a different experience if people were allowed to choose their own path. Then they would be much busier with making choices (left here, right there) than with experiencing the landscape. Ultimately I would like to convey the feeling I had in the middle of that dark meadow in Friesland; the experience of amazement, of insignificance, of wonder. That sublime feeling is mine, but I am willing to share it."

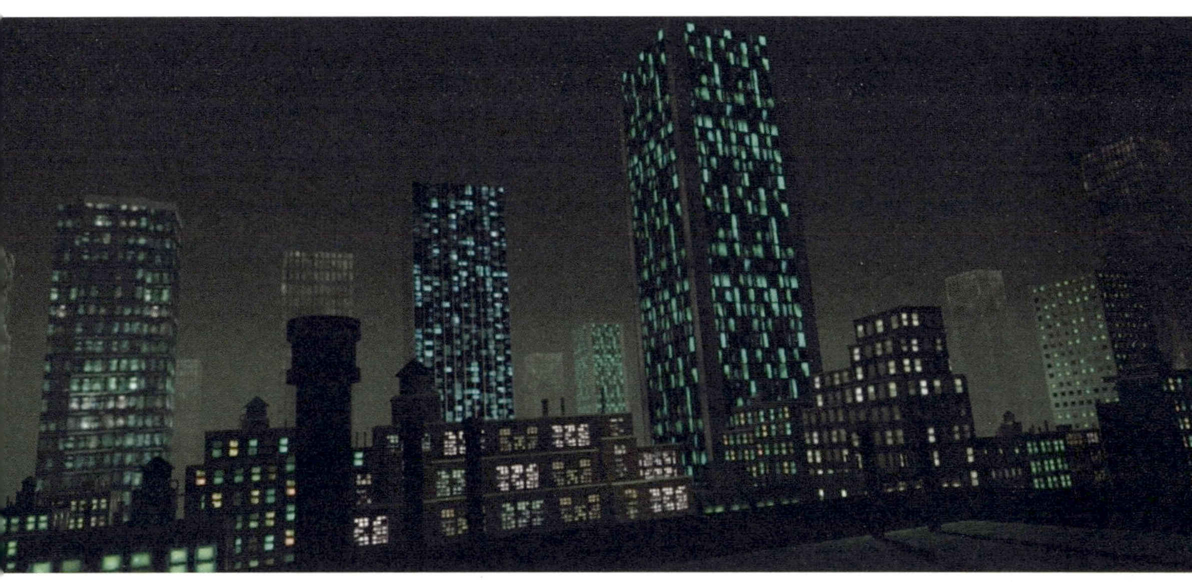

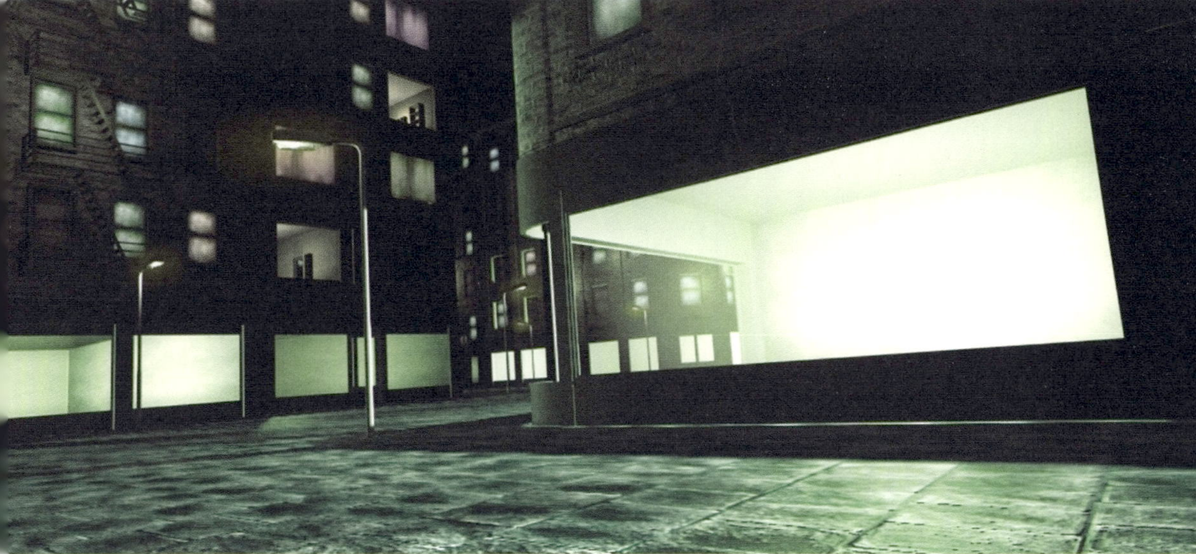

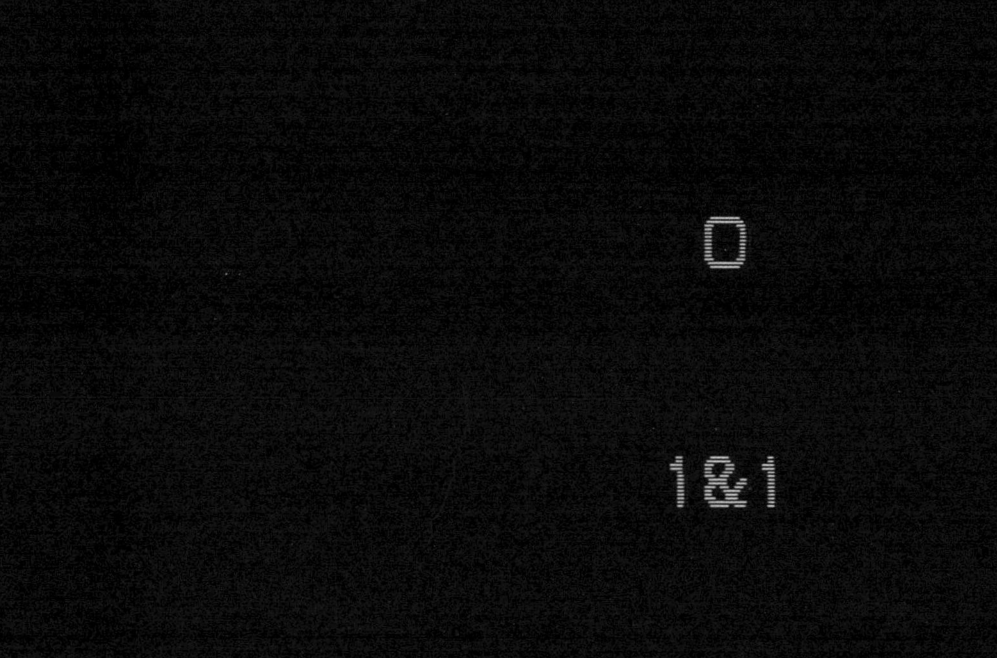

Karl Klomp
Quotes I like

Marshall Mcluhan
If it works, it's obsolete.
(1963)

Norman White
Mistakes help us transcend the original idea.
(2003)

Kim Cascone
The medium is no longer the message in glitch music:
the tool has became the message.
(2000)

Marshall Mcluhan
First we shape our tools and then tools shape us.
(1967)

John Glenn
Literally, a glitch is a spike or change in voltage
in an electrical current
(1962)

Iman Moradi
...they exhibit themselves in the surface of other media
perhaps as a layer of visual communication that shows something
has gone wrong. They are sub media.
(2004)

Walter Benjamin
Even the most perfect reproduction of a work of art is
lacking in one element: its presence in time and space,
its unique extistence at the place where it happens to be.
(1936)

David Zicarelli
I would only observe that in most high-profile gigs,
failure tends to be far more interesting to the audience
than succes.
(1999)

Jonas Salk
Life is an error-making and an error-correcting process.
(1914-1995)

Zen Proverb
If you understand, things are just as they are;
if you do not understand, things are just as they are.
(unknown)

Failures for sale *An Interview with Karl Klomp by Natalja Oosterbaan*

Karl Klomp is interested in mistakes, particularly technological ones. In his studio there are equipments and computer components, wires, transmitters, monitors and mixers of all sorts. For his final examination project at the Interactive Media and Environments course, he made a collection of modified video tools. With the aid of such home-made tools he creates and cultivates technical imperfections, known as 'glitches'. These are faults which everyone is familiar with from their everydag encounter with the media, such as interferences in the image or annoying repetitions.

And these are the very sorts of technical problems that Karl Klomp finds interesting. A fault prompts us not only to gain insight into the purpose of something or the way it works, he feels, but it also feeds our inventiveness and our associative capacities. What is more, faults and imperfections have an aesthetic very much their own. He therefore uses them consciously as a stylistic device.

Karl Klomp uses his 'distortion tools' during his public audio-visual performances. Together with the musician Tom Verbruggen (Toktek) he makes live improvisations, with Verbruggen providing the sound, and Klomp providing the visual accompaniment with his home-made equipment. He also offers

Image below: *Karl Klomp, MNKdiss, 2004, Gritch*

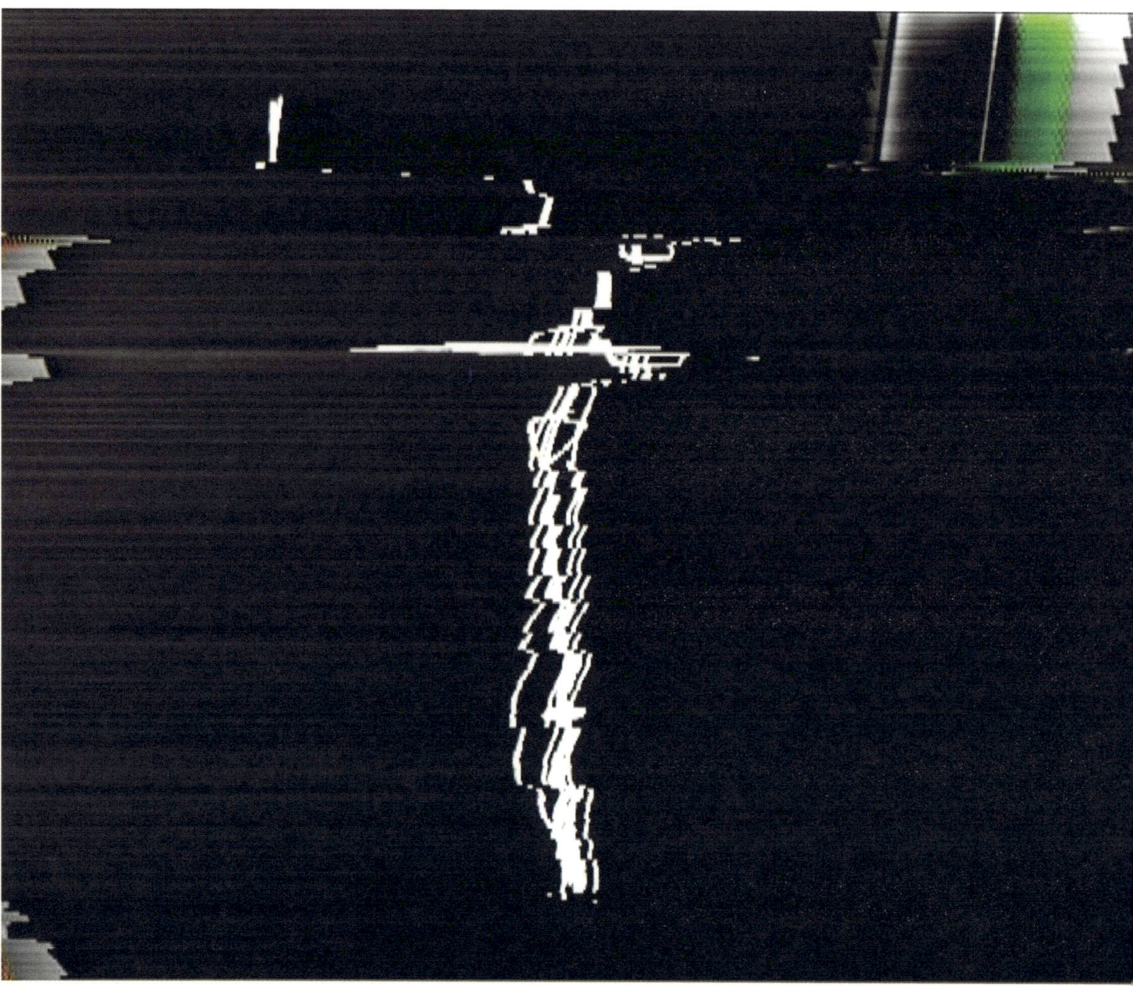

his equipment for sale on the Internet, on sites for selling second-hand stuff as well as on his own site: www.glitchism.org.

The project for your final examination contained your modified tools. Can you tell me what these exactly are? *"They are little pieces of equipment that form existing circuits. Such a device often consists of a box with four or five rotating knobs and a few push buttons and switches with which you can create a video effect. A signal goes in, you process it and a signal goes out. By connecting these hardware tools to an existing video image you can influence it. This is called 'circuit bending'. I alter the tools myself, and in my view this usually results in an improvement. But there lies the sticking point, since from a technological point of view this is often not the case. While technology companies try to eliminate faults, I bring them into the equipment again. I botch up a video image with them by introducing noise or interference. That is precisely what I am concerned with. I am looking for my own aesthetic of disturbance, for there are thousands ways to disturb a signal. These devices were originally intended for video editors and VJs. I am also a VJ or live visual artist myself. I create live images and this is what these devices were built for. In my work the 'tool' is the interface, the mediator between soft- and hardware, and my equipment."*

Image below:

Karl Klomp,

DNW-66, 2006,

Tool

What sort of visual distortions do you end up with in your search for an aesthetic of disturbance? *"There are two*

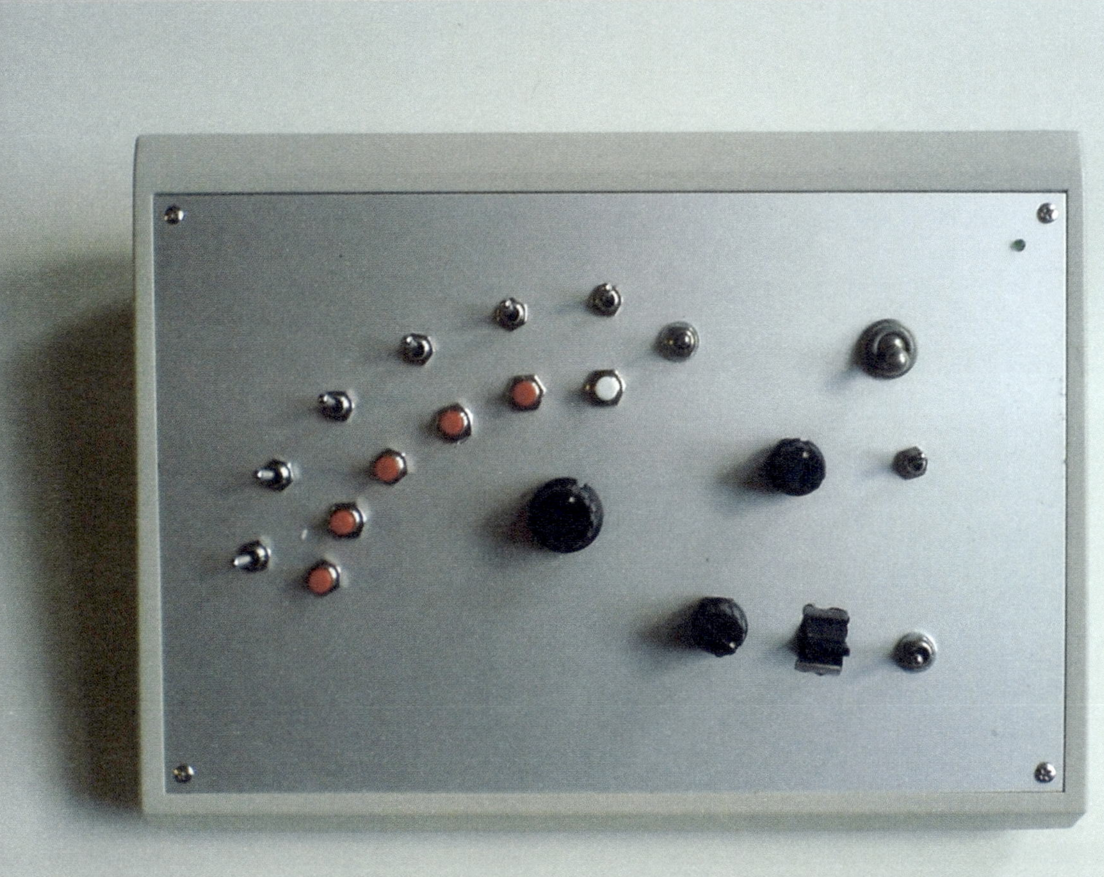

types of distortion techniques: one that generates an image and one that manipulates the image. I make both types of devices. These are video character generators that are normally used to add text to video images. I use them in such a way that the characters they generate spring all over the place.

The interferences I introduce with my pieces of equipment can vary from all sorts of noise to disturbing stripes, or even figurative forms. I have a preference for minimal signs that have something nervous and fickle about them. Signs and forms that are alternately abstract and figurative and together form an illogical whole. The effects do not have to be easily controllable or usable as a direct translation of sound. I rather like to challenge myself through effects that are difficult to employ.

What I often do is mix the disturbances with my own black and white animations. I choose black and white because I want to refer to the graininess of traditional analogue film and the dust and scratches you can see on it. Just like the glitch, such disturbances of the image represent a particular aesthetic and visual vocabulary for me. I want above all to keep my images as minimal as possible, with as little distraction from the distortions as possible. This is why I choose black and white images.

Chance plays a role in the process of searching, although I am consciously looking for something, and maybe you than cannot call it chance. The term serendipity could be more adequate: unexpectedly finding something useful while you are not specifically searching for it. Just as some discoveries came about as a result of mistakes, I let my fantasy and associative capacities be fed by mistakes and coincidences, and am constantly looking for new outcomes.

The interference images I look for, are also connected with the sound that Tom Verbruggen creates during our performances. Sometimes it is melodious, other times it is impulsive and whimsical. Part of our performances is a twenty minute improvisation in which we sit opposite each other and 'fight' with sound, image and equipment. Sometimes I use my effects to visualise his sound, other times to create the very opposite image.

These decisions can stem from rational, or from unconscious associations.

Emotionally I sometimes end up in a sort of trance. I find it particularly interesting to cause surprises during such performances. Many performances are too predictable for me. At a drum and bass party I can predict exactly when a break is coming; you can tell it from the attitude of the DJ or from the behaviour of the crowd or by listening to the beat. I try to deviate from this. In my view, the challenge and the aesthetic effect also lie in the mistakes that are made and how the other responds to them."

What do you mean by 'mistake' and what do you find so interesting about technological mistakes? *"With 'mistake' I mean an external action that has to do with equipment, and with human 'failure'. I still do not have a final definition of 'mistake', and that is what keeps it exciting and challenging. I often make use of faulty images that everyone recognises as such from everyday reality, like computer images that get stuck or become immobile for a moment instead of running smoothly. Or an unexpected repetition of images which you get in the background when you shift a window too fast on the computer. In any case, I want to show that, in my view, mistakes have an aesthetic of their own.*

With virtually all public performances, failure rouses more interest than success. It also makes us more alert, since an unexpected rupture in a structure compels attention. A mistake or failure inspires us to gain insights into the aims of something. Technological mistakes provide insight into technology, giving us an indication of how something should or should not be done. Moreover, they stimulate our fantasy. Loss of control creates a vacuum in which you have to come up with initiatives yourself. For me, failure is synonymous with being human, given that the electronic nowdays is usually perfected. I use failure and mistakes as a deliberate stylistic device. Making mistakes during a live performance shows that you are not just playing a preprogrammed piece. Perhaps it does have to do with 'mastery' or 'professionalism'; we are not afraid of failure during our performances. Improvisation means we have space for things to happen and that is when mastery comes into the picture. The questions then are: How do you deal with these events and what happens afterwards? How can you use your 'mistakes' as your style?"

What sort of work did you made while studying at the MFA Interactive Media and Environments course? *"During my studies I built and rebuilt a lot of small appliances: software, joysticks and video mixers. One project involved a video mixer which I had completely opened up. You could clearly see the central chip and the resistors and the little capacitors hanging on them. I wanted to show the complexity of such an appliance. It was inspired by the work of Peter Vogel who makes large audio installations consisting just of wire, resistors and electronic components. These form individual circuits, inspired by the circuit of a loudspeaker. Instead of making it flat and small in a box, he made it into something spatial. I made a similar circuit, but then using a video mixer. It is a kind of illustration of what I am busy with. On seeing it, you almost understand how it works, without really having knowledge of it."*

How does your work relate to that of 'predecessors' in image manipulation and tool creation? *"My work has parallels with that of artists like Nam June Paik. He also made his own equipment and used it to create his own images. His audio-visual works have a lot of humour, but they are*

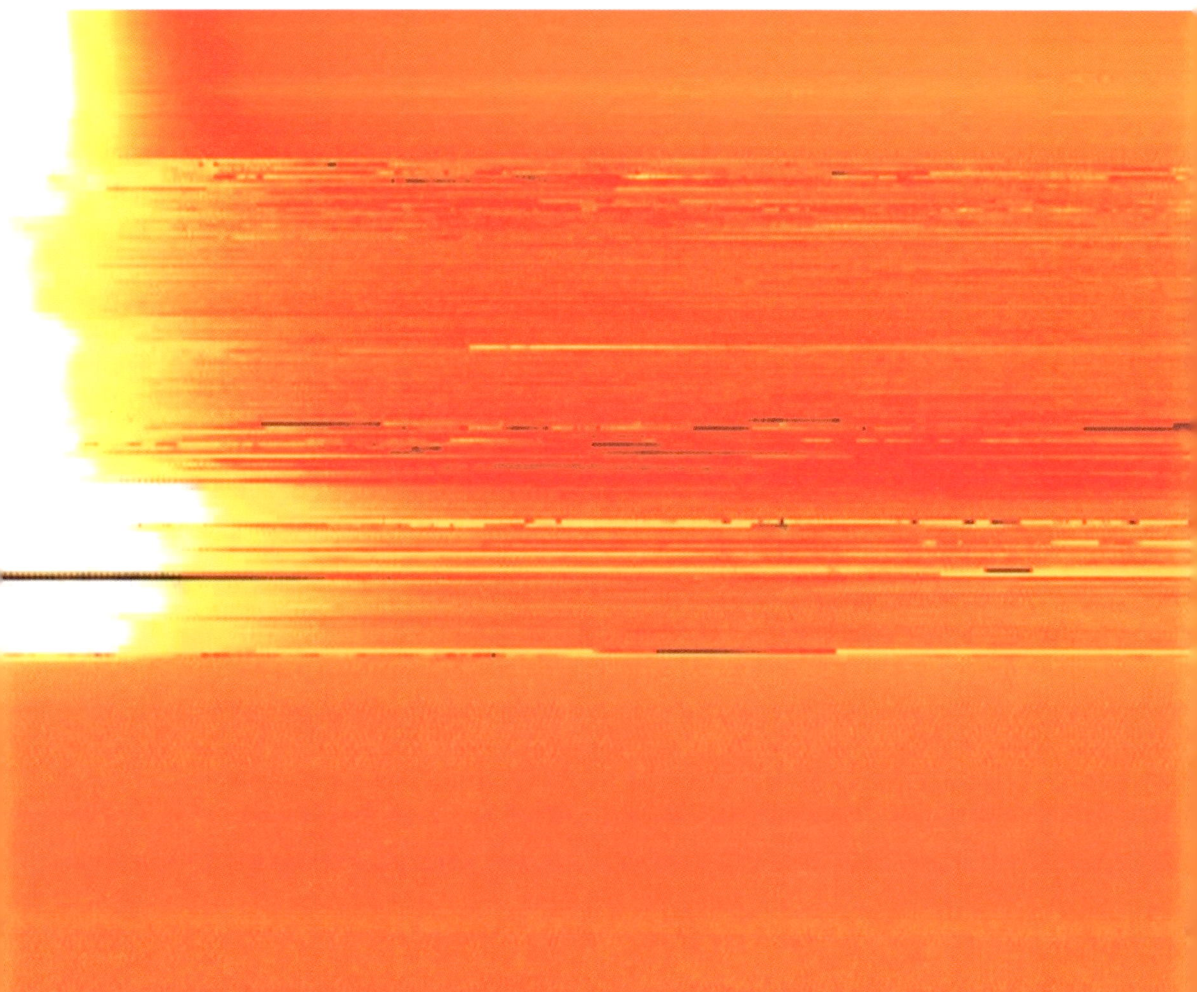

Image below:
Karl Klomp,
Die-Struct,
2006, Gritch

more focussed on the medium of video, while
I am more interested in the tools themselvs
and use video as the final result.

Steina and Woody Vasulka also make their
own equipment and have done many experi-
ments that were later labelled as video art.
What my work has in common with theirs is
that it is often an experiment, an improvisation. I am also indirectly indebted to John
Cage, the American avant-garde composer,
who expanded the boundaries of music. He
included the sounds of the environment in
his work, turning them into music. Profit-
ing from his breakthrough work, I take the
liberty to experiment with all sorts of sounds
and abstract images and to use them within
a composition."

**In your thesis you state that: "The tool
is the message". Can you explain this
quotation?** *"The quotation is from Kim
Cascone's 'The Aesthetics of Failure', in*
which he proposes that the medium is no
longer the message in glitch music, but that
the tool, the means, has become the message.
Mistakes are shown for the sake of their own
value. In music this results in a stretching of
the boundaries of what counts as music, but
it also ensures that we have to look critically
at our notion of what is or is not a mistake.
The sentence "The tool is the message" is
connected in my work with glitch images, in
the sense that I am referring to the use by
musicians of the results of a digital system's
mistakes. I apply this use of mistakes in
analogue systems and in my own work.

You can represent this quotation by thinking
of the imprint that a hammer makes in the
wall when you miss hitting a nail. The message is the imprint in the wall, but this is
directly linked to the tool that was used. Just
as the hammer is the messenger, so too with
glitch, the interference device that causes

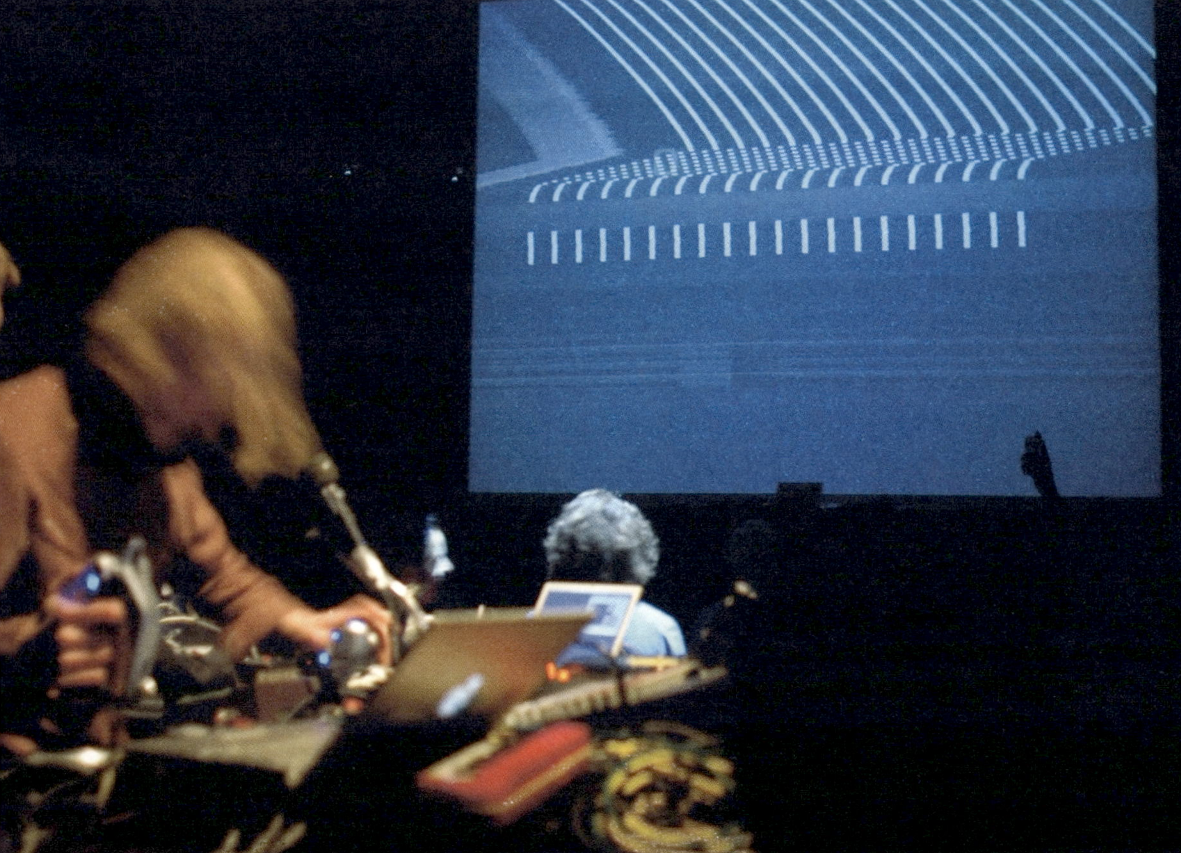

Image below:

Karl Klomp, Sonic

Act, Paradiso,

2006

*the noise, becomes the messenger. So for me
it is not so much the resulting image that is
the message, but the medium whereby it is
obtained. This tool is both the messenger and
the message in my work."*

**Do you already have an idea how you
will go on in your work?** *"I'm thinking of
working towards my own sound, so that I
can work completely individually. I have also
recently printed glitches onto cards. These are
pictures of the images that I make in connection with sound. On the one hand I want
to disconnect myself more from sound and
work more visually, on the other hand I want
to investigate the musical side more, instead
of working together with a musician for
this. However, I have not yet found the right
form, so fortunately there is a long voyage of
discovery in front of me.*

*I would also like to make a sort of new nota-
tion system: video notes like music notes.
I select one effect and make this a function
that people can use. Via Ebay I am selling
all the tools that I am not able to use myself.
They are selling very fast, for an average of
a few hundred Euros. I am not selling them
as a concept or an art work, but as practical aids. There is a market for them and the
charm of my work is perhaps also precisely
their practical applicability. So for me the tool
is the message."*

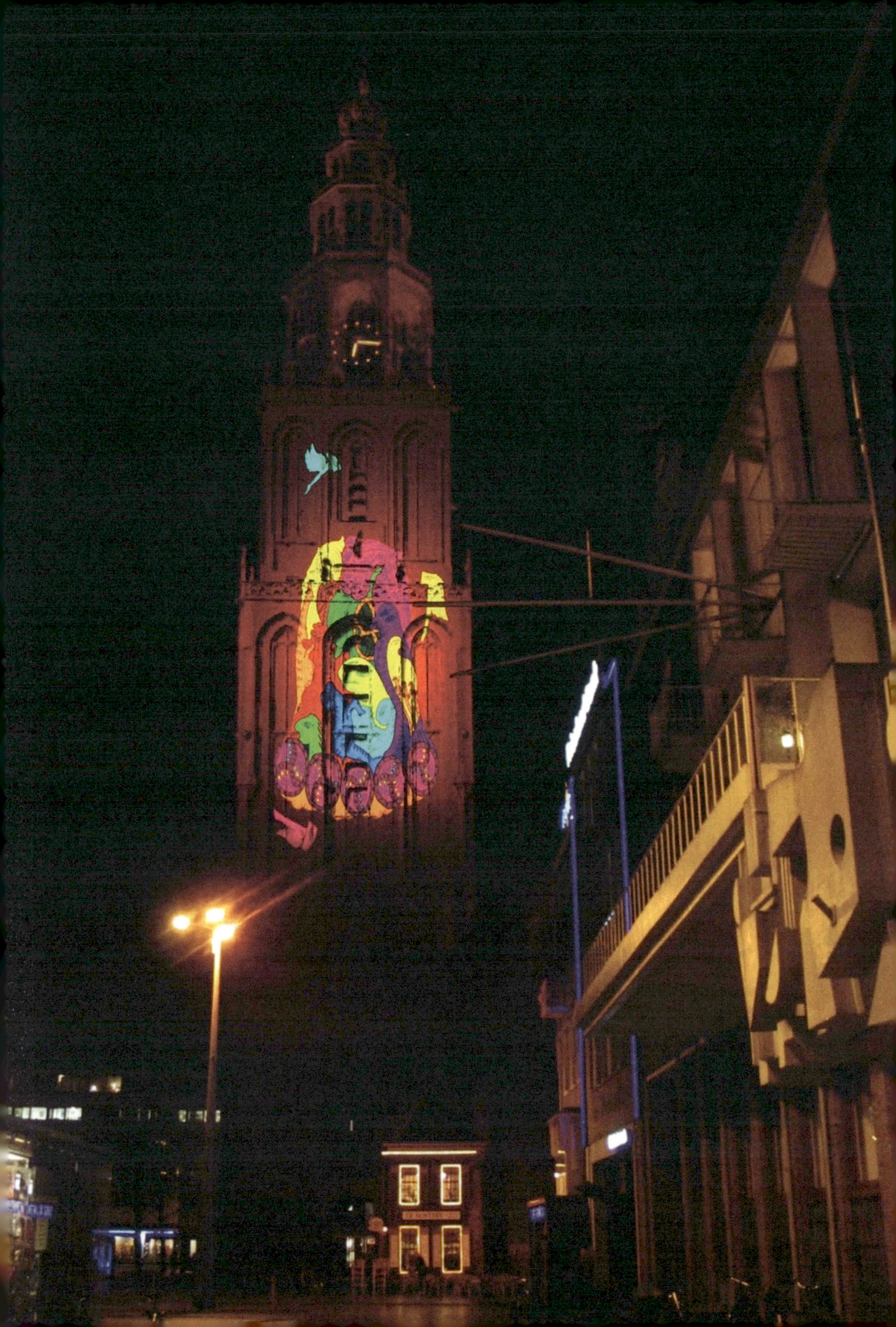

Xinjian Lu

Teaching the audience a lesson

An interview with Xinjian Lu by Jakob van Stolk

Xinjian Lu came from China to study in the Netherlands. For one year he studied at the MFA Interactive Media and Environments course. He is a member of a Chinese family of farmers, so being an artist and getting a proper education is a luxury for him. This makes him even more determined to become a good artist and designer. During the year he stayed in Groningen, he developed a concept for projections on the walls of the Martini Tower. Although everybody in Groningen knows the tower, only few people are aware of its history and its importance for the city. Xinjian Lu wanted to revive this history and inspire future generations to learn more about their cultural identity. Unfortunately, the project could not be executed while the artist was in the Netherlands, but he is still trying to realise it.

Left image:

Xinjian Lu, Projection on Martinitower, (photomontage) 2006

Considering your background, what was your first contact with art? *"I grew up in a very small village. There was nothing regarding to art. No books, no museums; only some paintings of traditional painters. Sometimes my family asked painters to decorate their furniture and we had some old-fashioned paintings in our house. They depicted legends and other stories. I liked the shadow plays they performed in the village. Artists played with beautiful, painted puppets before a white screen. They showed stories about Chinese history and moral dilemmas; we did not have television. Nowadays shadow play is disappearing, because of the new technologies.*

One day, my teacher asked me if I wanted to go to the university to follow a drawing program. I wished to become an artist, but did not know how to achieve it. When I found out there was a place where I could learn all this, I knew there was a future for me. But my family was very poor; they did not have money for my education. There also were no painters or designers in the family who could teach me, and my parents did not have any experience with sons who wanted to be artists. They only knew that most artists are very poor. In their eyes a practical study would have been better, so I would make a good living, and in the end I could support them when they grew old. This attitude is very common in China. Nevertheless, I was stubborn and wanted to be a painter. When my parents saw how determined I was, they stood by me and sustained my study at the university. I graduated from the Nanjing Arts Institute in the year 2000."

When did you come to the Netherlands?
"In 2004 I studied for one year at the Design Academy in Eindhoven, following an industrial design program. I wanted to go to the Netherlands because I like Dutch designers such as Studio Dumbar and a friend of mine, who was studying in Eindhoven, told me how good education was there. In China they do not experiment in art schools; they are more concerned about the commercial aspects of art. Therefore the quality of art is very poor. Now they are beginning to understand that it is not good for art students to do only commercial work. In Europe, people are freer to do what they want, so the Chinese universities learn a lot from looking at Western art from Germany and the Netherlands. In the year I studied at the Frank Mohr Institute, I learned a lot about myself. I am a designer, but I noticed that I am also interested in art. Some people say I am a designer, others say that I am an artist. The academy in Eindhoven was really about design, while the MFA Interactive Media and Environments course focuses more on being an artist. I would like to combine both professions, that of artist and of designer.

*When I started in Groningen, I had set myself some goals I wished to achieve. I wanted to make a series of graphic designs with basic software such as Photoshop and Illustrator. I also wanted to present drawings in the public space to see how I could express myself in a kind of public art. My hope was to intertwine media, design and environment with each other, in order to create a new, experimental and conceptual public art. I designed three different concepts to achieve my goals. First was **Shadow Play**. In this concept my objec-*

tive was to modernise the traditional shadow play which I saw in the village where I grew up, so that it will not disappear in our times. Shadow play is part of the Chinese culture and folk art, but it is very old fashioned. Most of the traditional performances follow a fixed story and a fixed sequence of scenes. The viewers can only watch the play passively; they do not have the opportunity to intervene in it. With the new digital techniques it is possible to let the viewers change the order of scenes, so they become the actors themselves. I wanted to realise a projection with the help of a computer program in which the viewer could make up his own story, be an active player. I designed two possible installations with two different effects. In the first installation, a special computer captures the shadow of the person in front of it, and projects images in that shadow, so you will see a colourful shadow of yourself. In the second installation, your shadow is also captured by the computer, but this time it projects the same shadow next to you on a white screen. When you move the shadow will follow you."

Image below:
Xinjian Lu, Image for projection on Martinitower, 2006

Right image:
Xinjian Lu, Image for projection on Martinitower, 2006

The history and the culture of a country are important themes in your work. Your second concept, the *Magic Mirror*, is also about history, but this time it is your own. This work is the answer for a very personal problem: your baldness. During your childhood you have been teased a lot because of this. So you decided to design a mirror, with the help of a computer program, in which the viewer could see himself with or without hair. Why did you choose to put this very personal experience out in the public space? *"When you see yourself in the mirror, you ask yourself: am I perfect? But what is perfect and what is imperfect? Everything can be perfect or imperfect, in different times and spaces, because people have different views; it all depends on our perspective and imagination. Children think it is strange when another child does not have much hair, although he cannot do anything about it. With **Magic Mirror**, I wanted to teach the audience about how it feels to be bald or to have hair, so they*

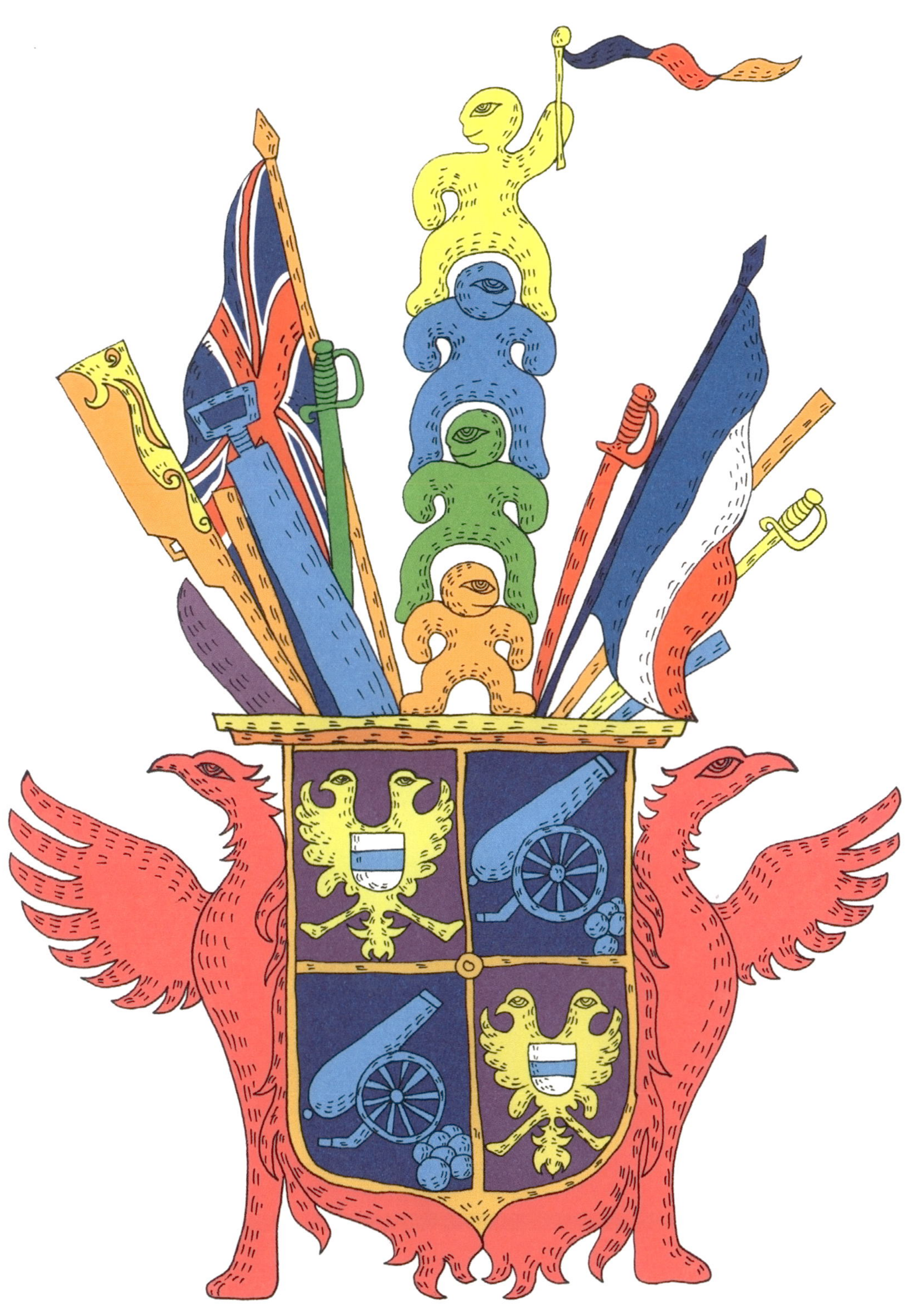

would understand it better. A bald person in front of the mirror will see himself with hair and a person with hair will see himself as being bald.

With my work I want to teach the audience something; I am very idealistic.

In the **Martini Tower Project**, *my third concept, and the one I finally developed, I wanted to show people the importance of history. History is part of culture and therefore part of your identity. If you lose history, you will forget who you are and where you came from. The Martini Tower is the symbol of the city of Groningen, a monument, a landmark, a part of a religious building, and it used to help to protect the city. We do not have such towers in China; there are other architectural styles. The towers we do have, do not stand in the middle of cities, but on the borders. Nobody really realises, but a tower like the Martini Tower 'experienced' a lot during its existence. I think it is sad that it stands in the middle of the city, while only few people know its history."*

In order to show the history of the Martini Tower, you chose ten stories to project on the walls of the tower. What kind of stories did you choose? *"With the help of a Dutch friend I researched the history of the tower, but also the symbols, which are present in and on the church. I selected ten stories which I thought were important to know for the people of Groningen. I liked these stories and they were not too difficult to transpose into drawings. I made drawings about the first building of the tower in the thirteenth century, about Saint Martin, the patron of the tower, and his horse you still can see as weather vane at the top, about the new building of a tower in the Gothic style in 1469, completed in 1554. I also made drawings about people who made a bonfire in the spire of the tower as a celebration after the Spanish army left in 1577, and about the two attacks on the city, which the tower survived. First in 1672 when the English, the French and some German bishops besieged Groningen, and second when the Canadians attacked the city to liberate it from its German occupiers in April 1945. I wanted to project these drawings on the walls of the tower, so citizens could see some aspects of*

the history of their city. Next to the drawings I would project a short explanatory text, so the audience could read which stories were shown in the drawings. I simplified the drawings on purpose, so viewers could understand them better.

Image below:

Xinjian Lu,

Images for

projection on

Martinitower,

2006

Right image:

Xinjian Lu,

Projection on

Martinitower,

(photomontage),

2006

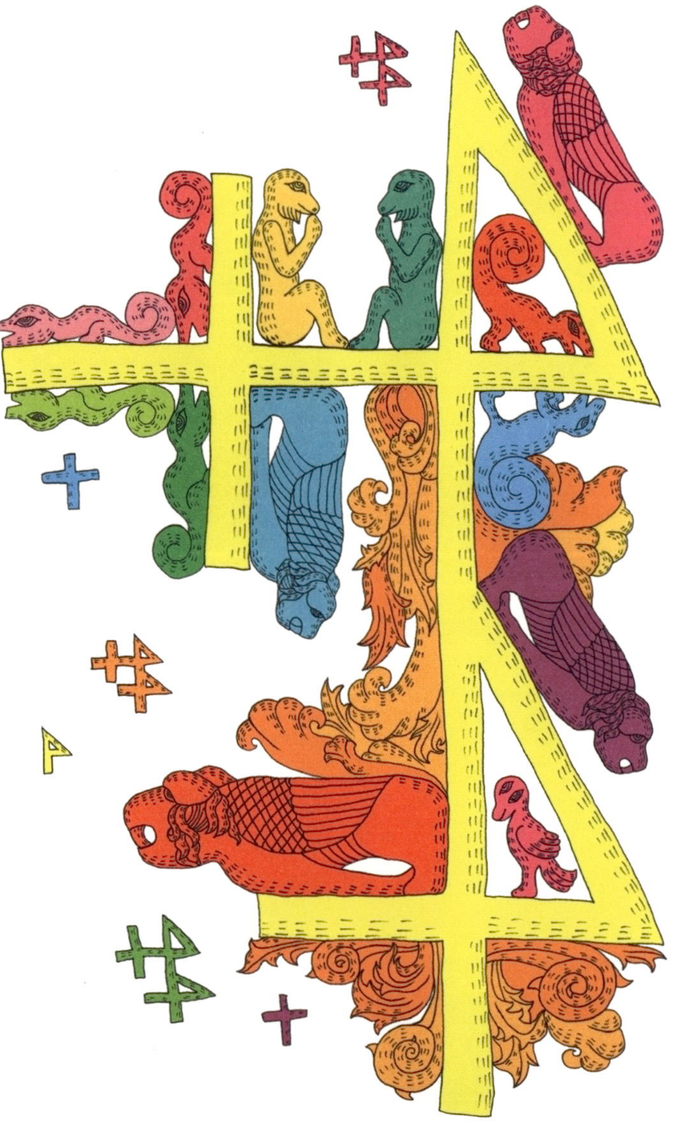

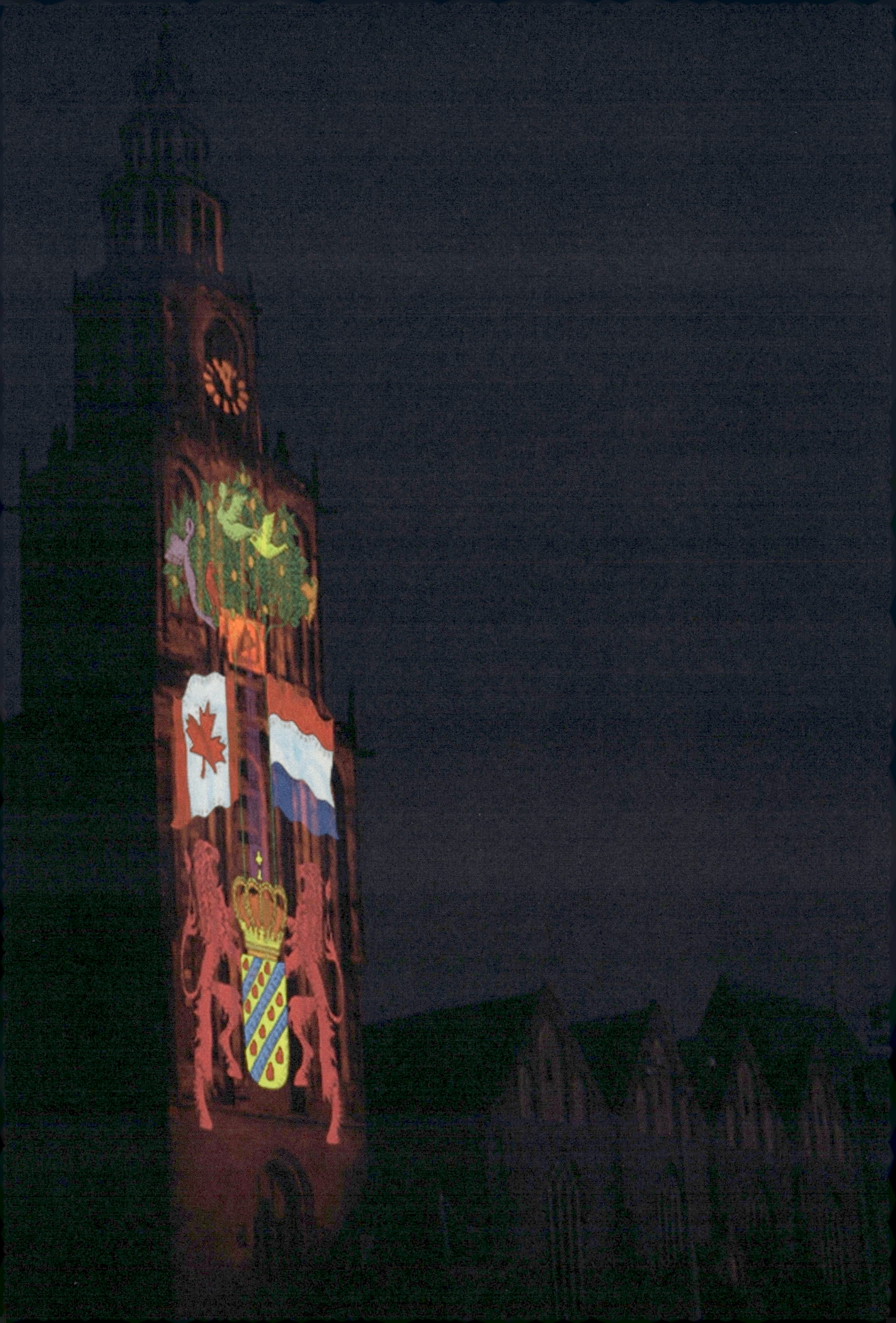

*Unfortunately, the project could not be
executed. To get a clear image on the tower,
I needed a very powerful projector which
was very expensive. I wanted to realise the
projection on august the 28 of 2006, when
the city celebrated the liberation in 1672 from
the English, French and German occupations.
Because of the amount of money and the
different permits I needed to make such an
event to happen, it did not work out. It is still
my dream to realise it; maybe next year."*

You are inspired by the work of the artist and architect Jorge Orta (Argentina, 1953). He also makes projections on the walls of important buildings and monuments. For instance, he made a projection on the wall of the Cathedral of Chartres in 1994. What is the difference between his work and yours? *"At that particular project, Jorge Orta worked with religious symbols to create a spiritual experience for the viewers. I also use symbols, but I do emphasise the history of Groningen and the tower more. The Polish artist Krzysztof Wodiczko makes as well huge projections on walls, but his work is a critical reflection on politics. I use the same techniques as those artists, but for another purpose; our works have different meanings.*

These days people are not interested in history any more; they seldom read about it. In order to teach the audience, I want to project drawings on buildings for everybody to see history. This will be far more effective then showing art works in a museum. Moreover, these projections of drawings about history, on ancient and important buildings, will make history more alive. This way I hope to inspire next generations to learn more about their cultural heritage."

MFA Painting

Alumni Rachel van Balen
Sibylle Eimermacher
Saskia Koops
Alex Winters

'Artistic research' – Production of art or production of knowledge?

Margo Slomp

Last summer, three theses by students of the Hanzehogeschool in Groningen were nominated for the 2006 Hannie Schaft prize.[1] One of the authors was Alex Winters, who graduated from the MFA Painting course at the Frank Mohr Institute in June 2006. In his thesis entitled: *Toe (te gaan) gang-kelijk. Het zichtbare en het onzichtbare, (Ac-cess-ible. The visible and the invisible)*, he reflects on his work in three different sorts of texts. The literary-poetic texts on the left-hand pages take the reader along and through a series of real and fictitious areas in his work. Leaving one area, we enter another together with the artist: from time to time we have to stoop, then climb up the stairs or onto a table. On our way, we encounter drawings, cupboards and visitors, turn on or turn off a lamp and look for the passage to the next area. On the right-hand pages, Alex Winters presents his ideas on the development of his work, the procedures he used and the possible interpretations. The reader can fold out these pages. In the inside pages created in this way, the artist presents a number of topics which are relevant for his work and his working methods, such as paradoxes, the attraction of mathematics, the charm of systems, the possibilities of executing his ideas, perception and an inquisitive line of thought. By way of 'evidence', he has added a number of discussions of the work of other artists.

Unfortunately, Alex Winters did not win the Hannie Schaft prize.[2] One important criterion for the prize, the level of social commitment, probably played a role in this. It is easy to imagine that the jury found it difficult to measure the immediate social relevance of reflections directed mainly on the artist's own artistic practice. In any case, the jury proved to be divided with regard to the decision, as the chairman told my colleagues after the prize was awarded.[3] Some of the members objected to the inconsistent way in which philosophical theories were used. However, within the criteria for the thesis of the MFA Painting course, this does not have to be an insurmountable problem. The ideas of others must be correctly rendered, but in the end it is about the way in which they are processed within an individual artistic system. Logical consistency is not always the most important aspect of this. Furthermore, during the last stage of the study the thesis and the visual images are developed at the same time, and during the examination the two are presented and judged together. Although the thesis of Alex Winters has an independent quality, it achieves its true significance only in relation to the work which is presented.[4]

The artist as researcher

The interconnection between theory and practice in art has been the leading principle for the educational approach of the MFA Painting course for more than ten years.[5] In this vision, the artist's practice is 'theoryladen' and is both supported and directed by practical and theoretical starting points. Individual working methods and an individual artistic system are developed in the course. The develop-

[1] At the start of every academic year the Hanzehogeschool Groningen awards a prize to the student with the best thesis in the previous year. Alternately this is the Hannie Schaft prize (social commitment) and the Hanze Innovation prize (groundbreaking practice-oriented research). Both bachelor and master theses can compete for these prizes. Source: http://www. hanze.nl/home/

[2] The 2006 Hannie Schaft prize went to Rixt Nicolai and Anne Kruijsen for their thesis **SportieFit**, *a design for a programme of movement for obese children aged ten to twelve.*

[3] No report by the jury was drawn up in 2006, so that the precise reasons are not (or no longer) available. Source: Hanzehogeschool Groningen,

Marketing & Communication department, February 2007.

[4] The jury was not able to see the visual work of Alex Winters because they arrived at their decision after the presentation of the final examination. His thesis consists completely of text and does not contain any visual material of his own work or that of others.

[5] Katalin Herzog wrote an essay every year from 1998 to 2004 in the catalogues for the final examination, exploring aspects of the education at the MFA Painting course. In 2005, an anthology of the seven essays was published, which can be read as the reflection of the educational approach of the MFA Painting course. K.E. Herzog, **Show me the moves. Essays for the MFA Painting of the Frank Mohr Institute,** Groningen 2005.

45

ment of ideas is not only promoted by the lectures at the University of Groningen, but also by a theory programme in which discussions and talks with tutors and guest tutors about topics in art theory play an important role.

During the first years of the course, the tutors were regularly confronted with a strong protest from the art world against what was felt to be an undue emphasis on theory.[6] However, the tide has turned in that respect. The idea that theory is an inextricable part of artistic practice is now widely accepted in art education and integrated in the structure of the advanced courses and in the workplaces. The way in which this is done – with programmes of guest tutors, programmes of lectures or research projects may differ, but the image of the artist exploring theories and actively engaged in the theoretical discourse forms the basis of the programmes.[7]

'Artistic research' is the new magical word in current artistic practice, in which theory and an enquiring mind appear to play a self-evident role. In an issue of *De Witte Raaf* devoted to artistic research, Camiel van Winkel adds a number of critical notes to the 'inflationary' use of the term research in connection with the artistic process.[8] The term evokes associations with scientific precision and general applicability and appears to be used in order to raise artistic practice above the individual concerns of the artist. An artist no longer simply 'makes' his work, but is concerned with the acquisition of knowledge and engages in 'research'.

Publications, symposiums and debates in the last few years reveal that describing artistic practice as a research activity is based on two important starting points. The first refers to a necessary attitude of research among contemporary artists. Henk Slager, the dean of the MaHKU, Utrecht Graduate School of Visual Arts and Design, states that: "Isn't it true that the currently dominant culture of non-material production requires new types of artists, [...] flexible enough to organize their artistic activities ad hoc? [...] Based upon a critical and investigative attitude, they also search for novel media combinations and variable collaborations with different fields of knowledge." [9]

Anke Bangma, head of Visual Arts at the Piet Zwart Institute, is not so much interested in describing contemporary artistic practice, but does see artistic research as a platform for cooperation: "I would propose considering research as a particular institutional structure, or framework [...] which delineates as well as limits and excludes certain possibilities for artistic practices."[10]

The second starting point of 'research in artistic practice' is the assumption that the work of art contains knowledge and – following on from this – that the production of art can be made equivalent to research, just as we know it in the sciences. I will return to the big step in these ideas at a later stage. At the moment it is particularly important to note that in this way an attempt is made to approach the sciences. Amongst other things, this is the result of the reorganisation of higher education and the related 'academisation' of the arts. Recently, there has been a division into bachelor's and master's degrees at Dutch universities and institutes of higher education.[11] These two institutes are therefore becoming increasingly similar and this development is continued in the plan to introduce doctoral

[6] *The criticism often concerned the importance of the thesis in the examination. Herzog presents this sort of criticism in the article 'Clear Reason and Dark Emotions'. Ibid., pp. 39-45.*

[7] *For the different ways in which this is done, see inter alia the websites of the Sandberg Institute (www. sandberg.nl), the Piet Zwart Institute (http:// pzwart.wdka. hro.nl), the Post St. Joost (www. poststjoost.nl), the MaHKU (www.mahku. nl) and the Frank Mohr Institute (www. mohr-i.nl).*

[8] *Camiel van Winkel, 'Flexibele multipliciteiten. Het discours over onderzoek in de kunst', (Flexible multiplicities. The discourse on research in art), in:* **De Witte Raaf,** *volume 21, 2006, No.122 (July/August) pp. 2-3, 2.*

[9] *Henk Slager, 'Discours de la Méthode', in: Annette W. Balkema and Henk Slager (eds.),* **Artistic Research. Lier en Boog. Series of Philosophy of Art and Art Theory,** *no. 18, Amsterdam/ New York 2004, pp. 34-38, 34. This issue of* **Lier en Boog,** *reports on a two-day symposium on 'Artistic Research' in the Maison Descartes in Amsterdam in 2004. Since 2004, there has also been an European network for artistic research (EARN) which organises seminars every year. In addition, the MaHKU organises the annual Dutch Artistic Research Event (DARE) every year since September 2006.*

[10] *Anke Bangma, 'Observations and Considerations' in: Ibid., pp. 126-134, 128.*

[11] *In 1999, the European ministers of Education signed a declaration in Bologna in which they agreed to arrange the organisation of higher education in Europe together. The distinction between undergraduate (bachelor) and graduate (master and/or doctoral) degrees is an important aspect of this. Source: Bologna Declaration, www.bologna-berlin2003. de/pdf/bologna_ declaration.pdf The organisation of higher education, amongst other things, has been worked out in the so-called Bologna Process by means of two-yearly conferences in different European countries. England has been responsible for the coordination since 2005 and the next conference will take place there in 2007.*

degrees for artists as well, as this already takes place, for example, in England, Sweden and Finland.[12]

The discussion on how these doctorates should be designed is becoming more topical because the Bologna Process plans to conclude the reorganisation of higher education in 2009. In that year, the introduction of a PhD. for artists should become definitive throughout Europe. However, before the nature of the doctorate to be introduced in the arts is worked out in greater detail, it is useful to start by formulating the basis for this, the artistic research, in the structure of master's degrees. Here, artistic research can be clearly described without any confusion with scientific research and can be clearly placed in the context of artistic production.

Practical and theoretical finding out

Artistic practices are not uniform. In the MFA Painting course, we are mainly confronted with artists who adopt an individual practice in the studio.[13] This does not mean that they are solipsistic or hermetically operating artists. The training focuses on ensuring that students adopt an open artistic practice, in which they clearly relate to the social, cultural and theoretical environment.

Artistic research plays a role in the different stages of the development of these students. If artistic research is conceived in the sense of 'finding out', close to the concept of research, which refers to 'a precise examining, tracing, exploration', it is important in every artist's practice.[14] After all, an artist has a great deal to find out when making a work of art. Amongst other things, he must examine how the idea is transformed into an image and should be developed further; what materials, techniques and procedures he wants to employ; what impact he wants to achieve on the viewers with his work; which aspects of the subject should be emphasised in the work; what cultural materials he will use, what symbols and metaphors he will apply; whether and how the work forms a part of his oeuvre; where and how he wants to and is able to present his work and whether and how this should be accompanied by any text.[15] Viewed in this way, research focuses on making and developing the work of art and ideally the artist will have already formed a basis for doing this during the bachelor degree.[16]

In the MFA Painting course, the research is also focused on developing an individual artistic system. The thesis which students write in the last stage of their course is a collection of images and texts which provide an insight into their working methods and artistic development. Interests and sources of inspiration which form the basis of their artistic production and the artistic goals and theoretical starting points of their work are reflected in this. In addition, the students explain how they see their relationship to the viewers and make statements on the sort of artistry they are aiming for. The texts in the thesis can be very varied in terms of genre and character. Depending on the ideas and abilities of the student, the thesis can comprise both poetic texts and essays, as well as more discursive texts. The thesis is an essential part of the final examination because it contains the artist's theory of the student in its totality.[17] Therefore the visual work and the thesis are presented at the same time and

[12] *An artist can gain a PhD. for example in Great Britain or at the Helsinki School of Art (Finland) or the Malmö Day School of Art/Lund University after an average course of four years. In general, this means that the student produces both visual work and a written text.*

[13] *The other two courses at the Frank Mohr Institute are more often concerned with artistic practices other than the individual practice in the studio. In these practices, technical research (Interactive Media and Environments) and working in joint productions (Scenography) often play a more important role.*

[14] *'nauwkeurig nazien, nagaan, nasporen', in E. de Ru (ed.)* **Wolters' Woordenboek Nederlands Koenen,** *1989, p. 854.*

[15] *The idea for this view of artistic research and the summary of the aspects of this research is taken from conversations with Katalin Herzog on 12,1,2006 and 1,22,2007. She also helped me with advice in writing this article.*

[16] *Our experience at the MFA Painting course shows that these basic skills are admittedly often present, but that they must be further explored and be more consciously applied during the master's degree.*

[17] *Katalin Herzog took this term from H Paetzold, 'De relatie tussen kunstenaarstheorieën en filosofische esthetica', (The relationship between artists' theories and philosophical aesthetics), in 'K. Aarts et al. (ed.),* **Ik geef mijzelf de horizon,** *Amsterdam 1992, pp. 9-16. In her article, 'Bête comme une peintre' she described how the MFA Painting course interprets the term 'artist's theory'. K. Herzog, op. cit. (no. 5) pp. 17-21.*

are assessed in relation to each other.

Many people, both in the art world and in science, are still very suspicious about the texts of artists. This seems to be incompatible with the great emphasis which is now put on research, and the ideas and theories related to art. It can be understood better when we see the light in which the written words of artists are – unfortunately – still often seen.

According to the philosopher of science Gerard de Vries, texts of artists are often uninteresting. He does not consider the artists' views about their own work very useful either: after all, he does not believe that the work will improve as a result.[18] The Flemish philosopher Bart Verschaffel also comes to the conclusion that as a rule it is best for an artist to keep as quiet as possible about his own work. He considers that texts by artists are by definition defensive, apologetic and even deceptive.[19] In their characterisation of texts by artists, both of these authors are clearly thinking of discursive texts, in which artists justify their own work and/or try to explain their work.[20] However, this view ignores the diversity, functionality and often the poetic potential of artists' texts.

Since 1998, forty-nine artists have graduated from the MFA Painting course. This means that by now there is a considerable body of theses. The diversity amongst these is so great that it is not possible to do justice here to the many different forms in which they have appeared over the years. The theses of the students whose work is shown and described in this book show already four different approaches. As indicated at the beginning of this article, Alex Winters presented an exploration in language of the spatial experiences of his images. Many – though not all – of his texts have a literary or poetic character. On the other hand, Sibylle Eimermacher writes more discursively about the relationship of her work (paintings) to different views about the moment of tension in photography. Saskia Koops links a number of texts about her work and themes by reflecting her artistic development in the adventures of Dorothy in the film *The Wizard of Oz*. Finally, Rachel van Balen presents a kaleidoscopic collection of short reflections and poetic texts based on elements and themes in her work. For all the theses, the collection of texts and images provides an insight into the starting points, fascinations and inspirations, objectives, and positions taken by the artist, in other words, into the artist's theory.

As the majority of the theses have shown over the years, artists certainly are able to speak and write about their own work. This does not mean that the different texts should be seen as documents in which the work is explained or interpreted in a definitive way. The texts are not a justification of the visual work, but supplement it and give an insight into the ways of thinking and working methods of the artists concerned. They can serve as a basis for interpretations by others or by themselves. The thesis is not a treatise on art history either. The process of writing serves to clarify the students own ideas and to gain insight into the personal working methods.[21] When this is done well, the work certainly does improve, because the knowledge and insight that is acquired at a certain moment is then used in subsequent work.

[18] Gerard de Vries. 'Beware of Research', in: Balkema and Slager (eds.), op. cit. (no. 9), pp. 16-18, 18. De Vries considers the most important difference between scientific and artistic practice to be that in the first, the producers and people carrying out research are also those who discuss the results. By contrast, he believes that in the arts producers are only concerned with the production, while critics, viewers and curators carry out the discussions. According to De Vries, the practice of artists would have to change to really achieve artistic research, in the sense that artists should become actively involved in the debate. For the reasons he gives in the text, he does not consider it desirable to change this. Thus, in this respect, De Vries reveals an outdated vision of artistic practice, which was pointed out to him by the participants in the discussion at the symposium 'Artistic Research' ('Elements of Discussion', in: Ibid., pp. 27-31, 30).

[19] Bart Verschaffel, 'De toekomst van het hoger onderwijs in Vlaanderen: een 'doctoraat in de kunsten'?', (The future of higher education in Flanders: a 'doctorate in the arts'?), in **De Witte Raaf**, op. cit. (no. 8), pp. 10-11, 11.

[20] Although it is probably going too far to describe discursive texts in which artists justify their own work and/or try to characterise that work, as being 'deceptive', they are admittedly very often not particularly clear or interesting. Fascinations, starting points or results of the process cannot automatically be explained and cannot be uniformly interpreted either. Admittedly the artist is the first interpreter of his own work, but his own interpretation is not more important than anyone else's. With the help of the written language the artist can provide an insight into his working methods and the theory that was adopted, but this requires a freer approach to the genre and an arrangement of the texts. Also see: K.E. Herzog, 'The artist and his theme', in op. cit. (no. 5), pp. 45-50, 48.

[21] K. E. Herzog, op.cit. (no. 17), pp. 17-21.

Artistic research, as the term is understood in the MFA Painting course, therefore always serves a work of art in particular and the development of an oeuvre and artistry in general. Therefore the practical and theoretical 'finding out' which students pursue during the course always results in the production of art.

Production of art and production of knowledge

Many supporters of 'research in artistic practice' justify their approach to scientific research, amongst other things, by stating that both result in knowledge. In his discussion of the discourse of research in art, Camiel van Winkel justifiably asks what type of knowledge the work of art produces and to what extent this can be reproduced and generalised.[22] He does not answer his own question very clearly, but it is evident that the knowledge in a work of art cannot comply with these criteria. Although the work of art does contain knowledge, this is of a different nature than that of the knowledge in science. Knowledge in art can best be characterised as singular, open to interpretation and experimental.[23] Unlike a scientist, an artist does not look for general truths in his work, not even for temporary truths that apply. What he is looking for are possible truths; with his work, he makes proposals, as it were, for 'other possibilities'. As in the sciences, human reality is the starting point for art, but it is not concerned primarily, as it is in science, with the laws of nature and the conventions of culture. In art there is an expansion of human reality, by creating new, poetic connections. These dreamy and poetic worlds cannot be transformed into techniques to process and control reality; at most they can provide an unexpected vision or another view of reality, or explore different possibilities for being and thinking.[24]

Unlike some of the supporters of artistic research, Camiel van Winkel does not consider that the theory incorporated in the work of art can easily be transformed into knowledge that can be explained. This reveals an important characteristic of the cognitive aspects of art, as these are incorporated in the work of art which above all contains aesthetic information. These forms of knowledge are contained in the work of art because of the cognitive aspects of images and the use of cultural material, the use of symbols and metaphors, and possibly of language. However, all these aspects appear through the subjective vision of the artist who uses them in the work of art and processes them in order to achieve the desired effect. The work of art can then be interpreted to reveal both the aesthetic and the cognitive elements in relation to each other.[25]

In the structure of the MFA Painting course in particular and in the master's degrees in general, artistic research can be clearly formulated. It is a 'finding out' focusing on the artist's own practice in the context of obtaining a masters degree in higher education. Therefore it concerns "exploring or extending the content of the bachelor degree which is acquired in close interaction with professional practice and with (applied) research in the available relevant reservoir of knowledge".[26]

As indicated earlier, in writing the thesis the student develops and formulates his artist's theory which he or she is using at that mo-

[22] *The way in which results can be generalised and reproduced are important aspects in the natural sciences, which puts forward hypotheses about the laws of nature. These are tested by means of practical tests and the results are then subjected to verification and falsification. Theories in this branch of science compete with each other and the acceptance of a new theory automatically entails the rejection of the last theory. In contrast, in the human sciences the focus is on identifying, describing and explaining the inner world and the culture of people and one concentrates on interpretations of what is produced, the artefacts. Although it is also important to generalise results in the human sciences, different interpretations do not always displace each other. It is possible that they can co-exist (source: Michiel Leezenberg and Gerard de Vries,* **Wetenschapsfilosofie voor de geesteswetenschappen (Scientific philosophy for the human sciences),** *Amsterdam 2005, p. 29. Because art is a cultural product, conflicting theories in art (sometimes even within the ideas and work of one artist) are not unusual and works of art cannot be verified or falsified. So it is probably better to look for correspondences with the human sciences.*

[23] *This characterisation comes from Tuomas Nevanlinna, lecturer in the theory of art at the Helsinki School of Art in Finland, and a participant in the symposium 'Artistic Research' in 2004. Tuomas Nevanlinna, 'Is Artistic Research a Meaningful Concept?', in: Balkema/Slager (eds.), op. cit., no. 9, pp. 80-83, 83. Several authors provide comparable characterisations of knowledge in works of art. For example, Camiel van Winkel cites Henk Borgdorff, lecturer in 'Artistic theory and research' at the Amsterdam Institute of Higher Education for the Arts, who refers to 'situated, implicit knowledge' (Van Winkel, op. cit., no. 5, p.3).*

[24] *This view on art, closely corresponds to the view adopted by Katalin Herzog which was important for the formulation of the educational approach of the MFA Painting course of the Frank Mohr Institute.*

[25] *See K. Herzog, 'Wie is er bang voor interpretatie? ('Who's afraid of interpretation?') in:* **Kunstlicht,** *19 (1998) 2/3, pp. 33-39.*

[26] *From: 'Formele criteria masterniveau naar HBO-richting, Rapport*

ment. The preparations for this have already been carried out in
the theory programme and the discussions with other students and
the tutors. Therefore during the course there is a forming of theory
and a development of knowledge, which is applied for the benefit of
practice as part of the artistic research. This research does have some
similarities to some of the aspects of scientific research and certainly
makes use of the results of this to arrive at new ideas, but it does
not lead to a theory which is generally applicable. It emphatically
concerns *artistic research* which results in works of art and the related
artist's theory.

*Commissie
Franssen',
('Formal criteria
for the master's
degree to Higher
Education,
Franssen Com-
mission Report),
September 2001.*

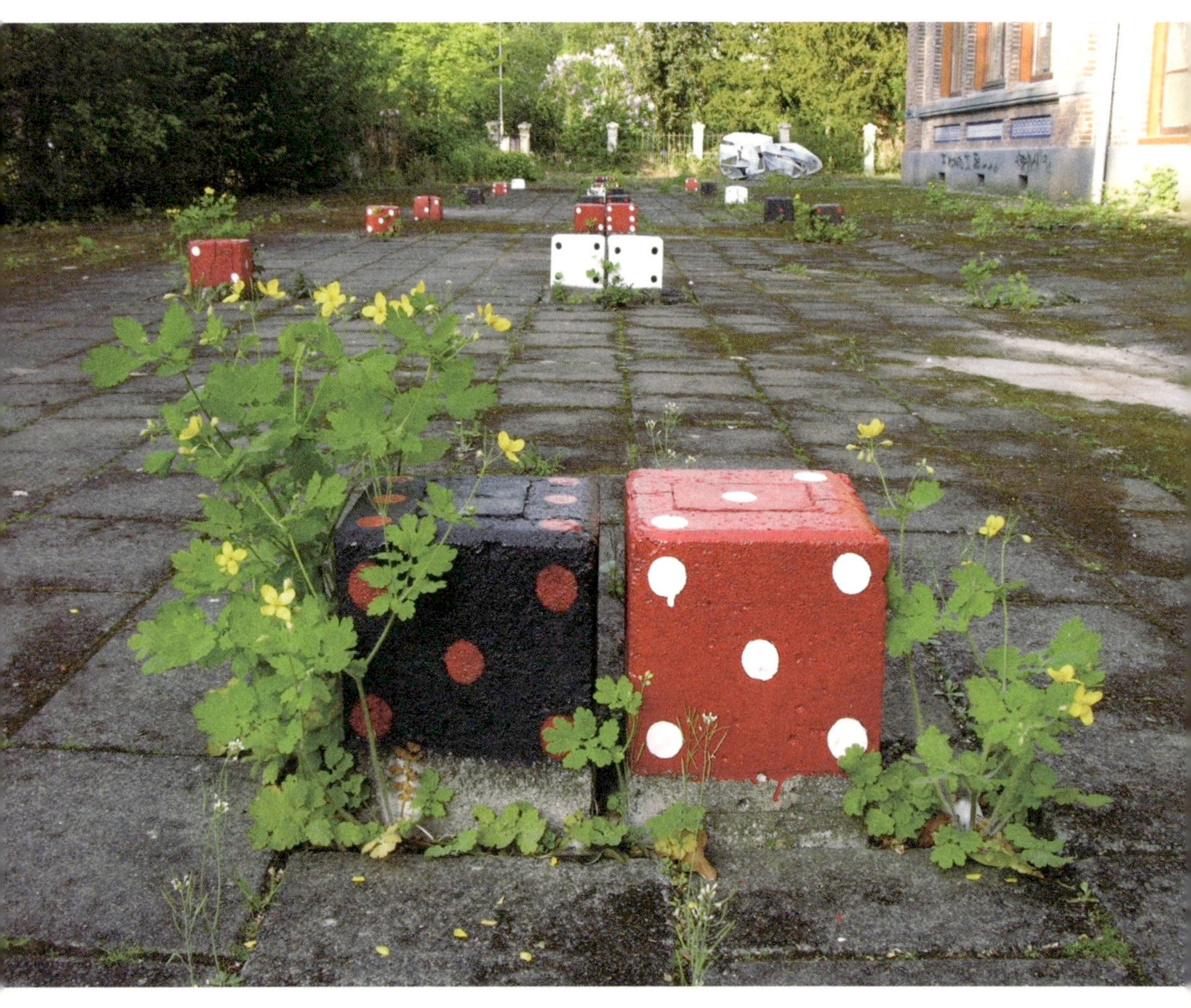

Rachel van Balen
On the way

The path begins
To take a direction
Gets going, from here to there

A bend, a pot-hole, a bridge, a mountain
There and back, and always further away

There is here and then was now
Earlier and later pass without cease

Either/or or both/and?
Having your cake and/or eating it?
Excluding neither
So just make off with it!

Left and right, up, down
What's the nicest way to travel? asks today

Blowing with the wind, flowing like water
Or against it after all?

See, something is glowing-glittering-glistening there,
Like a mirage, or a weather-mermaid
Is it truth, or a dream? All and/or nothing?

The path continues with a broader beginning
Filling itself with what I might or might not invent.

Left image:
Rachel van Balen, Stilstand in Beweging, 2006, Enamel on concrete, mirrors, Noorderbinnensingel, Groningen

The complex game that is called life *An interview with Rachel van Balen by Natalja Oosterbaan*

Everyone has occasionally wondered about the surreal game they have ended up playing in their life. What are the rules exactly and who made them? Rachel van Balen does not easily let go of this subject. Since her training at the Minerva Academy, she has ponderd on the characteristics and backgrounds of the 'rules' which we impose on ourselves in our everyday lives. To what extent are they determined by the culture and age we live in? And to what extent can the comparison with a game be upheld? In her work Rachel van Balen looks for metaphors to express the elements of games in life. Sometimes she finds them in nature, sometimes in her own life or imagination. Other themes include her preoccupation with primeval forms and her own subconscious. The exploration of these different themes has resulted in a great diversity of work: direct representations of what the artist sees in nature, and translations of this into a personal and symbolic imagery, or an abstract rendering of an examination of the self.

You have many interests. Are some of them more important than others?
"Despite the different starting points, I do believe there is a central theme in my work and that is my interest in the way in which humans function in this world. My focus is on the laws, the rules of behaviour and life which man has drawn up in order to survive. I attempt to find visual metaphors to express

this. I am interested in this theme because it shows something about the core of mankind, the aspect of our beings which is separate from fashion and cultural differences, and which ultimately connects us. This interest is also the result of the search for my own identity.

I want to explore which applicable truths prove to be temporary, and which are permanent, universal and related to who we are as human beings. I try to gain insight into this theme by reading sociological and cultural studies, by looking at images which people used in the past, and by looking at the structures and forms of life in nature. Then I try to represent my findings and ideas of these things; literally or symbolically, in the hope that I can also inspire others by this."

A number of metaphors recur in your work, such as 'life is a game' and 'the world is a board game'. Can you tell me more about this? *"I see life as a game, with rules, some of which are basic and others which are subject to change. Just as in a game, in life there are the conscious actions of pawns; in this case, human beings. Both in a game and in life, every square on which one can stand or every direction one can take, entails consequences. There are risks, traps, and obstacles, there is bad luck and loss, or good luck, chances, and gains. Just as there are well-worn paths in a game which we have to follow, society and culture directly or indirectly provide a number of paths which we must and can follow. In society there are laws, moral rules and rules of conduct, cultural rules, family rules, and so on.*

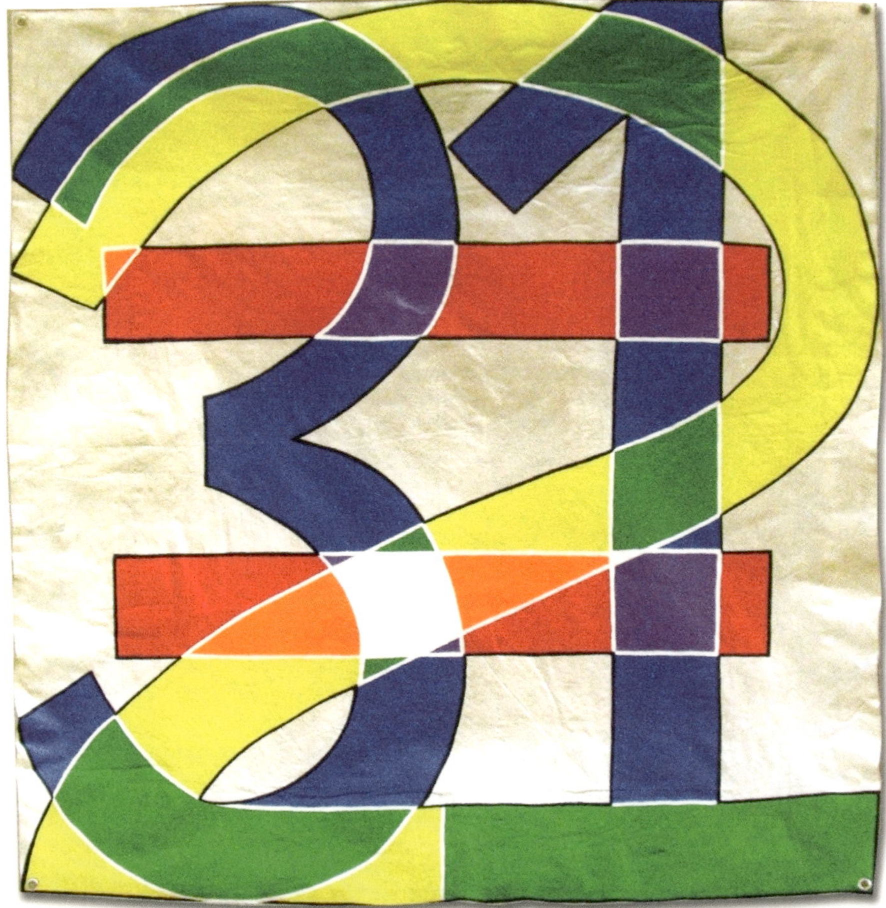

Left Image:

Rachel van Balen, Is Gelijk 2007, Acrylic on canvas, 100 x 100 cm.

In my work I use the metaphors: life is a game, and the board is the world or human life. For example, I show aspects of life in a schematic form and I make them visual in the form of a game. In other words: I use the imagery and colours of games to represent an idea or a view about life in general. This imagery can refer to children's games or computer games and to the imagery of maps. Sometimes I also literally add toy objects to the installations. For the aspects of games which I see in nature, I apply the same procedures.

The rules of games are for me like the rules in our lives, and I relate the characteristics of both to each other visually. In most games chance or luck plays a decisive role, for example, dice can be totally decisive. In life, combinations of circumstances, which may or may not be coincidental, can have a decisive

influence on the course of lives. The power of this could be called destiny or fate. In my work ocasionally I use rolling or still dice to express this. Dice as a symbol for chance, or for destiny, if you like.

For me, every game is like a painting, a min-iature world which shows a different view of reality. They operate as a small universe within our own existing world, just as this occurs in our lives. They only come alive when you start to play; otherwise they are only theory. As every game has its own specific combination of rules which are ultimately derived from reality and the human mind, every game provides a possibility of gaining insight into certain aspects of the human mind and life."

Was it immediately clear to you how you wanted to represent this in your work? *"It was actually quite a long search*

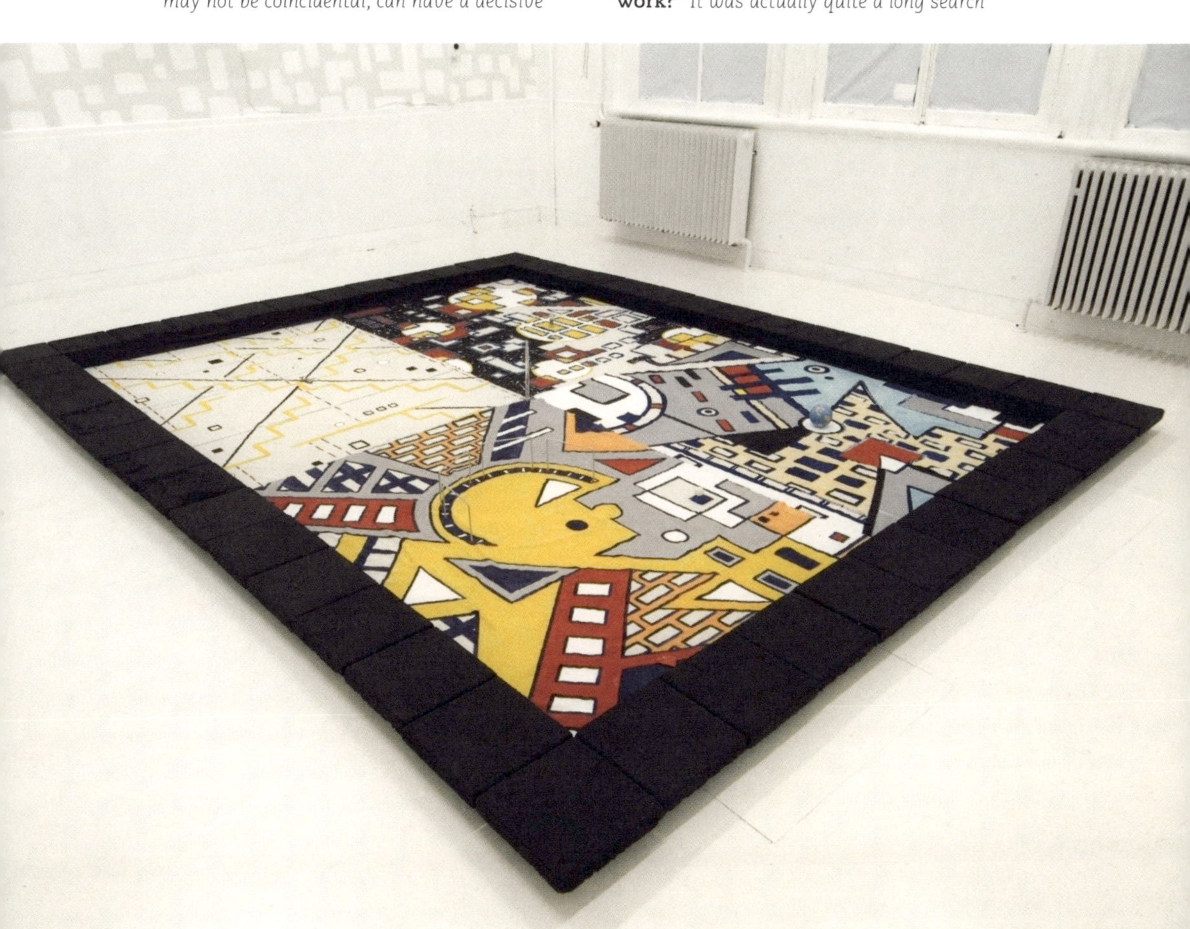

and really I am still searching. At the MFA Painting course my tutors, like my Minerva tutors before, did not consider my work uniform enough; I work in very different styles.

On the one hand, I made realistic works directly from nature, on the other hand, I also produced work based on my ideas about nature for which I developed a personal imagery and metaphors. These are usually more abstract and diagrammatic, sometimes almost like cartoons. In addition, I am interested in metaphysics and I make works related to this, reflecting my own artistic vocabulary and symbols. I also build three-dimensional installations.

Although I am aware that my work is very diverse stylistically, I have come to the conclusion that I need these different styles to represent my themes. Moreover, I love

having the freedom to determine the rules in my work, and so to be able to express myself, exactly as I want to."

In your thesis I read that your work Island is a reflection of your search for the metaphor: life is a game. It strongly reminded me of the urban grid and the dynamics of a city. Can you tell me something about this work? *"For Island I was inspired by the excursion to New York. The starting point was the structure and dynamics of that city; the visual and spiritual effect which the metropolis had on me. I tried to reduce this to a collection of signs and symbols, typical characteristics, such as the grid and the profile of the buildings. But I also represented the dynamics of the traffic, amongst other things. I then showed these characteristics as the elements of a game: in geometric images and in primary colours on a canvas divided into four planes. This is reminiscent of the rugs for children showing a traffic lay-out on which the children can drive their cars and can build their own miniature town. It is also reminiscent of complex topographic systems, such as a map of continents, or a map of the stars.*

With this work I tried to grasp reality, and reduce it to something essential, almost to a new world. Noticing the visual similarities to a game, I hope that the viewer will be able to form new associations and relationships between both. For example, between the earthly and human dynamics and the game of survival, as it is played in a 'fast' city such as New York."

How is the element of a game expressed in your work for the final examination: Stilstand in Beweging, (Stationary in movement)? *"When I was working for my final examination, this work accompanied Island. From the space where Island was located, you could see it outside through an open window. The geometric structure of the paving stones on the square in front of my studio, reminded me of Einstein's statements about time and space*

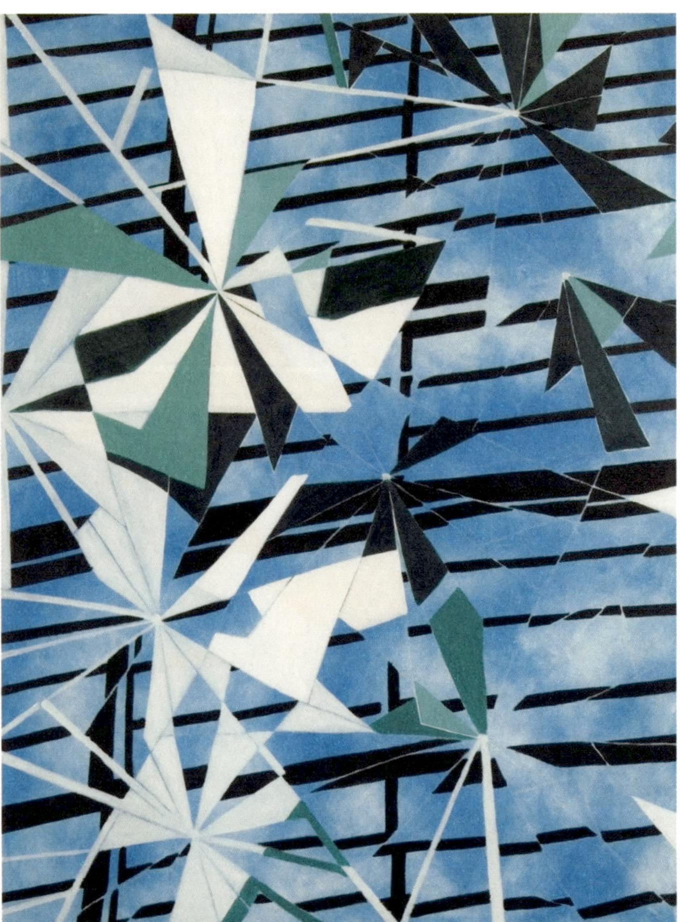

and of the basis of the universe. I painted dice on the posts which were already there in the contrasting colours red, white and black. The posts were quite short, and therefore the dice appeared to be lying on the ground. They are mainly arranged in pairs or groups of three, and sometimes they stand on their own. Plants grow around them and between the paving stones.

This work can be seen as a symbol for life in which the dice are the people. The different number of dots on the dice represents the

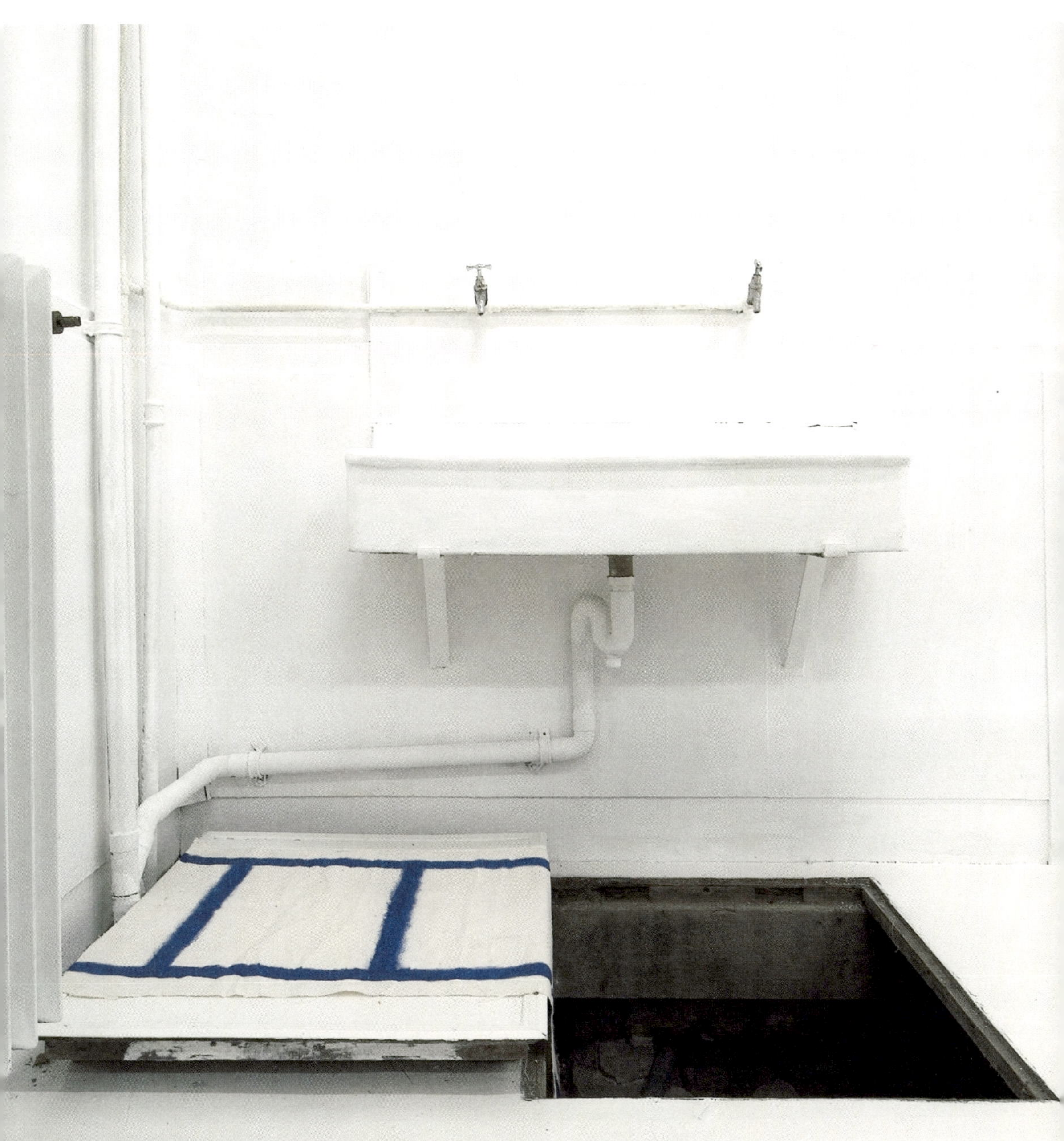

different views on reality. The colours red,
black and white refer to the human races
and the groups of dice can be symbolic in
regard to our multicultural society or to our
tendency to associate with the same sort of
people. However, I also opted for these three
colours because I associate them with the
hard, competitive aspect of existence, the
game of survival. In this way they symbolize
the apparent random nature of life - the op-
portunities which we are given, but also the
risks that we run with every step we take,
every decision we make. I use them as visual
metaphors for this 'game element' of life.

The dice have been placed in nature because
in the end we are also subservient to nature,
no matter how much we would like to control
it. If we are unlucky, we could die today, as
a result of illness, an accident or natural
disaster. I wanted to represent this aspect of
chance, or even fate, amongst other things.
Just as we throw dice to determine how to
continue in a game, we make decisions every
day which decide our fate. There is a sense
of uncertainty because the dice should be
rolling, but here they are frozen; the game
seems to have come to a stop. This makes it
even more noticeable how the plants continue
to grow playfully around and between the
stones. I wanted to show that in the end we
cannot control nature or conquer it, no matter
how calculating we are when we play the
game of life.

I like to see children playing around my work.
In their games they often confirm my ideas
about human behaviour, and sometimes
about the rules of survival. It is precisely
because they are not yet aware of this themselves and respond in a basic way in that respect. To me, this actually reveals something
of the essence of who we are as people."

**You see yourself as someone who can
show the viewer certain matters and
can reflect and open worlds. How important is this aspect in your work?** "In
my observation of the world, of life, man and
nature, I notice things and I see relationships
which I want to show and explain. I try to do
this in different visual ways; this is an important aspect of my work. I think it is interesting
and good to refer in my work to the wealth of
the existing, but often concealed reality. In this

way I hope that people will be able to look at
the world, at life, at other people and nature in
a new and more open way."

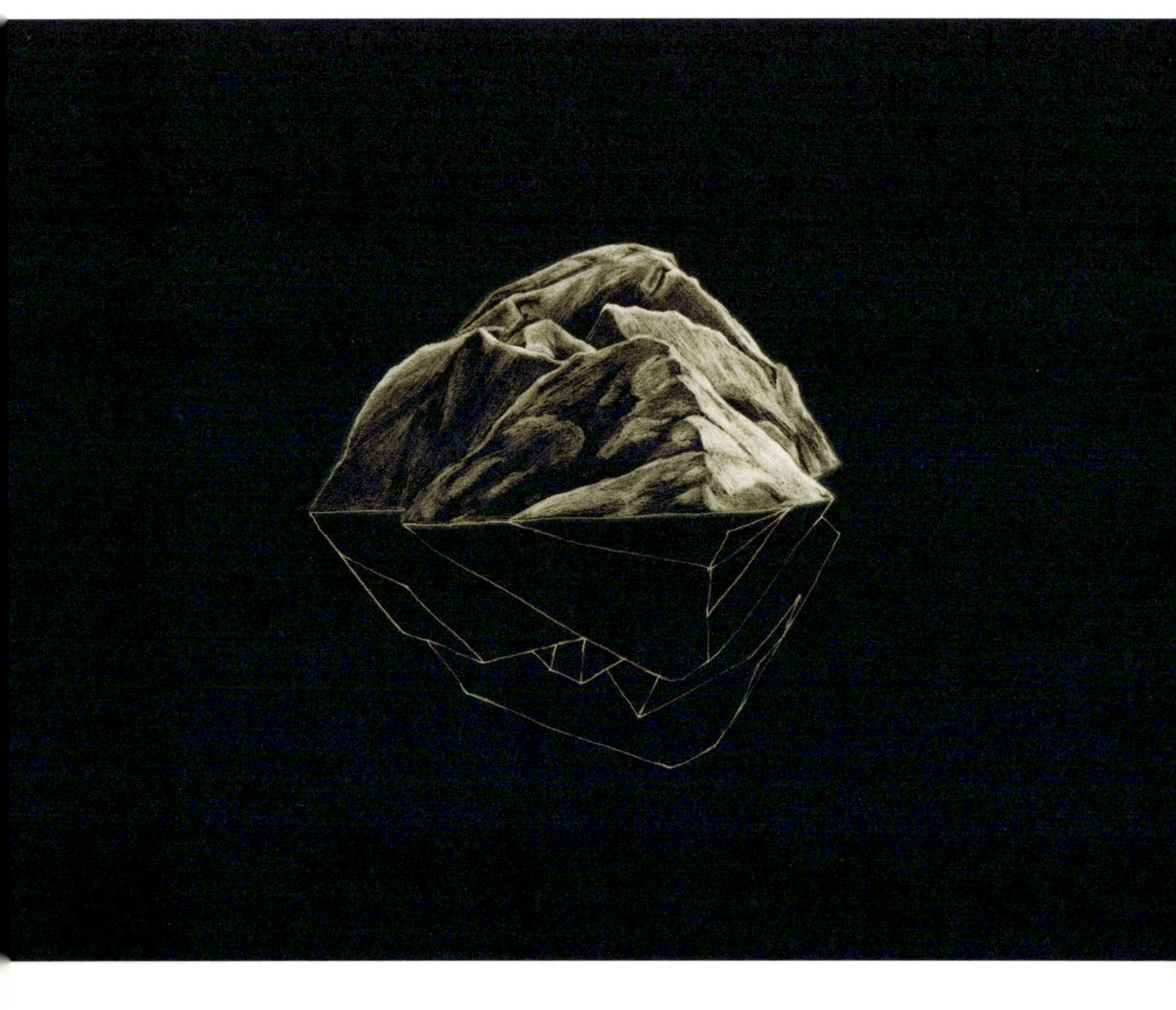

Sibylle Eimermacher
About my work

The image as a phenomenon which can disappear from one moment to the next, plays an important role in my work. For me, it is about the material quality of painting versus the intangibility of the ephemeral image of the new media.
I take the figures and objects in my paintings from pictures on the Internet, from films and computer games. The images which circulate on the web are usually exchangeable and remain in a virtual space for a short time. Objects which we encounter in computer games, slide past us because of their immaterial quality. This also happens in the game, *Deer Hunter*, in which we ride a horse into virtual space to shoot deer. This game was the source of inspiration for some of my paintings.
In my paintings and drawings I try to give a place to these volatile images without a 'home'.

Looking for the meaning of art, through doubt
An interview with Sibylle Eimermacher by Josien Beltman

During her studies at the MFA Painting course, Sibylle Eimermacher was mainly making paintings. Before embarking on the Frank Mohr Institute in Groningen, she studied at the AKI, the Academy of Art and Design in Enschede, where she worked in various media: drawing, painting, film and installations. Her desire to concentrate on one thing and tired of discussions about which discipline suited her best, led to her spending two years with painting. Animals and houses seem to glide through her pictures. The surroundings of the objects are often indeterminate and a unity of time and space appears to be lacking. The artist describes the atmosphere in her paintings as 'uncanny'. In a former barracks in the woods near Laren, where she now has her studio, along with a number of ex-fellow students, she talks about the indefinable atmosphere in her work.

Left image:
Sibylle Eimermacher, Mountain 3 2006, Digital print, 20 x 30 cm

The 'uncanny' is a familiar term from psychology and art, but what does the term actually mean for you and what exactly is the 'uncanny' aspect in your work? *"For me, the 'uncanny', in German 'das Unheimliche', is something inexplicable; it is beyond our power and cannot be 'grasped'. It changes everything familiar, what is "Heimlich'. If you are in your house, for example, and you suddenly hear all sorts of noises that you have never heard before, you have a strong feeling of discomfort, while your common sense says that you are imagining it. It is an indefinable feeling.*

In my paintings the 'uncanny' is caused on the one hand by the presence of something familiar and on the other hand by the presence of something unfamiliar. As a result the viewer can feel a bit uncomfortable when looking at the work, since he does not exactly know what he is experiencing. In the work **Fire,** *for example, one sees a fire in the middle of the painting. At first the viewer recognises the familiar form. But the dark blue colour of the flames, the cold aura and the unidentifiable surroundings, endow the fire with qualities that one is not familiar with."*

Other elements that determine the 'uncanny', and which you often mention in connection with your work, are 'fleetingness' and 'instability'. Can you indicate how you try to achieve these effects? *"I often look at film stills. They evoke associations of ephemerality and instability. In my paintings I use effects derived from these stills, like cropping. This creates the suggestion that all sorts of things are going on outside the painting, which one associates to movement and fleetingness. In the painting* **Mit Huhn,** *for example, a large white form pushes into the picture from above. This is a shadow - white and light instead of black and dark - of an object outside the image. Shadows are also used in this way in horror films, but after a while one sees what is coming; it is quite obvious that something is about to happen. In my paintings I try to subtly indicate that there is perhaps also something outside the picture. There is a further sugges-*

tion of intangibility in that objects appear to hover - they have no shadow and so they are surrounded by emptiness. Some objects, like the chicken, in the painting mentioned above, seem immaterial because of the transparent, fluorescent, negative colours, which makes them intangible.

*Instability likewise ensures elusiveness, since the viewer does not know where to look. I create instabilities in my paintings by means of what I call 'forced symmetry'. There is an impression of symmetry, but it is not exactly right. In the case of the painting **Fire,** the fire is in the centre of the picture with on either side two ovals. On closer inspection, they are not placed at the same distance from the pictures edges. The viewpoint of the beholder begins to falter - his gaze can go to the right or to the left - thus giving rise to instability."*

Are you consciously concerned with the role of the viewer? *"In the second year of the MFA Painting course, I started to think more about the connection of the viewer to the picture. Because of this it also became easier to arrive at instability. One of the first pieces in this manner is **Horse in Space.** The head of the horse, which is seen from behind, occupies the place of the viewer, who by this is incorporated into the work. But in the background there are different perspectives: one looks into the space from above and head-on. This instability is experienced more powerfully as the viewer is drawn into the work. Later I made the painting **Mirror** in which I broke up the viewpoint with the result that this work is even more unstable. The beholder now occupies two viewpoints, having not just one horses head to identify with, but two. Yet confusing the viewer is not the main aim of my work."*

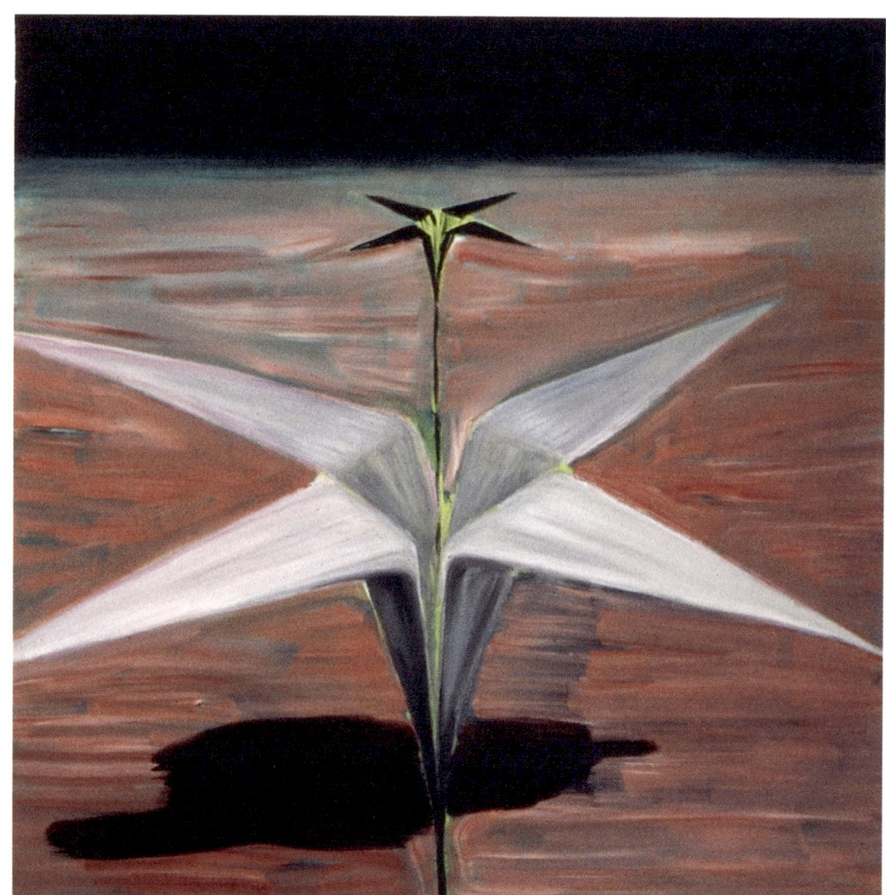

If that is not the main aim, then what is your work really about? What processes do you want to set in motion on the part of the viewer? *"It is more a question of doubt giving rise to an unstable way of seeing, resulting in an uncertain, intangible atmosphere. Art is not meant to make people look at familiar things; it is showing something new. I want my paintings to make a new experience possible for the viewer. But the viewer would have no access to the work if the content was completely 'strange', if there were no recognisable elements. That is why it is necessary that a painting possesses something familiar and something unfamiliar. On the one hand the viewer has a point of contact and on the other hand he has a new experience because, for example, things are put in a different light.*

In my thesis I refer to the theories of the semiotician Barend van Heusden. In his view art has no definite meanings; it is the beholder who endows it with meanings. The beholder's doubt motivates him to search for 'solutions' to this 'problem of meaning' that the work of art is. He is thus constantly comparing his expectations with what he actually sees and looks for the meanings of the differences. He might ask himself whether he finds the fire [in Fire] an attractive source of warmth. Or maybe he finds the image repellent. 'Instability' is usually not a pleasant feeling. Looking for an explanation for the instability is a way of getting rid of the unpleasantness. In my work I leave the viewer in a state of doubt by not incorporating any clear references in my paintings that would explain things. So the viewer has to keep searching for possible meanings."

Image below:

Sibylle Eimermacher, Fire 2006, Acrylic /oil paint on canvas, 125,5 x 161 cm

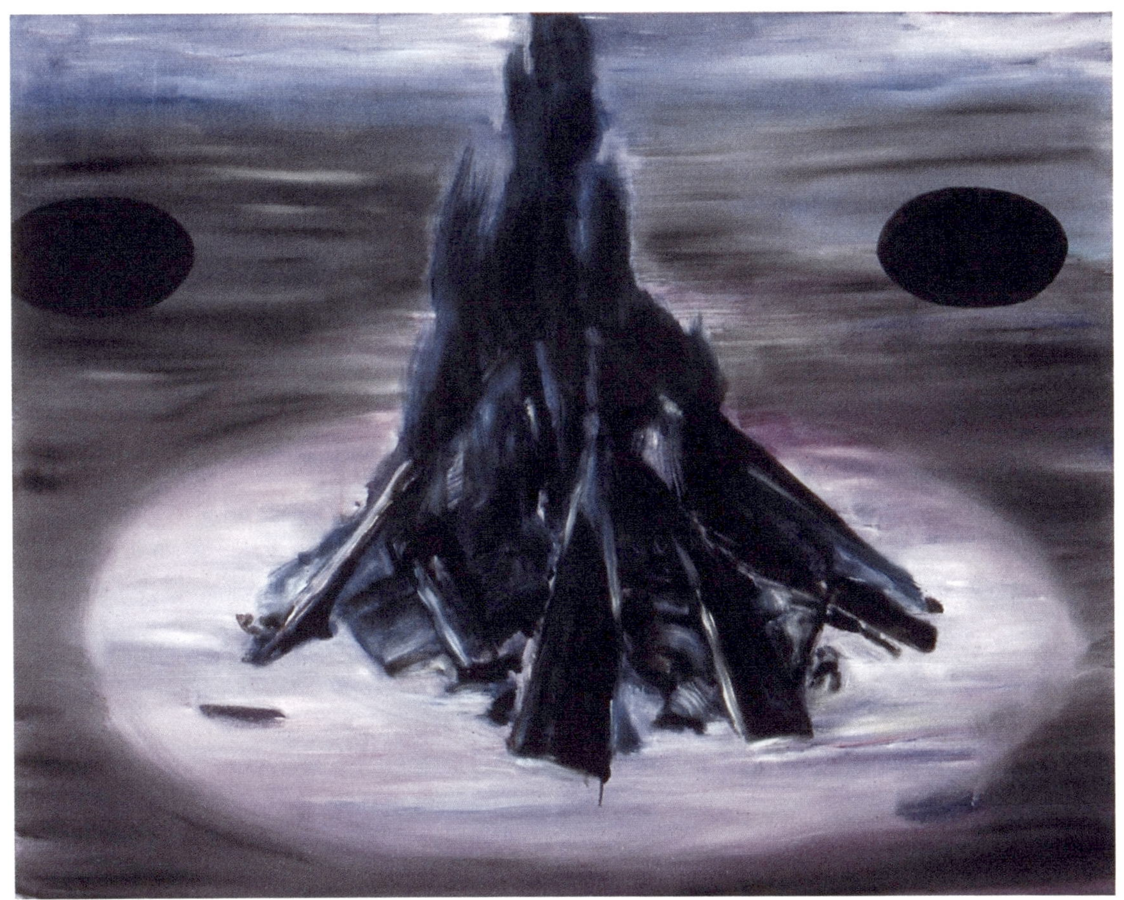

Many of the visual means you use, such as cropping, over-exposure and 'negative' colours, are derived from photography and film. Why have you chosen painting rather than those other media with which you could just as well produce an effect like 'elusiveness'?

"When I was still at the art academy, I used many media: painting, drawing, making films and installations. I have never really been involved with photography. In Groningen I started focussing on painting because I wanted to concentrate more on one thing. If you restrict yourself in terms of media you can concentrate more on the content and perhaps the work also becomes better. I also think I have more the viewpoint of a painter than of a filmer. The video works I made, for example, were more moving pictures than stories like in a film. I found painting the most difficult and hence the most challenging. If you are good at something, you all too easily do it automatically.

What I find particularly interesting is to catch things like 'fleetingness' and 'elusiveness' in a painting, because then you have the contrast between the materiality of painting - the paint - and the ephemerality of media like film and photography. And painting is more direct; that is to say, you make everything yourself, in contrast to a video in which you use images that you record with an instrument and which are thus perhaps less your own. The French theoretician and philosopher Roland Barthes refers to 'becoming an object' in connection with photography. If, for example, you make a portrait of a person (the subject) then this becomes the object in the photograph. When this person looks at the photograph, he is looking at himself from the outside. He knows that he is the figure in the photograph, but he also sees this person as an autonomous thing in the world of the photograph, as something strange that is separate from himself.

A painter has a larger part in the process of 'becoming an object' than the photographer, since it is his hand that puts the representation on the canvas. Not only does he make a picture, but he also determines the painting's own life, since he has more freedom in making it into something other than just

Image below:
Sibylle Eimermacher, Stage #1 2006, Acrylic /oil paint on canvas, 185 x 120 cm, Photo: Harold Koopmans

Right image:
Sibylle Eimermacher, Horse in space 2006, Acrylic/ oil paint on canvas, 140 x 156 cm

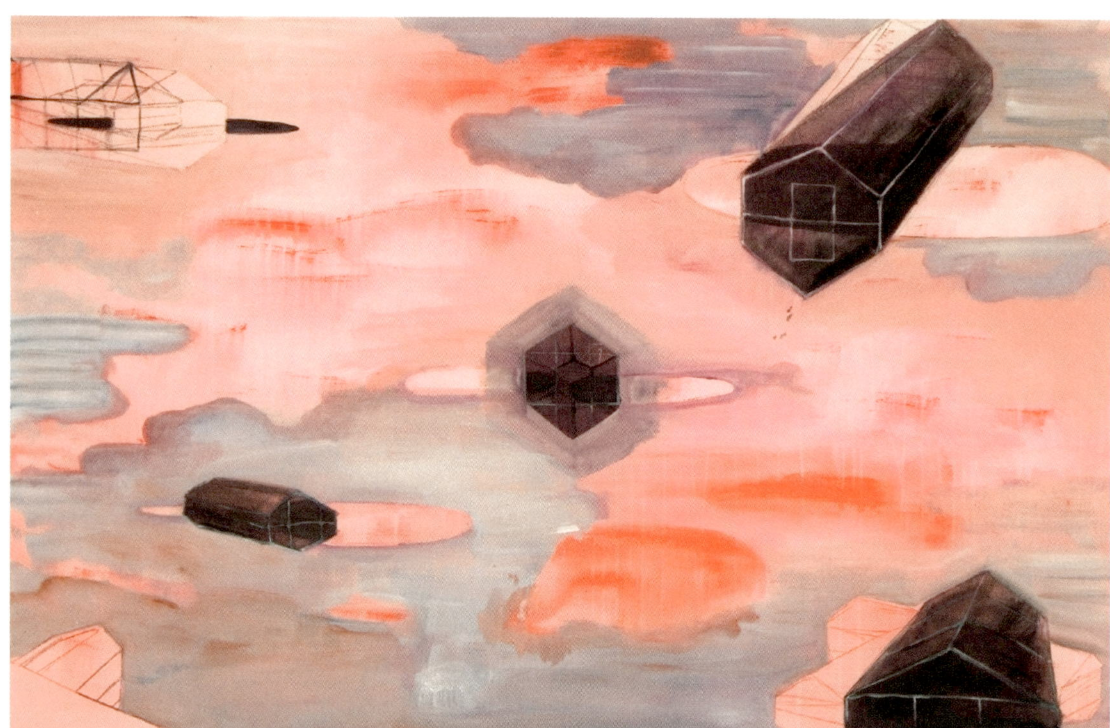

a representation of a person. A painting is a new creation that is made in response to something, and so it is never a proof that something actually looks like that."

When you start on a new painting, how do you go about it? *"The starting point of my work is nearly always a photograph that I pick up from the Internet or a film still. The painting* **Huisje** *for example, was inspired by a scene from Tarkovsky's film* **The Sacrifice** *and the pattern in* **D.'s House** *refers to the carpet in the film* **The Shining**. *I choose the image that comes closest to an image or idea in my head. Or while searching, I find an image that evokes a new idea for a painting. From a collection of images or starting from a particular atmosphere, I then create a new image by cropping it and making a collage. This forms the basis for the painting, but during the process of painting anything can change. Sometimes I take photographs of the painting while it is in progress, and then I use Photoshop on the computer to see how it works if I change the colours, before making any changes on the canvas. In this way I also arrived at a new colour scheme. In the beginning, for some time I was using the same, mainly sweet colours. At the end of my first year at the MFA Painting course I made digital scans of my paintings and reversed the colours so they became like the colours of a photographic negative. As a result, I*

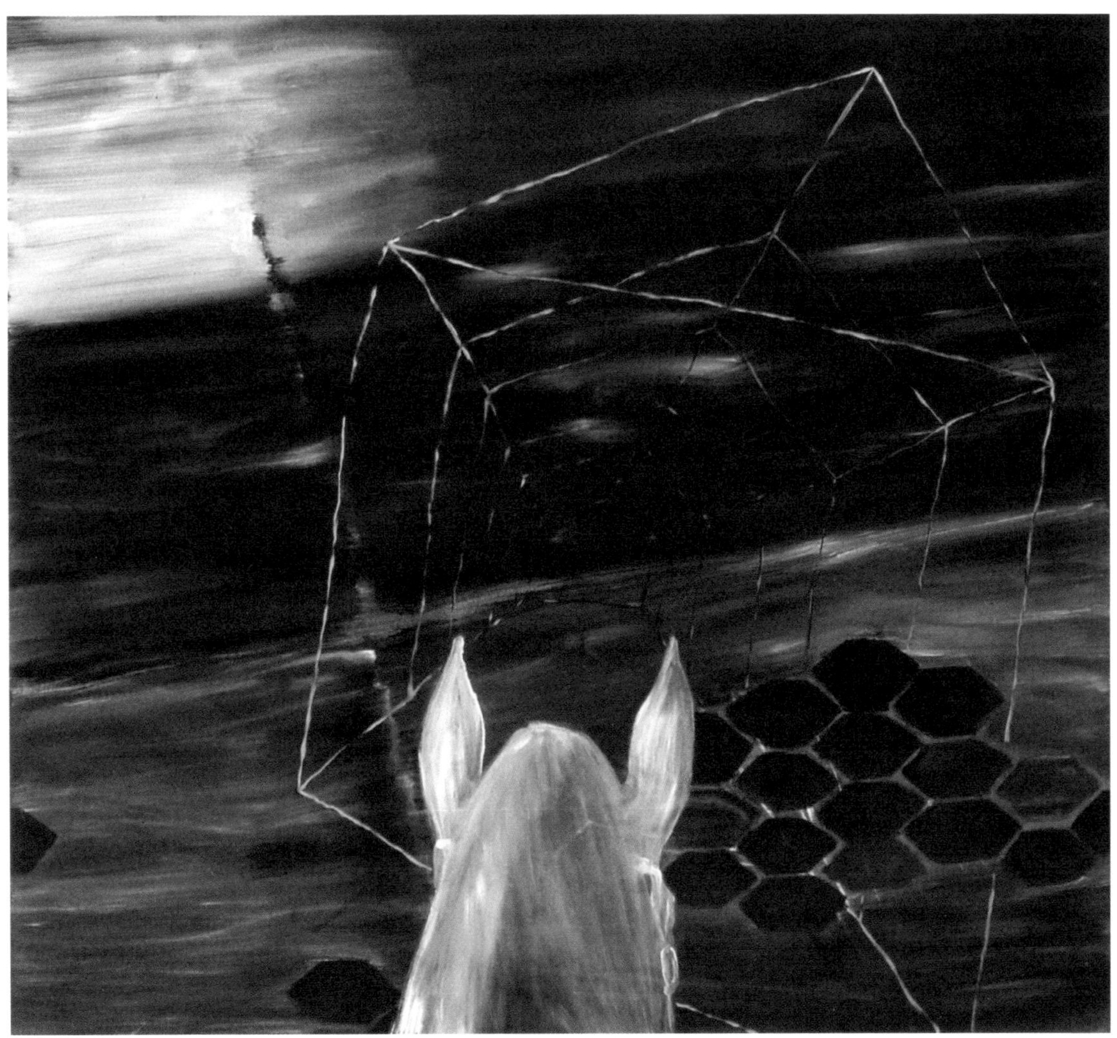

started using colours I had never actually used before. These new, cold tones and the effect of 'reversing', whereby the objects seem to be fluorescent, also contribute to an 'uncanny' effect."

You already said that you search on the Internet for pictures of animals and houses among other things. There is a striking absence of human beings in your work. *"In the past I have painted portraits of people, but when you portray people you have to deal with aditional things like how they are dressed and from which time they come. This is not the case with animals; they are just the animal they are. The deer in my paintings, for example, have those big, empty eyes that you can look through. I treat them as 'figures' rather than as personalities. Maybe the representation of animals also has something to do with the intangible. People often have pets and they love them, although in general the animal could not care less. This is especially the case with rabbits. You might love your rabbit a lot, but at the same time you never really get to know it, and you have no idea what is going on in its mind, since the animal is in its own world.*

I also like it when there is something apocalyptic in the painting. The occurance of only animals in my work has to do with desolation and emptiness; as if there are no longer any people living. And allthough people are not seen, their traces are still present in, for example, the empty houses."

Where does your fascination with the 'uncanny' come from? *"The 'uncanny' does not have so much to do with a specific memory or a particular experience for me. It is more a general feeling which everyone knows. It is also intangible - like all feelings, it seems. I do not know whether I experience alienation in my daily life more than the average person. Everyone has probably had the experience that something was suddenly striking and that you then would see it differently. And every artist is involved with showing 'ordinary' things in a different light; letting people look at reality in a different way."*

Would you say that the 'uncanny' has to do with a feeling of emptiness you experience yourself? *"It certainly has to do with my own experience of emptiness and intangibility. During holidays, I was quite often in desolated places like mountains and deserts. There you can feel very small and lost in the landscape. This is a tranquil feeling which I can long for.*

But the 'intangible' is also a reflection upon the feeling of life nowadays. Because of all the media in our everyday life, we get too much information and cannot observe everything. With the fast, busy traffic and the ephemeral media like films and computer games, a lot passes us by. As far as the 'intangible' is concerned, I think it is challenging to be involved with something that you cannot grasp, and then to try to represent this in a painting you can actually touch."

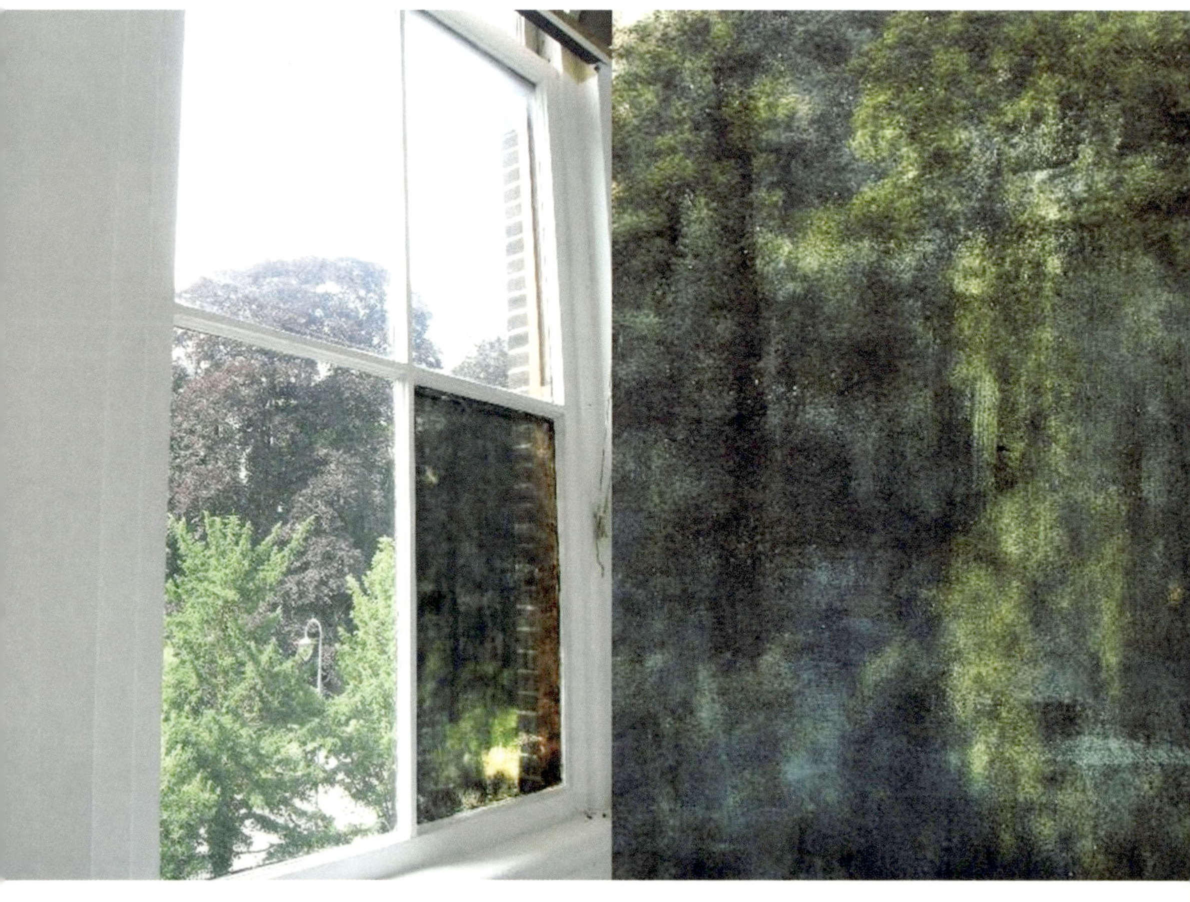

Saskia Koops

I lie in my bed and I can't sleep. It's the evening and I'm almost six years old. It's dark. There's a small window above the bedroom door. On the landing the light's on behind the door. My parents are downstairs. I'm all alone. The light in the hallway shines into my bedroom and that makes it slightly less dark.
Suddenly the room seems to come to life. There is a wall on my right. I can see it and I can also touch the wall. When I look at it, I see various pieces of torn wallpaper. The wall is purple, very dark purple, but through the damaged areas I can see that there are many other different colours underneath. In addition, I see landscapes and cities in the shapes created in this way. What is there behind the purple? What is there behind the other colours? I start to pull on the loose bits of wallpaper.
I'm convinced that if I pull at it long enough there will automatically be a hole, the wall will disappear and I will be able to look in the room next to mine, or perhaps, even better, I can enter another world. So I go on tearing and tearing.

I would pick and pull at it endlessly, and every time I would lose myself in this activity. I was sure of it, there was more. It was not possible that the world ceased to exist at my wall …

Capturing time *An interview with Saskia Koops by Jakob van Stolk*

What do Dorothy, the heroine of the film *The Wizard of Oz* (1939), and Saskia Koops have in common? At first sight nothing. For those who do not know this classic film, the little girl named Dorothy is stuck in boring Kansas and is longing for a nicer place elsewhere. Her wish is granted when a cyclone hits her town, and her house, with Dorothy and all, is lifted up and deposited in another place. From one moment to the next she is transported from colourless Kansas to the fantastic 'Land of Oz', somewhere over the rainbow. There she meets the Scarecrow, the Cowardly Lion and the Tin Man with whom she travels to the 'Emerald City'. It is a journey full of excitement and adventure.
In her thesis Saskia Koops descibes her own journey in the two years she has attended the MFA Painting course. Like Dorothy, she is now on the way to her 'Emerald City'. She has been able to free herself from a paralysing, critical attitude and is open to new ideas and to commentary on her work. She now sees herself as "someone who has switched from acting in an intellectual way to thinking in activity."

Left image:

Saskia Koops,

Black Window,

Enimal paint on

window, 2004.

(right: detail)

What does this statement mean exactly? *"I am very curious by nature and I read many art books and go to many exhibitions. This way I acquired a large frame of reference, which is both an advantage and a disadvantage for me. One disadvantage was that I rather let myself be impressed by the artists around me. For me, a work always begins with looking and experiencing. At a certain moment I realised that my head was so chock full of information from books and exhibitions that I could not 'see' any longer. I was thinking much too much about what my art should consist of and why I do the things I do. As a result, I felt I knew even less. Because I compared myself too much with other artists, I ended up doing nothing. But through the discussions at the MFA Painting course and the reflection they offer, I was able to get this craving for accountability out of my mind. In this course they force you to adopt a position. Because you start conversing with people who have a completely different view of your work, you are shown other points of view. The Frank Mohr Institute offers you chances and possibilities that you do not have if you are alone in your studio, and so your development accelerates.*

I have learned to take the liberty to do things my way. I now see more of a thread in all the things I have done and made in the past. Even though the work I did in the beginning looks very different from what I am making now, I can see that the basis is the same. I want to offer the viewer something that emerges from my own amazement. So to come back to that statement - previously I thought too much and this got in the way of doing things. Now I am doing a lot and my ideas are formed by that."

In 2002 you made a work in Galerie Sign, and in 2006 you made a new version of it in Kunstruimte 09. The one piece stems from the period before the Frank Mohr Institute, and the other was carried out after your graduation. In both places you made the exhibition-history of the galleries visisble by creating a complex play of lines on the walls. Are there big differences between the two works? *"At Sign the piece was called **Spiegel Mij** (Groningen 2002, black and white latex paint). The version in Kunstruimte 09 is called **K0920042006**. Both pieces were based on the idea of looking at and experiencing the place itself. What does it look like, what is its function and what is so special about this particular place? Galerie Sign has existed for fourteen years. For each*

year of its existence I made a map of the walls showing the outlines of every exhibited work. I then assembled these fourteen maps into a single one, and masked off its lines on the walls, while I painted the rest of the walls black. When the masking tape was removed, the history of the space became literally visible. After three weeks I painted the walls white again so that the next exhibition could leave its traces on the walls and write a new piece of history. People found it too bad that I painted over the walls again, but this temporariness is an important part of my concept. For me it is as though time has been stopped for a moment during the exhibitioon. Not only the past, but also the present and the future become visible: you see the passing of time. As soon as the walls are painted white, time and space coincide again.
I applied the same concept in Kunstruimte 09, but this time I used transparent varnish on a white wall. When you enter the space, you do not see the lines immediately; there are works by other exhibiting artists hanging on top of

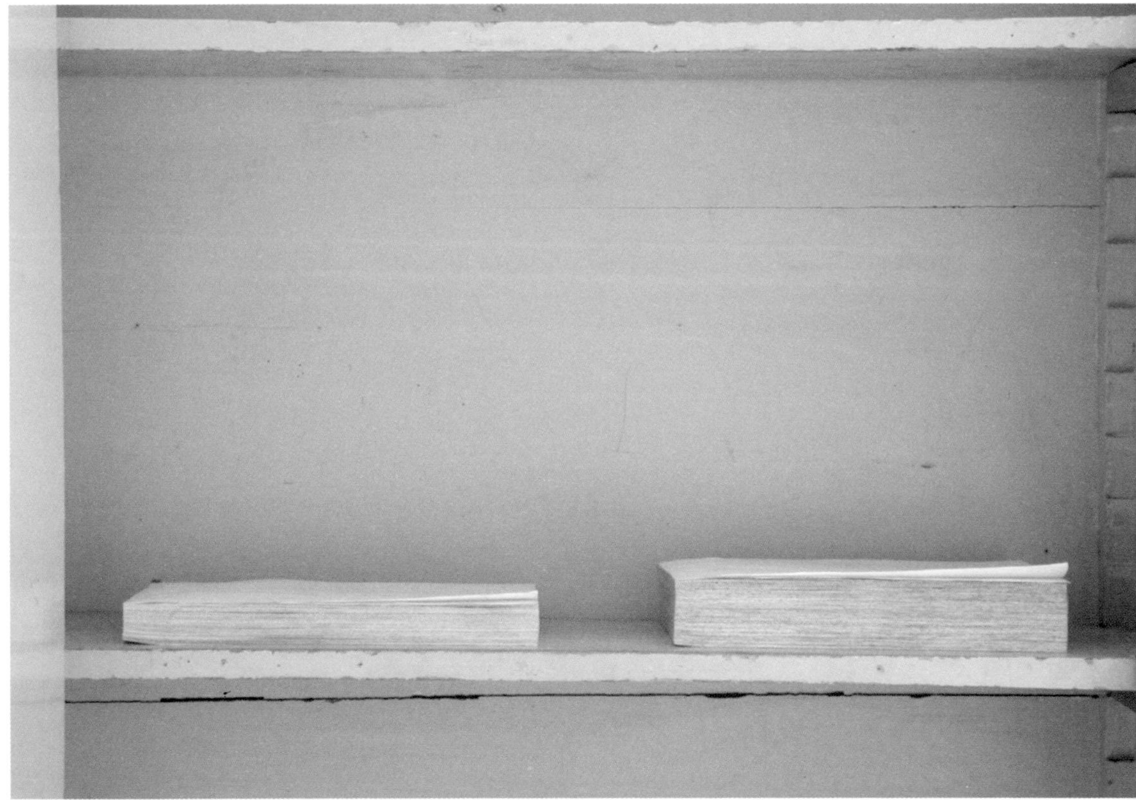

the lines, and you only see the lines when the light falls on them from a particular angle. This piece is like an apparition. It remains in the background, but it seems from comments by visitors that once they have spotted the various lines, this is all they are able to concentrate on, so that the works of the other artists fade into the background. Thus the major difference between the pieces in Galerie Sign and in Kunstruimte 09 has mainly to do with how the work is executed. The lines are less prominently present at Kunstruimte 09, and so a totally different experience is created. The function of the work is also different. Martijn Schuppers, who curated the exhibition at Kunstruimte 09, asked me to make a basis for the exhibition. My lines literally connect the other works with each other, while at Sign the piece stood completely by itself.

For both versions I used the photographs that the gallery owners have made of their exhibitions over the years. Their way of seeing was the basis for a work of art that expresses my ideas about their location, but which also plays with the way in which viewers look at art."

In your thesis you mention the Swiss artist Rémy Zaugg (1943-2005) and in particular his work *Constitution d'un tableau, 27 esquisses perceptives, gravures, 1963-1968* (1990) as one of your sources of inspiration. Why did this work make such an impression on you? *"I first saw this piece, as well as other works by him, at the Witte de With Centre of Art in Rotterdam. It consists of a series of fourty eight numbered sheets, in an edition of fifty copies. On each sheet Zaugg gives a different description of the same painting by Paul Cézanne; the handwritten lines calling the painting to mind. The words in French function as quick notes describing the original painting: "ciel bleu, ciel cobalt, façade orange". What you see is a registration of the artist's gaze. Registering, remembering, observing and seeing coincide here in a fascinating way. I was so overwhelmed by*

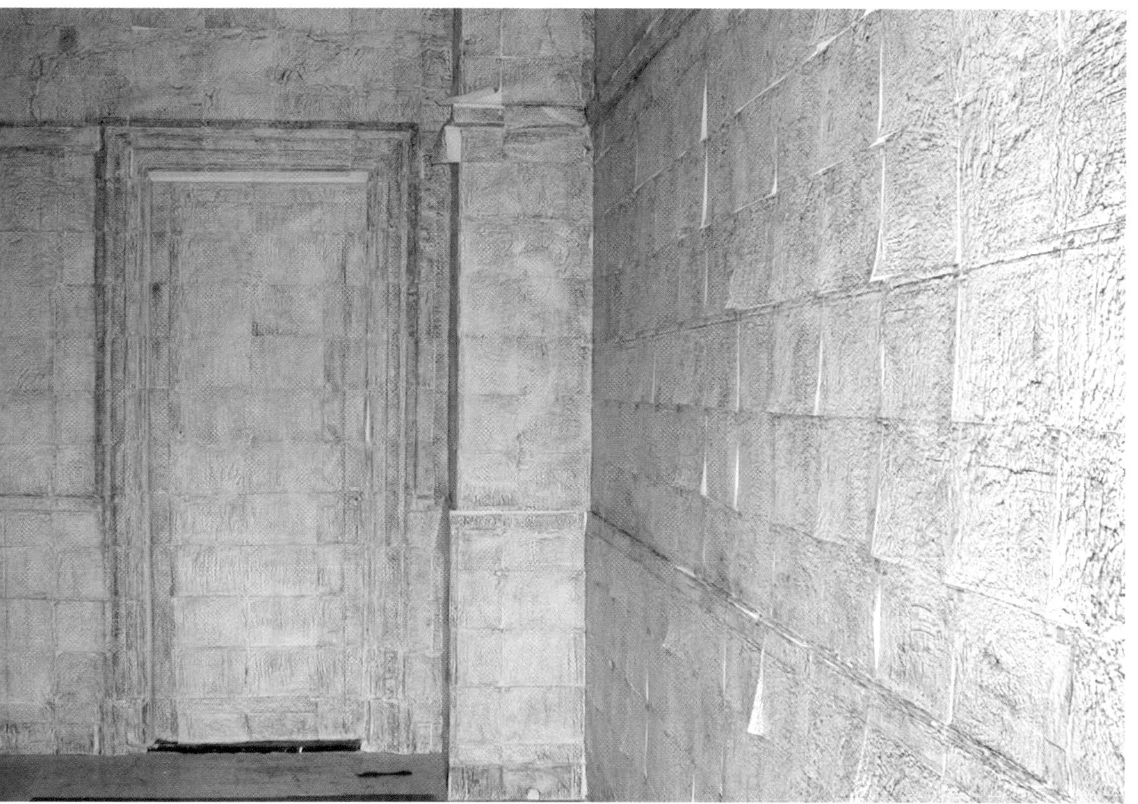

this work, while at the same time I saw how far away it was from my own work.

Rémy Zaugg is describing a painting in words, evoking images and associations in the viewer; he wants you to see according to his way of seeing and at the same time he allows you to see details that you might otherwise not have noticed. Since he provides fourty eight different descriptions of the same painting, it becomes clear that ways of seeing differ not only per person, but also per moment. Something that is each time the same is also each time different. And while you are looking at the descriptions by Rémy Zaugg of a painting by Cézanne, you form an opinion not only about Zaugg's way of seeing, but also about the original work by Cézanne. It is precisely this layering that fascinates me. He is playing with the viewer's experience, their way of seeing, but he gives them the freedom to interpret the work of art in their own way.

For me, the work of Rémy Zaugg is an experience in seeing and discovering. He is one of the many artists I have come across in whose work I recognised something, or became curious about something. He has made it possible for me to see and experience art in a different way."

Your project for the final examination, *Wall Work III* (Boteringesingel 14 Groningen, studio 7, 2006, paper and

graphite) consists, like *Siegel Mij* and K0920042006, of a space that you have transformed into a work of art. Here too you represent the history of the place. By wallpapering your entire studio with white A4 sheets and then rubbing over the paper with a graphite, you charted the space, but at the same time you also freezed the studio in time. *Wall Work III* was preceded by two earlier versions. Are all these pieces separate from each other or were you working towards a particular climax or final result? *"The first two versions were also snapshots in time of studios: my studio at the Frank Mohr Institute Wall **Work I** (Boteringesingel 14 Groningen, studio 18, 2005, paper and graphite) and my work place in New York, **Wall Work II** (41st Street New York, studio 312c, 2005, paper and graphite). The first version came about because I changed studios at the Frank Mohr Institute and I realised what a beautiful and interesting studio I had left behind. I wanted to take the space with me. By numbering all the pages covered with rubbings and binding them, I ensured that a space of about 20 square metres was transformed into a book measuring 21 by 29.7 centimetres. This is a book in which a process, an action is stored, and it is a space that you can take everywhere with you. I repeated the proces in my studio in New York, but the smaller space and the different texture of the walls meant that a completely different work of art came about. I presented **Wall Work I** and **Wall Work II** in their final form as a book. With **Wall Work III** I deliberately started rubbing on the sheets of paper a day after the opening of the graduation show. So instead of a snapshot in time, the people saw me tracing the walls gradually, sheet by sheet, like the making of a film. The sheets of paper function as a sort of filter that makes the traces*

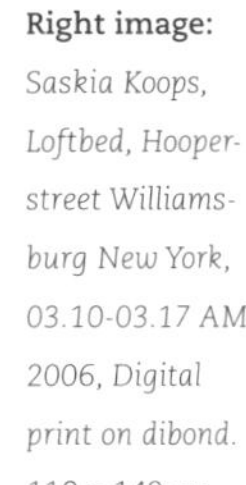

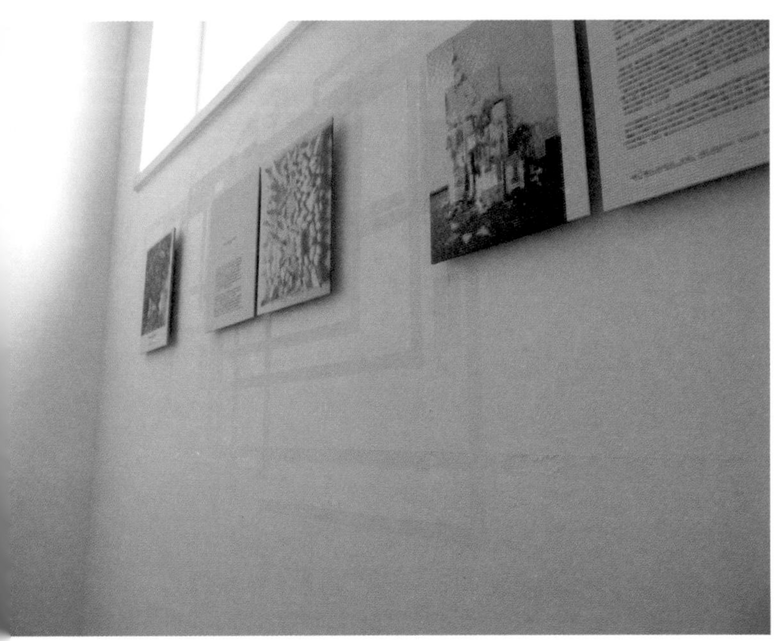

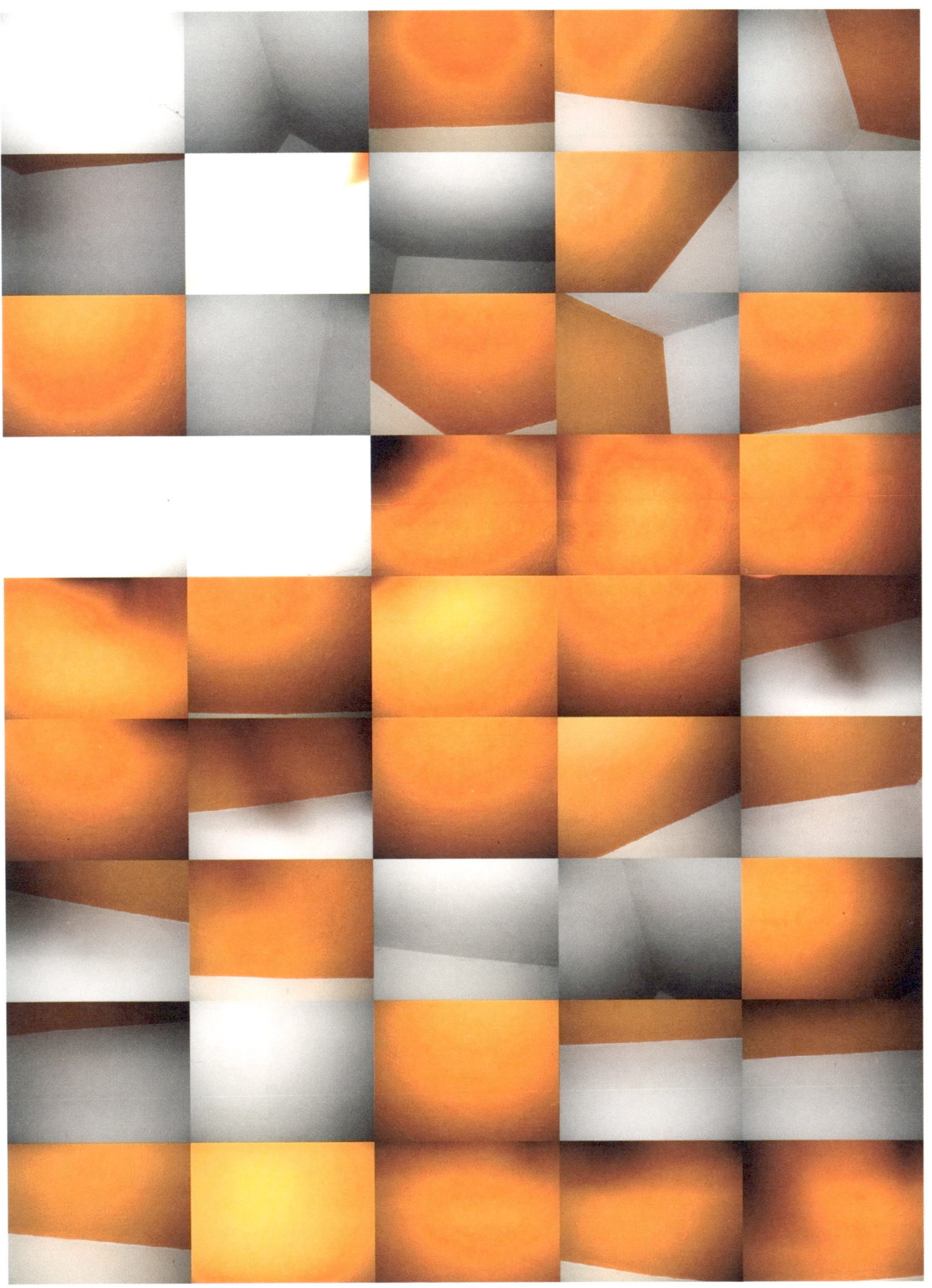

on the walls visible, so that the passing of time and the duration of the action can be observed. This is a slow kind of art. Visitors to the exhibition told me that by watching me mapping the walls, they calmed down, while everything around us goes so fast. They felt they were joining in in my action and were thereby literally lifted out of time."

Image below:
Saskia Koops K0920042006 2006, Mural in gloss latex paint, Exhibition: °BSTR°CT, Kunstruimte 09, 2006. Other works by: Twan Janssen, Stage Property # 061201:" Catalogue", Work in progress 12 parts 2006, plastic on aluminium, Courtesy Torch Gallery, Amsterdam, Martijn Schuppers: #0607, 2006, Acrylic, alkyd and oil paint on polyester canvas, Courtesy VOUS ETES ICI, Amsterdam.

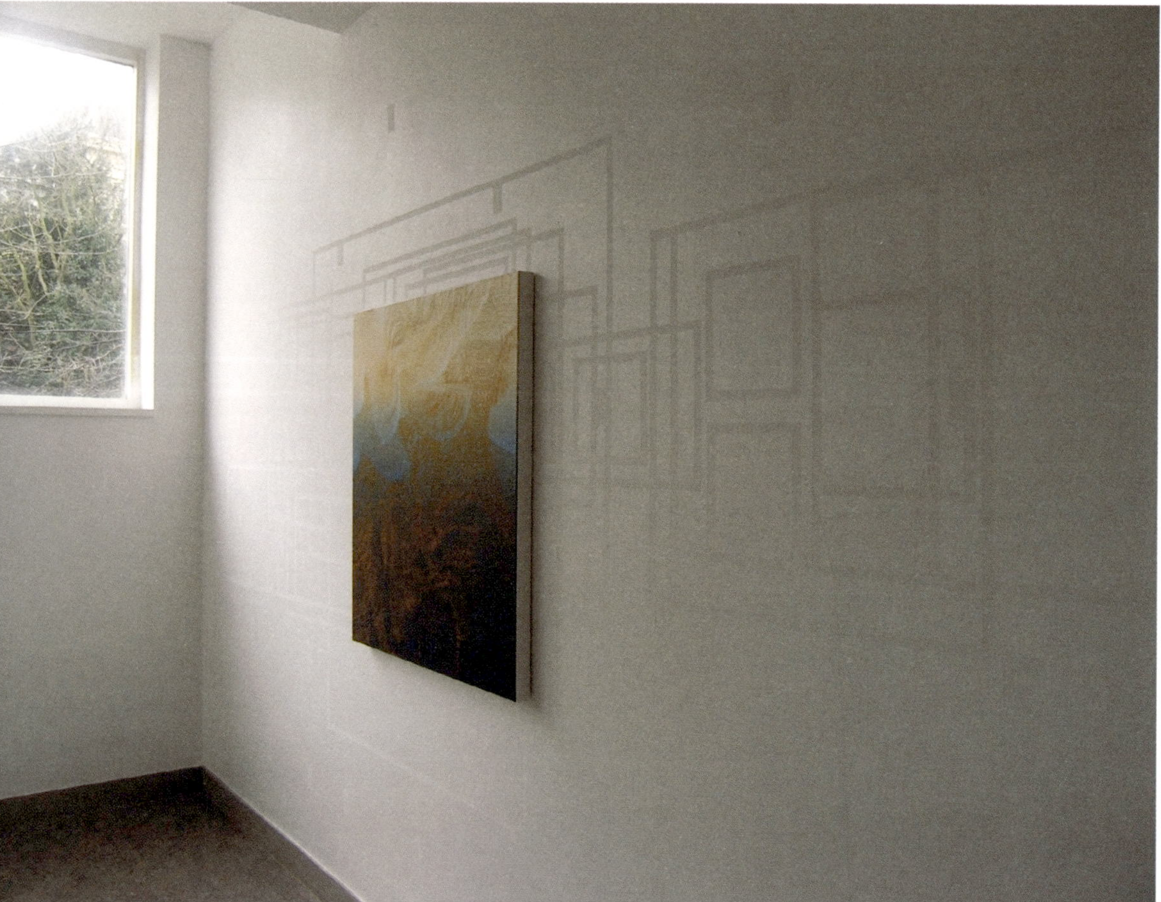

Image below:
Alex Winters,
13V, 2006,
Lambda-print
on dibond, 76 x
80 cm, Courtesy
Galerie Fons
Welters

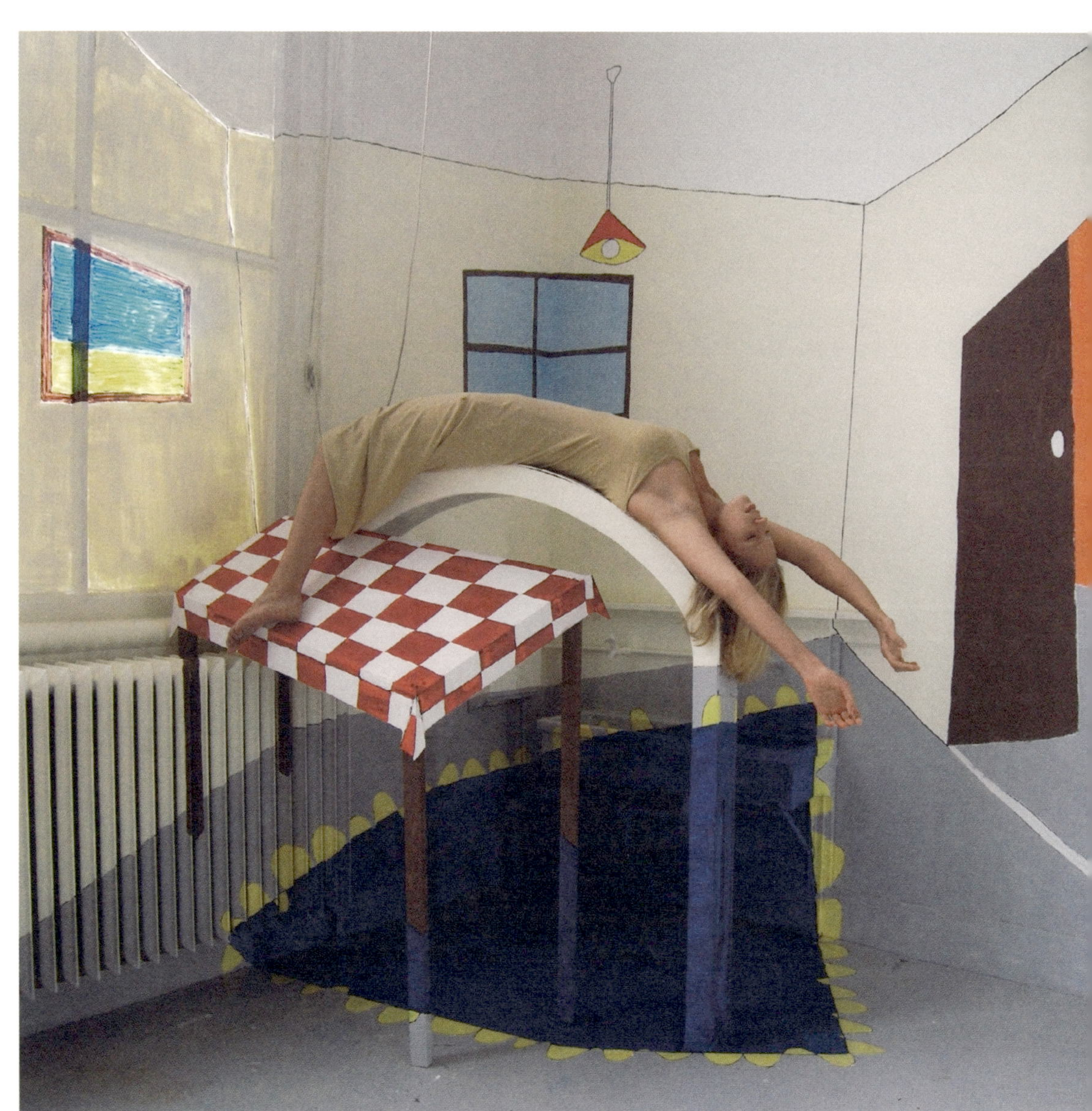

Alex Winters

```
                    ROOM    L    /    R    /    M    /    B

I t       d                                                        A
 urn                                                                  The room
an        i     I          swerve,              but       collide.  b looks empty.
 d pl     n     The    pen    drops    out    of    my    pocket.      Very far
ace:            It     falls    on    the    ground    and          s    away.
 Twi      a     I      move    it    over    the    wall.           e
ce/             A      door    is    drawn    and    opened.          Something:
 tim      l                                                                is
es/       i                                                         n  dominant.
 det      n     I                            continue:             c  The room
ail.      e                                                             stays
          .                                                        e    empty.

Fol             Standing    in    a    space,    I    look.           I fall off
 low      T     Looking    for    a    pen,    I    find    it.        the table,
step      u     Meant              is              drawn,              the wall,
 s a      r     the          space          I          posses.     o  the plinth.
lon             The     body    follows    it    in.                  A roaring
 g t      n                                                             sound.
he        e
 wal      d     I                        stumble:                   f
l fr                                                                   Curved
om s      f                                                            lines
 hou      l     Trying    to    fail,    I    succeed.             across the
lde       a     Again         and             again.              back-wall
r-wi      t     Trying    to    fail,    I    repeat.             a  of seeing.
 de.
          i     Action          after          action.            w Woman gives
Loo             A    logic    born    of    necessity.                  in, in
 k t      n                                                        a splendour,
hro             However    it    is        different.                in osten-
 ugh      p     Seen      from      my      rooms.                 r    tation.
/ l       e     Closed         in         cache.
ook       r                                                        e  Adorned
 pas                                                                  being /
t; w      s     I                        wallow:                   n in colour,
all       p                                                        full of seeing
 and        e                   Wal                                e and giving.
ed          c                 k roud in
ge.                         circles. Assimi
            t               late the space and                    s  The door;
De f        i               take it with me. Wal                     flat and
 act      v                 k round in circles.
o pl        e               Assimilate the sp                      s     shut.
 ace      .                   ace and take i                         The table-
                                t with                                   cloth
                                 me.                                     lays /
                                                                   .    stays
                                                                       behind.


I     s     e     e     W     h     a     t     t     o     s     e     e     .
```

Aimlessness as a logical instrument *An interview with Alex Winters by Jakob van Stolk*

For his final examination Alex Winters made *Room 3* and *Room 14*, respectively an installation and a video work. These two works are characteristic of his oeuvre. The artist combines three-dimensional spaces with two-dimensional planes and uses simple materials to achieve this. *Room 3* consists of partitions on which he has drawn windows, heating appliances and light switches, amongst other things. These partitions have been placed in the space in such a way that you are led through it via narrow corridors. After a while, you are able to recognise the shapes on the walls: the artist has drawn the studio that you are in on the walls with simple lines. However he has turned the space around, cut through it and pushed it together. In the kitchen next to the studio, you can watch the film *Room 14* in which Alex Winters has drawn the same kitchen on a wooden floor. In the film you can follow how he draws the space, and at the same time, it is possible to check how accurately he does it.

Both works lead to surprise, tension and confusion. *Room 3* has a slightly claustrophobic effect because of the rather narrow corridors. It is certainly confusing; the artist has extended the floors onto the walls so that the two-dimensional plane merges with the third dimension. This works so well, that when the girlfriend of the artist recently wanted to mop the floor, just before the opening of the graduation show, she also started cleaning the partitions, without noticing that she was doing so. *Room 14* seems to be an ordinary representation of reality, but when you look closely, you see that the artist omits certain elements from the composition and actually emphasises other details, playing with different perspectives. Thus Alex Winters draws the viewer into his creative process: through his eyes you are looking at a space which fascinates him.

The experience of the viewer is part of your work. Do you want the viewer to feel that he is in your place? *"Everyone looks at a certain space in a different way; I want to show the viewer my view of this room. The details fascinate me in this sort of space, and I want to show those details to the public. The interesting thing about details is that you notice them only when they are removed. As soon as you start to focus on the detail, it loses its meaning. You cannot emphasise details. I solved this problem in* **Room 14** *by showing the process of drawing in a video, so that you see the details which were worth showing. In this way, I involve the viewer in my space and in the things that fascinate me. But I also want to lead him out of the space again. At the end of the performance, I saw a piece out of the floor and climb down through the hole I have made. It is only then that the viewer, frightened by the sound of sawing, can see that I am sitting on a raised area above.*

I have now carried out this idea in three different locations. I started at the DeFKa [Department for Philosophy and Art] in Assen. I then presented it as a work for my final examination, and I have also performed it at the Fons Welters Gallery in Amsterdam. These three versions had the same duration as it took me to make the different drawings. I also leave all the films running continuously so that visitors can come into the film at an arbitrary moment. **Room 3** *is a literal translation of the concept of 'showing the viewer around in my vision.' At the same time, I also give him the freedom to determine which route he will take. I do not want to impose anything. Nevertheless, I have noticed that a certain route, or the order in which you look around, can greatly increase the impact of the work and the viewer's experience of the space. A long building process works also very well in the performanc: in this way, I create a sort of distance and perhaps also an element of objectivity. A work of art should not be served as a ready-to-eat meal: you should work towards something slowly."*

How do you work? *"I always start with the space itself. I do not know exactly what I am looking for beforehand, but it emerges automatically while I am looking around.*

*I do not have a specific end result in my head.
The idea is constantly changing, or in other
words, I never know exactly when the end
has been reached. Nevertheless, an artist
has to decide at a certain moment when it is
time to stop. Sometimes, another work also
emerges from a process. I am not so much
looking for a particular experience which
a viewer must have, or an emotion which
he should feel. Many of these elements only
appear halfway through the creative process
or afterwards. I look at a room in a certain
way on the basis of my own view and logic.
The viewer does not have to notice the same
details as I do; perhaps he will not notice
certain details at all, or he will actually see
things which I did not see. I only give some
indications."*

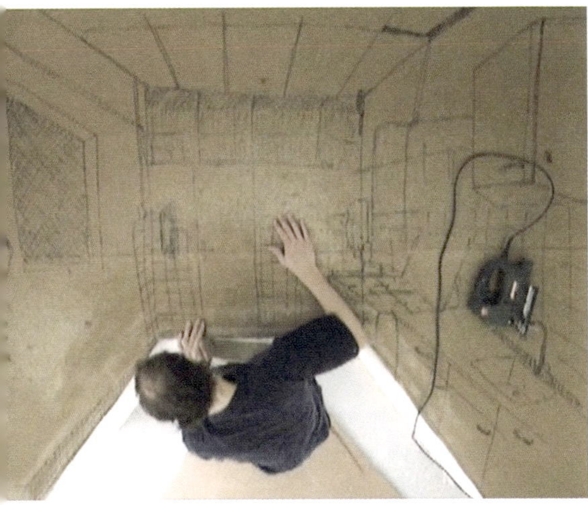

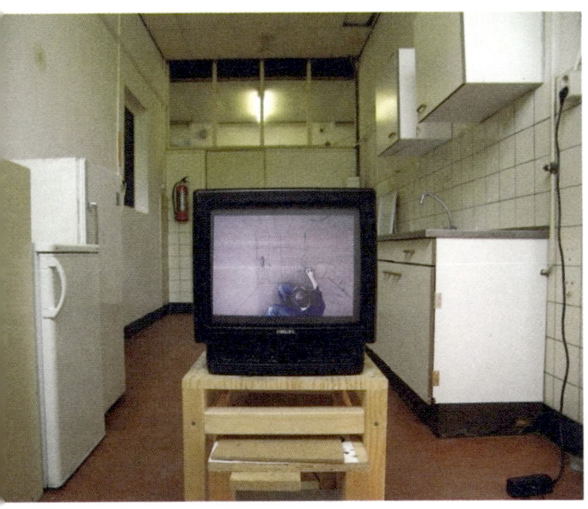

In the introduction to your thesis,
you noted that in writing it, you were
inspired by the Flemish poet and writer
Paul van Ostaijen (1896-1928) and the
American writer Mark Z. Danielewski
(1966). This is particularly noticeable in
the design; the words and letters are
spread across the pages. As you say
yourself: "The text becomes a picture,
every detail is important, even if its
presence and intention are not always
equally clear." You also indicate the difference between someone who thinks
in images and someone who thinks
in language. A thinker in images may
find that his ideas twist and turn, have
difficulty with formulating ideas, and
see connections which another person
would not see. You clearly see yourself
as an 'image thinker'. What does this
mean for you? *"My ideas do twist and
turn. I talk too much and not clearly enough,
but I am also very consciously working with
language, despite a slight degree of dyslexia.
My grammar is not good; language is not my
strongest point. But I deliberately include this
in my thoughts and writing. It is not the case
that I have images in my head which I then
translate into a text. It is more that there is
a world of difference between what I think
and what I actually write down. Language
is just as much a material as paint, but I
use language differently. I deliberately did
not use any pictures in my thesis, in contrast
with what everybody would probably expect.
I described the images in my head, as a sort
recipes, so that I can evoke these images in
the reader through language. In this way my
thesis is a 'linguistic' work on the one hand,
and a 'visual' work on the other hand."*

In your thesis you play with rules. Normally we read a book from left to right,
one page after another. In your book,
we first have to read all the left hand
pages, then the right hand pages, and
then we have to fold out the right hand
pages again. Repetition also plays an
important role. You describe the same
space nine times, but each time you focus on different details. The reader has
to follow you into your world in order to
understand it all. A 'language thinker'

has to follow you into your world of images, even if you describe that world in language. With the definition of the 'image thinker', you absolve yourself from any criticism. This happens to be the way you are, so we cannot criticise you for this. Is this Alex Winters the 'image thinker' against the rest, who are 'language thinkers'? *"I would like to be 'normal' in the usual way. Nevertheless, 'being normal' is not such a good thing either because it is imposed on you from outside. The majority of people call themselves normal while they are just as different for me as I am for them. Suddenly you belong to a minority, the misunderstood, because they say so. I do not understand that and I do not want to un-*

derstand it either. By playing with the rules, I am playing with the limits of normality. In my thesis I write: "In my work it is my truth which is used purely in accordance with my own rules." Nevertheless, I am constantly changing these 'rules'. For example, I decided for myself that I never wanted to work for longer than one hour a day. This rule reassures me, but at the same time I easily break it. I am not very consistent. I do not carry out the rule, but I do live by it. Rules are my starting points, but when I stack them all up what comes out is usually very different from what I had expected. For example, I once decided on my birthday to put all sorts of things on my bread that I like: peanut butter, liquorice and herring, like a sort of mathemati-

Both images below:

Alex Winters, Room 3, 2006, Latex & acrylic on wood, 275 x 700 x 500 cm, Courtesy Galerie Fons Welters

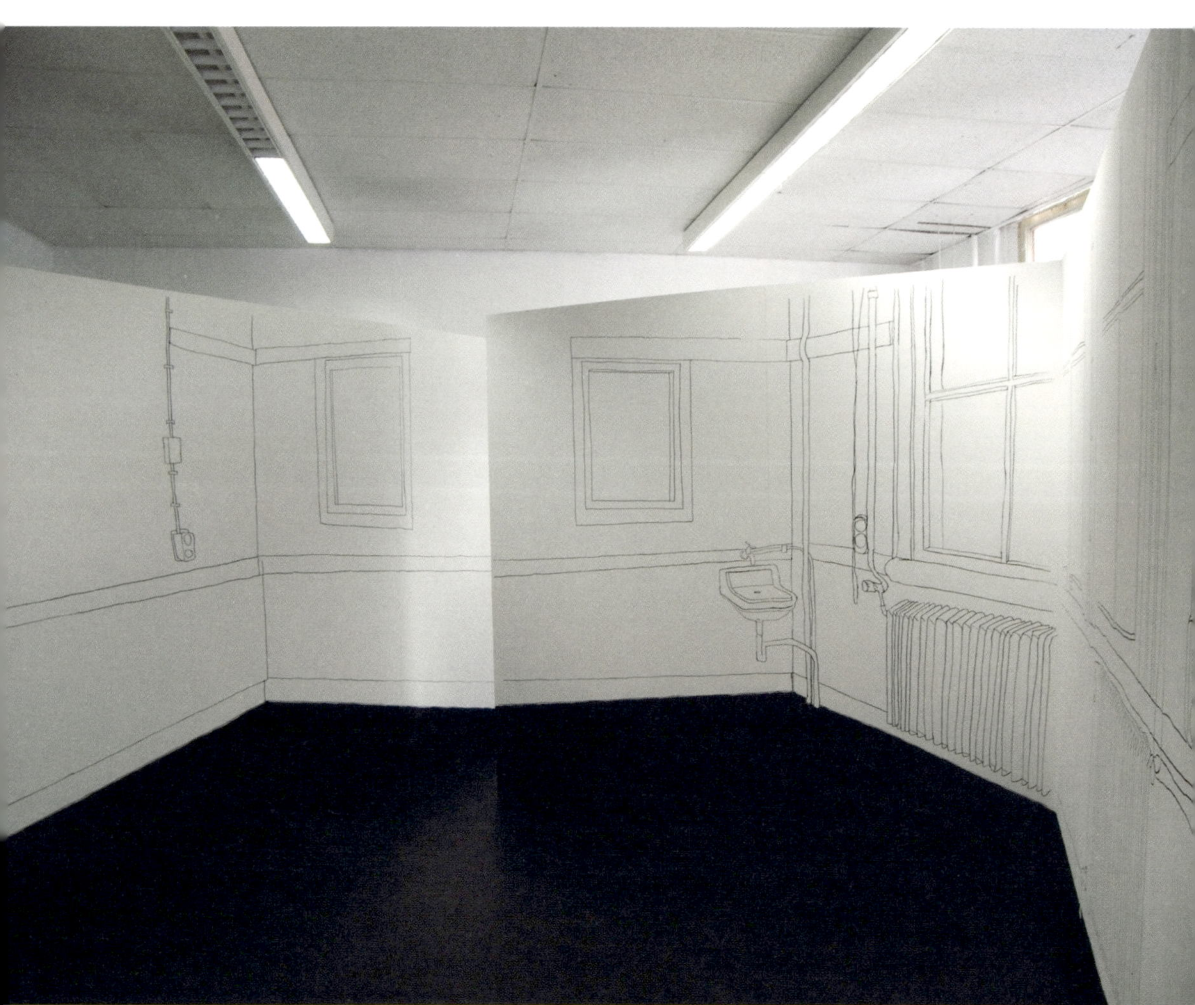

cal addition. Obviously, that sandwich was inedible. Nevertheless, in retrospect I thought it was very surprising because I like eating all those things, but when you put them together it is horrible: 1 + 1 = -3, or -4 or -5. It was a playful way of finding this out."

Both your thesis and this interview show me that you have got to know yourself very well in the past few years. You can talk about yourself and your work clearly and you are confident enough to start a work without knowing where the creative process is taking you. You make rules, but when necessary you bend or abandon them altogether. And you managed to use your 'problems' with language to your advantage. What did the MFA Painting course do for your creative development? Do you consider that you have grown during your training at the Frank Mohr Institute? *"I think I have become more focused, although it is obviously difficult to know whether this is a result of my training. I do think that the Frank Mohr Institute helped me to develop more quickly. After the Minerva Academy, I had reached a certain level and I used what I learned for two years. I could have continued in that way until I was sixty five, but that is not what I wanted. I went to the FMI with a number of empty boxes, and I said that I wanted to fill them. Now I think much more about how I want to do certain things. That is partly*

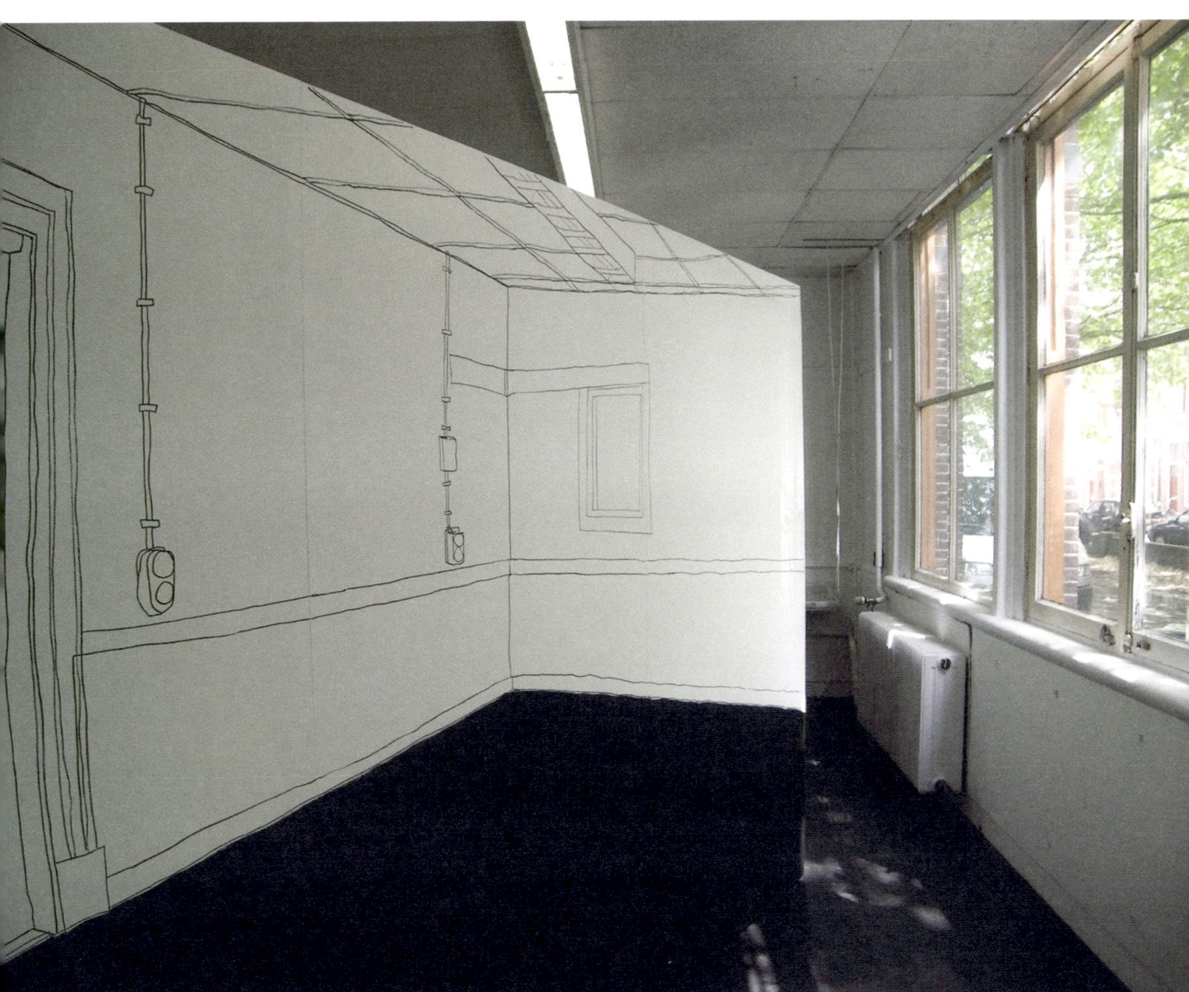

*because there were students in the last year
of the course who did not speak Dutch, so
English automatically became the language
used during the presentations. English is not
my strongest subject, so I had to think much
more about exactly what I wanted to say; in
that way you become more aware of yourself.
Another good thing about this sort of course
is the way in which the tutors reflect on your
work. I needed that. You start to talk to others and then you have to acquire a position
and defend it. You learn to talk much more
about your work. Your work leaves the studio
and you can learn from your mistakes. On
the one hand, you can safely experiment
within the walls of the institute, while on the
other hand, you are immediately judged by
your tutors. They keep you awake. For me,
the difference between the academy and the
FMI is that when I left the academy, I had the
sense that I could still decide to take an office
job. But after the FMI, I have now definitively
decided to be an artist."*

MFA Scenography

Alumni   *Marloes van der Hoek*
Wikke van Houwelingen
Marieke Küttschreutter

Research in theatre practice

Linda Nijenhof

"During their training, theatre makers should be prepared to reflect and carry out research into the professional practice. This is partly a question of 'attitude', partly a question of teaching some skills, and partly also a matter of showing them a way into the academic world. With the introduction of the Bachelor/Master-structure the climate for practice-oriented research will gradually improve in the next generations."[1]

This wish and prediction was expressed during a round table discussion which took place in 2003, and was devoted to 'practice-oriented research' in the world of Dutch theatre and dance.[2] According to the partners in this discussion, the moderate level of enthusiasm for this type of research was partly caused by the tradition of relatively short production processes in Dutch theatre practice. A production process of two months is too short to carry out research, and consequently there is usually little chance for any reflection on the working process and the methods used. To remedy this it would be necessary to break through these short cycles, and give a place to 'practice-oriented research' in the new master's degrees.[3] Within this context there is space, time and artistic freedom to devote attention to reflection and research.

The above-mentioned reference gives the impression that courses in the field of the dramatic arts (at least in 2003) still devoted insufficient attention to reflection and research. By coincidence, it was actually in 2002 that the Frank Mohr Institute in Groningen introduced a new course, the MFA Scenography. The development of an enquiring attitude and analytical skills are two set elements in the curriculum of the course. Furthermore, it includes following various series of lectures at the University of Groningen on the history of theatre, current developments in the theatre and the philosophy of art, resulting in a dialogue with students and lecturers from the university world. Is this the sort of thing that was envisaged by the participants in the round table discussion? Does this prepare a budding theatre maker for the 'practice-oriented research' in professional practice? And what is actually meant by 'practice-oriented research'?

Recently there are discussions on 'research in the arts', the 'artist as researcher' and 'practice-oriented versus scientific research'. Henk Borgdorff says that these discussions are held particularly in the world of the visual arts and design. In his view they are much less common in the field of the dramatic arts.[4] However, Lucia van Heteren points out that in recent years the term 'research' is increasingly explicitly used in descriptions of theatre practice.[5] According to Van Heteren: "Sometimes this notion appears to be synonymous with the creative process itself ('Every creative process is a research'), in other cases it appears to be concerned with a special form of theatre, a certain attitude of theatre makers or a specific use of theatrical media."[6]

In his article, 'Het debat over onderzoek in de kunsten', (The debate on research in the arts), Henk Borgdorff addresses the question of 'research in the arts' in detail. He divides practice-based research in

[1] *Laurien Saraber, 'Verslag ronde tafelgesprek praktijkgericht onderzoek in theater en dans', (Report on the round table discussion on practice-oriented research in theatre and dance), 4,25,2003, chaired by Bart van Rosmalen, http://www.fapk.nl/verslagen/Rondetafelgesprek25april2003.pdf, Consulted on 12,14,2006.*

[2] *Ibid.*

[3] *Ibid.*

[4] *Henk Borgdorff has been a lecturer in 'Artistic theory and research' at the Amsterdamse Hogeschool voor de Kunsten, (Amsterdam Institute of Higher education for the Arts) since 2002. H. Borgdorff, 'Het debat over onderzoek in de kunsten', (The debate on research in the arts), in: M. Bleeker, L. van Heteren, C. Kattenbelt, K. Vuyk, (ed.), Theater Topics. De*

[5] *Lucia van Heteren is assistant professor in theatre sciences in the course Arts, Culture and Media at the University of Groningen. She is also the co-founder of the MFA Scenography course at the Frank Mohr Institute and one of the composers of the series, Theater Topics. Ibid, pp. 9-14, 10.*

[6] *Ibid.*

the arts into three types: research *into the* arts, research *for* the arts and research *in* the arts.[7] Research into the arts has the artistic practice in all its aspects as its research object. The aim is to express valid conclusions about this practice with a certain theoretical distance. "Ideally the theoretical distance implies a division in principle and a certain distance between the researcher and what is researched. The rule which applies is the idea that the object to be researched remains unaffected, under the enquiring eye."[8] Within this type of research there are no interventions in the artistic practice. 'Reflection' and 'interpretation' are characteristic of this approach and this type of research is found above all in academic artistic disciplines, such as theatre science. Borgdorff calls this the 'interpretative position'.[9]

Research *for* the arts is applied research in a narrower sense. It is important that it is carried out to serve artistic practice. "The research leads to insights and instruments which can in some way be used in concrete practices."[10] For example, this could be an examination of live electronics in the interaction between a performer and light design. "The research provides the tools and the material knowledge, as it were, which are used during the creative process or in the art product."[11] Borgdorff calls this the 'instrumental position.'

The 'performance position', i.e., research *in* the arts, is a combination of artistic practice and research. The artistic practice itself is an important part of "both the research process and its result."[12] In this approach it is assumed that in the arts there is in principle no distinction between theory and practice. "After all, there are no practices which are not steeped in experiences, histories and opinions, and conversely there is no theoretical access to or interpretation of practice which does not contribute to making that practice what it is. Concepts and theories, experiences and insights, are interwoven with artistic practices, and this also means that art is always reflexive. Research *in* the arts now aims to articulate something of this embodied knowledge through the creative process and in the art object."[13] Borgdorff states that it is precisely the artist who can carry out this research best. As a result the above-mentioned division in principle between the researcher and the researched becomes blurred. This effect is increased because the research usually also serves the development of the 'artist-researcher'. However, Borgdorff argues that there are limits to this. "When the impact of the research is restricted to the artist's own work and has no significance for the wider research environment, the question can justifiably be raised whether this concerns research in a real sense."[14]

In the above-mentioned round table discussion, three different types of 'practice-oriented research' were also identified in the dramatic arts: 'the development of a personal signature', 'the pre-production research' and 'thematic reflections'.[15]

For the 'the development of a personal signature', the development of the maker is central. *Generale Oost* and *Gasthuis*, two theatre workplaces which particularly give theatre makers starting out an opportunity for practical research, state that research processes of these theatre makers have an individual character and focus on their own 'artistic profile'. More experienced theatre makers are increasingly able to relate research to their own environment or to developments within a style.[16]

[7] *Borgdorff bases the division into types of research on the threefold distinction made by Christopher Frayling: 're-search into art', 'research for art' and 'research through art', in: C. Frayling, 'Research in art and design', in: Royal College of Art Research Papers series I, London, 1993.*

[8] *H. Borgdorff, 'Het debat over onderzoek in de kunsten', (The debate on research in the arts), in: M. Bleeker, L. van Heteren, C. Kattenbelt, K. Vuyk, (ed.), Theater Topics. De theatermaker als onderzoeker, (Theatre Topics. The theatre maker as researcher) Amsterdam 2006, pp. 21- 39, 24.*

[9] *Ibid.*

[10] *Ibid.*

[11] *Ibid, 25.*

[12] *Ibid.*

[13] *Ibid.*

[14] *Ibid, 32. As in research into the arts, Borgdorff wonders what the difference is between artistic practice as such and artistic practice as research. In this respect he provides the following description: "Artisitic practice counts as research when the intention is to increase our knowledge and understanding by means of an original study of and with art objects and creative processes. This starts with questions that are relevant in the research environment and in the art world. Experimental and hermeneutical methods are used which reveal and articulate the implicit knowledge present in and characterizing individual works of art and artistic processes. The research process and the results are adequately documented and disseminated to the research community and the general public." Ibid, 33.*

[15] *The full name for this is 'professional research, thematic reflection.*

[16] *Yet experienced theatre makers could also benefit from more individually oriented research, for example, because in practice they do not always have complete freedom in making artistic choices. For example, time for research in the protected environment of a second stage of training could provide a solution. From: Laurien Saraber, 'Verslag ronde tafelgesprek praktijkgericht onderzoek in theater en dans', (Report of the round table discussion on practice-oriented research in theatre and dance), 4,25,2003, chaired by Bart van Rosmalen, http://www. fapk. nl/verslagen/ Rondetafelgesprek25april2003. pdf, consulted on 12,14,2006.'*

The 'pre-production research' is carried out in preparation for a production. It examines whether the intended artistic process is feasible. In many cases this form of research is the process of bringing together different theatrical means. Production companies are more often involved in this type of research than workshops.[17]

The 'thematic reflection' focuses more on specific themes, such as the position of 'theatre in society' or 'location theatre'. The choice of subject is inspired by developments in the theatre and can therefore be separate from the development of the maker's own productions. According to the partners in the discussion, it is paramount to choose for subjects which are important in the field.[18] The partners in the round table discussion did not talk about what these subjects might be.

A series of statements by theatre makers contained in *Theatre Topics no. 2*, reveals that many theatre makers see their work as a form of research. Again and again they look for subjects related to the problems of the contemporary age, they collect material, analyse it and cast it in an appropriate form.[19] Gerardjan Rijnders states: "It is certainly possible to indicate processes and moments in the theatre for which the word 'research' is appropriate. For example, this could be groups trying to develop their own new form of theatre during a series of different performances. Every new production refers to and builds on the last one. You could say that it is a matter of continuous research into an yet unknown almost utopian theatre."[20] Marianne van Kerkhoven states that there are many urgent and interesting research tasks which exist in the arts: "The new paradigm that we need in the artistic language can be achieved only in practice with a constant interaction between trying things out and questioning them, between creating and reflecting on what has been created. The repertoire of contemporary man is the world, and today the artist is one of its most passionate researchers."[21]

Following the outline given above of different types of 'practice-oriented research', I would like to return to the MFA Scenography course of the Frank Mohr Institute and to the question of how this course prepares future theatre producers to reflect and carry out research in their professional work. It would be interesting to discuss all the types of research which are carried out in the MFA Scenography. However, as this would be a study in itself, I will restrict myself to the 'research' in the context of the final theoretical work. What is the character of this work, do different types of 'research' emerge, and how do these relate to the 'practice-oriented research' described above?

The MFA Scenography is the latest addition to the courses of the Frank Mohr Institute, and was founded in order to provide students from art and academic courses with greater depth in terms of subjects and individual experience in scenography in the widest sense of the word.[22] The course is based on the assumption that the theatrical space does not exist only within the walls of a theatre, and that designing a set requires a different relationship to space than designing a flat stage, musical theatre, dance performances, or theatre performed on location. Virtual and film environments, theatrical installations and performances also require their own interpretation

[17] *Production companies particularly 'serve' independent theatre producers who cannot work on their own permanent structure, for whatever reason, and therefore need a place to work and perform for every production, as well as needing support for the production". Council for Culture, Cultuur, meer dan ooit. Vooradvies 2005-2008. Sector theater, (Culture, more than ever. Preliminary advice 2005-2008. Theatre sector), The Hague 2003, p.16.*

[18] *During the round table discussion it was noted that this sort of reflective research is often carried out in academic education, professional training and in umbrella organizations, such as the Netherlands Theatre Institute. Laurien Saraber, 'Verslag ronde tafelgesprek praktijkgericht onderzoek in theater en dans', (Report of the round table discussion on practice-oriented research in theatre and dance), 25 April 2003 chaired by Bart van Rosmalen, http://www.fapk.nl/verslagen/Rondetafelgesprek25april2003.pdf, consulted on 12,14, 2006.*

[19] *M. Bleeker, L. van Heteren, C. Kattenbelt, K. Vuyk, (red.), Theater Topics. De theatermaker als onderzoeker, (Theatre Topics: the theatre maker as researcher), Amsterdam 2006, p. 14.*

[20] *Gerardjan Rijnders is a director, actor and playwright. He works for the theatre, radio, film and television. Ibid, pp.16-17.*

[21] *Marianne van Kerkhoven is a dramatist with the Kaaitheater (Brussels) and HetNet (Bruges). She was the editor-in-chief of the journal **Theaterschrift** and was part of the editorial team of Etcetera, ibid, 19.*

[22] *The MFA Scenography course was founded in 2002 by Lucia van Heteren, Sjoerd Wagenaar and Petri Leijdekkers. The text on MFA Scenography is mainly based on and partly taken from: Beleidsnota, Frank Mohr Instituut 2005-2009, Visie, Onderwijs en Personeel, (Policy memorandum, Frank Mohr Institute 2005-2009, Vision, Education and Staff).*

of space. Therefore the student learns to design all sorts of possible spaces using his vision and imagination. The course programme consists of a combination of practice and theory, own research and practical projects. One of the starting points which was formulated when setting up the course was that practice benefits from theory: "The individual design, creation and execution of ideas require creativity, spatial insight and design skills, but also a theoretical insight. In the course, reflecting on their own work and the work of others is very important for students, and they learn to place both their own and other people's work in the broader context of historical developments on the basis of theoretical and historical study."[23]
Within various interviews with former students of the Frank Mohr Institute included in this publication the thesis is mentioned. The possibility of writing a thesis as a final theoretical work was recently introduced for the MFA Scenography course, in addition to the already existing practice of writing an essay. In an essay the student studies a subject in depth and writes a subjective treatise on it. The student could read texts on philosophy (of art) and (art) criticism, and study the work and ideas of other (theatre) makers to gain a greater insight into the subject. There is also room to reflect on the student's own work. These own projects are discussed in the light of the main topic. In an essay the student adopts a personal position and puts forward good arguments for it in relation to the subject, or argues for a specific approach in artistic practice. For example, Wikke van Houwelingen argues for visual theatre on the basis of four concepts, which are important for him in theatre: mystery, dynamics, spectacle and contrast. He states that: "I want to champion THE IMAGE, which admittedly serves what has to be expressed, but is equal to text and acting. I would like to fight for devoting attention to design. I call this visual awareness."[24] The choice for the subject of the essay is usually inspired by the student's own interests, occasionally the subject also corresponds to a topical debate in the theatre world. For example, this is the case for the study by Marloes van der Hoek into 'topical theatre'. In recent years the subjects of the essays have ranged from 'The interrelationship between football and contingency', 'Escapism' to 'Visual theater'.[25] In some cases an essay forms the theoretical support for a final production. In other cases the emphasis is more on expressing a personal vision, and the student's own work plays a role only in the background.
The essay particularly responds to the above-mentioned 'thematic reflection' as a form of 'practice-oriented research'. After all, this form of reflection focuses on specific topics. However, the fact that the choice of the topic is inspired by developments in the theatre, and can in principle be separate, for example, from the student's own productions, does not seem logical in the context of the MFA Scenography course. Practice shows that the research is always related, albeit to a greater or lesser extent, to the student's own work. However, even then, the topic can obviously be the result of development in the theatre and can deal with topics 'which are important for the field'. In contrast with the essay, the thesis expresses a strong reflective attitude to the student's own work.[26] Therefore a thesis contains reflections on the student's working methods, the sources of inspira-

[23] Ibid.

[24] Wikke van Houwelingen, *Zoeken naar levend decor. Een pleidooi voor beeldend theater, (Looking for a living set. An argument for visual theatre)*, Groningen 2006, p. 11.

[25] 'The interrelationship between football and contingency' is described in *Gott ist Rund, (God is Round)*, by Heiner S. Behrends, 'Escapism' is the subject of *The land of pure imagination* by Renske Vera de Kam and 'Visual theatre' is discussed in *Zoeken naar levend decor. Een pleidooi voor beeldend theater, (Looking for a living set. An argument for visual theatre)* by Wikke van Houwelingen.

[26] In the article 'Bête comme une peintre' Katalin Herzog explains how the MFA Painting course of the Frank Mohr Institute determines the content of the thesis. The ideas formulated here on the thesis are therefore taken from K.E. Herzog, *Show me the moves. Essays for the MFA Painting of the Frank Mohr Institute*, Groningen 2005, pp. 17-21, 20-21.

tion, the artistic goals, the theoretical starting points, the relationship to the audience, and the student's own position in the artistic field.[27] Theatre makers starting out in the MFA Scenography course are confronted in the preparation for the thesis with learning to analyse their own work and questioning and reflecting on their working methods, artistic goals, and so forth. Most of the time students find it useful to adopt an enquiring attitude. With the title 'I act', Marieke Küttschreutter wrote the following: "I'm increasingly aware that following my work, looking at and following the steps I take and the choices I make, make me more aware and more precise as a creator."[28]

The reflections, which are of a subjective nature, are related to reflections on the history of art, the theory of art and scientific reflections. While an essay is more of a running text, Katalin Herzog considers that a thesis, as practiced at the Frank Mohr Institute, is comparable to a file of texts and images. The texts differ in character. The students' own texts could be descriptions of their work, statements, critiques, analyses of productions or poetic texts. In the thesis also comments on texts and quotations of others could be included. In addition to texts, it is also possible to show the students' own positions, aims and sources of inspiration visually, while the design of the thesis should also correspond to the character of the work.[29] The research that is carried out in the context of the thesis both follows and guides; on the one hand, it describes developments retrospectively, on the other hand, it provides the material and insight that can be used in the future.

It was stated above that 'the development of a personal signature' takes place particularly in individually oriented research for theatre makers starting out. The thesis consists of individually oriented research by definition, and contains reflections on the student's own artistic practice. However, I am not sure to what extent a thesis makes a substantial contribution to a personal signature. Despite the fact that a thesis can also focus on (subject specific) topics, and can therefore be related to the 'thematic reflection' as a form of 'practice-oriented research', the choice of this sort of topic is more often inspired by the student's own work and interests than by 'developments in theatre that are important for the field'. Therefore the 'thematic reflection' in the thesis is emphatically related to the individually oriented research.

Not all the types of 'practice-based' research, distinguished by Borgdorff, are applicable. The research *into* the arts appears to be the furthest away from the research carried out in a thesis. After all, a distinction in principle between the researcher and the researched is desirable, and this does not tally with a theatre maker who reflects on his own artistic practice. Furthermore, making 'applicable', i.e., verifiable, statements about one's own artistic practice does not have priority in the thesis. Moreover it is not unusual for a theatre maker to intervene in the artistic practice while making the thesis. The research *for* the arts particularly appears to take place as part of the production process for a performance, for example, for the application of modeling and animation programmes in the design of a virtual space. Of the three types of 'practice-based' research distin-

[27] *Ibid.*

[28] *Marieke Küttschreutter, Bewerk, laat duren, manipuleer, maak zichtbaar, (Process, leave, manipulate, reveal), Groningen 2006, pp. 11-12.*

[29] *K.E. Herzog, Show me the moves. Essays for the MFA Painting of the Frank Mohr Institute, Groningen 2005, pp. 17-21, 20-21.*

guished by Borgdorff, the 'performance position', i.e., the research in the arts, appears particularly important. The maker 'examines' his own artistic practice, and the research in the thesis particularly serves the artistic development of the 'artist-researcher'. Borgdorff states that when the research serves only the maker's own work, and is not significant for the wider research environment, it is questionable whether this is research in a real sense. At the moment two MFA Scenography students are working, each in their own way, on a series of performances which are emphatically conceived as part of a continuing piece of research. Their intention is that their own performance(s) should also serve as case studies in this research. Insights obtained from the study of the theory and practice are processed in a visual form. This form is then analysed on the basis of a theoretical framework developed by the students themselves, the 'insights' obtained are processed again and so forth. It is not yet possible to say whether this will provide insights which are not only significant for the students' own work, but also in a broader context. However, it is clear to me that in addition to the research in the thesis and the essay, steps are taken in another type of research. At the time of writing this article it is not yet clear what the nature of this research is.

This account is based on my experiences as a tutor of theory for the MFA Scenography course at the Frank Mohr Institute. These are recent experiences and the field of theatre and theatre design is relatively new to me. Furthermore, there are only a small number of final theoretical projects on which I can base my views. Nevertheless, I have found that the nature of the research carried out is very diverse and has a strong individual character. This may be an obvious conclusion. Avoiding limitations and classifications is a characteristic feature of contemporary art forms, and therefore the research related to these. Instead of obeying criteria imposed in advance, art produces the criteria itself with which research should comply for each individual project, every time.[30]

[30] This idea is borrowed from Borgdorff. He describes the 'prevailing' idea that it is precisely this typical character of art and the research related to it that characterises the difference from scientific research. However, according to Borgdorff, this view is based on a 'specific and limited interpretation of what science is'. H. Borgdorff, 'Het debat over onderzoek in de kunsten', (The debate on research in the arts), in: M. Bleeker, L. van Heteren, C. Kattenbelt, K. Vuyk, (red.), *Theater Topics. De theatermaker als onderzoeker,* (Theatre Topics. The theatre maker as researcher', Amsterdam 2006, pp. 21-39, 25.

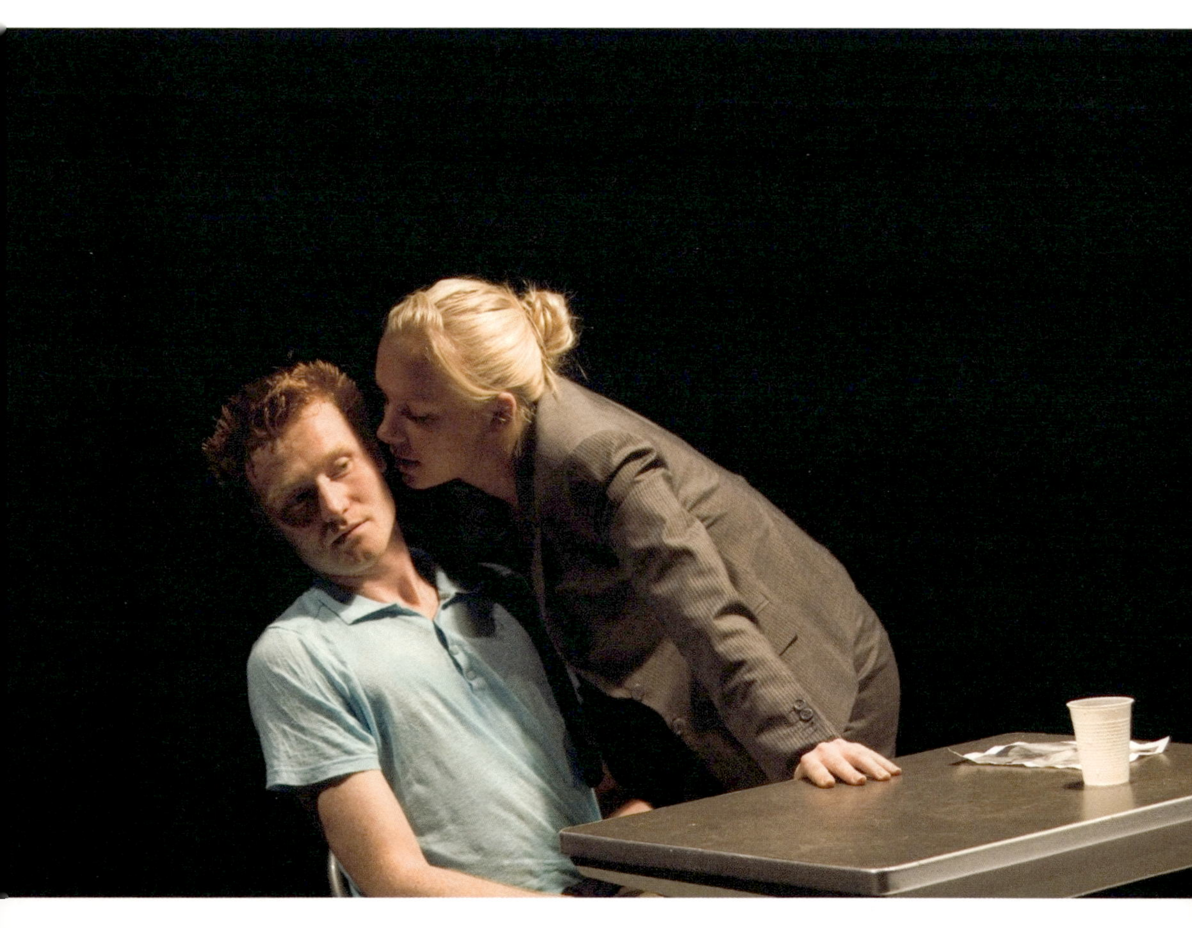

Marloes van der Hoek

The spectacle of current affairs
An interview with Marloes van der Hoek
by Natalja Oosterbaan

An illuminated platform on an otherwise dark stage stands uncomfortably lopsided, sloping downwards. On it is a school desk with a chair. Dark circular lines have been painted on the platform and one can also see dotted lines. They seem to be telling a story, although it is unclear what it is about. Then three persons appear: a young boy dressed casually, a young woman in a grey suit and a young man also in a suit. The boy sits down at the school desk, the woman is standing in the circle on the right. The second man stands in the dark behind the platform and watches the scene. Behind him appears a third man who silently observes what is happening.

All images:

Marloes van der Hoek, Snelcursus Onschuld, 2006, Concept, Text and Scenography, Photo: Harold Koopmans

This description concerns the beginning of the theatre performance: **Snelcursus Onschuld** (Quick Course in Innocence). The piece focusses on interrogation. The boy, who is the suspect, is summoned for a crime he knows nothing about. It is the woman interrogator's first day at the job, and she is determined to make him confess. In the continuation of the piece she changes tactics rapidly. The suspect is belittled and mocked, overwhelmed with detailed and suggestive questions, and then again spoken to sweetly. He is alternatively put at his ease and goaded to agitation. It has drummed into him that other people have made incriminating testimonies against him, but that there is nothing the matter as long as he confesses. His sense of responsibility and good character is taken advantage of, and he is spat upon. Everything passes off like a strange symbolic ritual, without becoming implausible or clichéd. A tense psychological game is played which becomes even more complex as the interrogation scenes alternate with scenes in which the interrogator herself is cross-examined by her supervisor who emerges now and then from the darkness.

Your final project *Snelcursus Onschuld* focusses on interrogation. What made you choose this subject and what are the theatrical possibilities of it?

"During my studies at the MFA Scenography course I became fascinated by stories about abuses in American prisons and the problems faced by the Dutch police and justice system. I read an article by Susan Sontag about the Abu Ghraib and Guantanamo Bay prisons, and the numbers of people, guilty or innocent, being detained there. In her article Sontag deals specifically with the phenomenon of arbitrary interrogation. She asks herself to what degree it is permissible for a society to sacrifice individual freedom for state security, and whether this actually does result in real security. I was affected by this and I started to think that an interrogation could be an interesting theme for a theatre project. It is a universal theme with great social relevance as it touches on many ethical issues. For example, it concerns the political debate about security versus the right to privacy, surveillance, preventive body-searches, interrogation methods and false confessions.

I got interested in the interrogation methods used by the police in questioning witnesses and obtaining statements. I started reading accounts of police interrogations and manuals, as well as transcripts of actual interrogations that had led to false confessions. In reading this material, it occurred to me that an interrogation is almost a ritual: a sequence of actions and questions with a clear purpose. The theatrical aspect of this dawned upon me. The interrogator performs almost like an actor, playing different roles aimed at getting the suspect to talk. I wanted to know more about how someone can be systematically manipulated to tell the 'truth'. This was an interesting paradox, and the following questions came up in my mind: Why do you tell lies in order to make someone else speak the truth, and what is the truth than? How can you still say whether or not justice is based on truth? And do statements acquired in such a way in fact still count as evidence? This whole area interests me, particularly the manipulative techniques that are used. It amazed me that there are manuals describing, almost scientifically, how someone can be manipulated.

> *Some of the interrogation techniques I came across have suggestive, almost lugubrious names. There is the 'Alice in Wonderland' technique, where the suspect is completely disorientated. Or the 'Wolves in Sheep's Clothing' technique. And the 'Good Cop/Bad Cop' routine which evereybody knows, whereby one of the interrogators adopts an aggressive attitude, belittles and threatens the suspect, while the other pretends to be sympathetic, friendly and understanding, so as to entice the suspect into taking the interrogator into confidence. There are numerous techniques that policemen can switch to, and for me that is where the theatrical aspect is involved..*

> *The interrogators are constantly taking on different roles and in this way creating theatre. The whole set-up as well is staged. The type of chair the suspect sits on, for example, is very deliberately chosen. Are you manipulating the suspect psychologically by having him sit in a really comfortable chair or on an unstable stool? And where do you then place it in relation to the interrogators? Thus it all has to do with staging. What I wanted to do was to represent my interest in this theatrical aspect of interrogation in a play, and at the same time to bring it up for discussion."*

How did you get from this starting point to a theatrical performance? *"The most important starting point for the piece were the interrogation manuals and transcripts that I studied. These served as the basis for the text. The main point I was trying to make was how stories and events can be reconstructed during interrogations; about what someone really remembers and what someone can start believing through inter-*

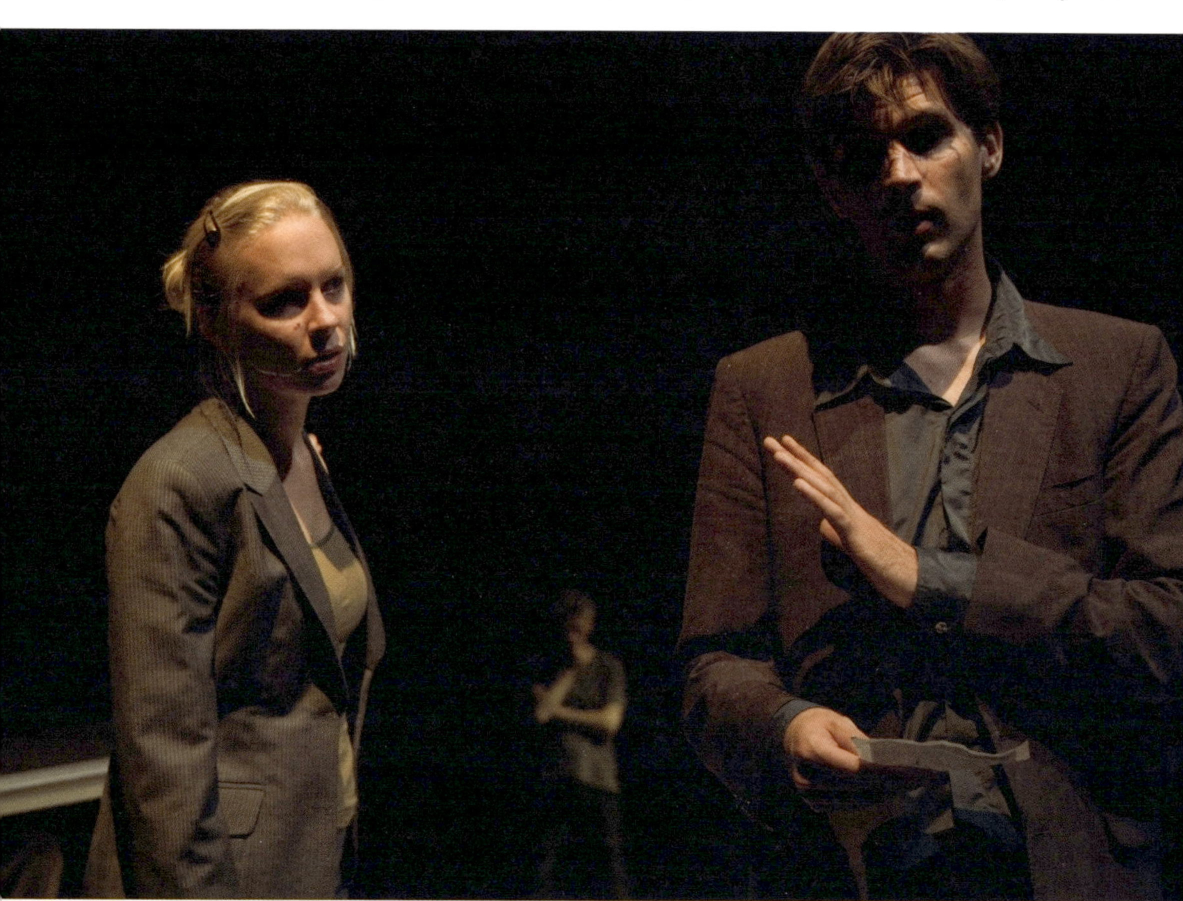

rogation techniques. On the basis of this my characters underwent an interrogation and a meta-interrogation. The meta-interrogation calls to account not only the interrogation techniques and the circumstances that are applied, but also the interrogator herself. In this way I wanted to introduce reflection into the piece."

How does the subject relate to the design of the piece? Can the sloping platform be seen as a symbol for the changing roles of the characters? *"Yes it does, but I arrived at first at that sloping form, because I wanted to get a strange perspective and a feeling of confinement appropriate to the situation. It made it more difficult for the actors to strike a pose and this physical effort corresponded nicely with their psychic condition. Since the surface is so white and so clearly stands out against the dark background, it also becomes a sort of*

dissecting table that the audience is literally looking upon. In my piece I dissect an interrogation, as it were. The circles and lines are derived from existing floor plans used during an interrogation. The circles indicate where the suspect, the witness and the lawyer are supposed to be seated in certain cases and the dotted lines indicate the desired lines of sight. I further wanted to keep the stage as sober as possible, without references to a Dutch police station, for example. That would have detracted from the illusion that this is a situation of all times and places. An illuminated stage is in any case a magical surface for me. Everything that lies or happens within it acquires extra emphasis and hence a new meaning. This is why an undefinable space on the stage seems to me to have perhaps even more power than a definable one."

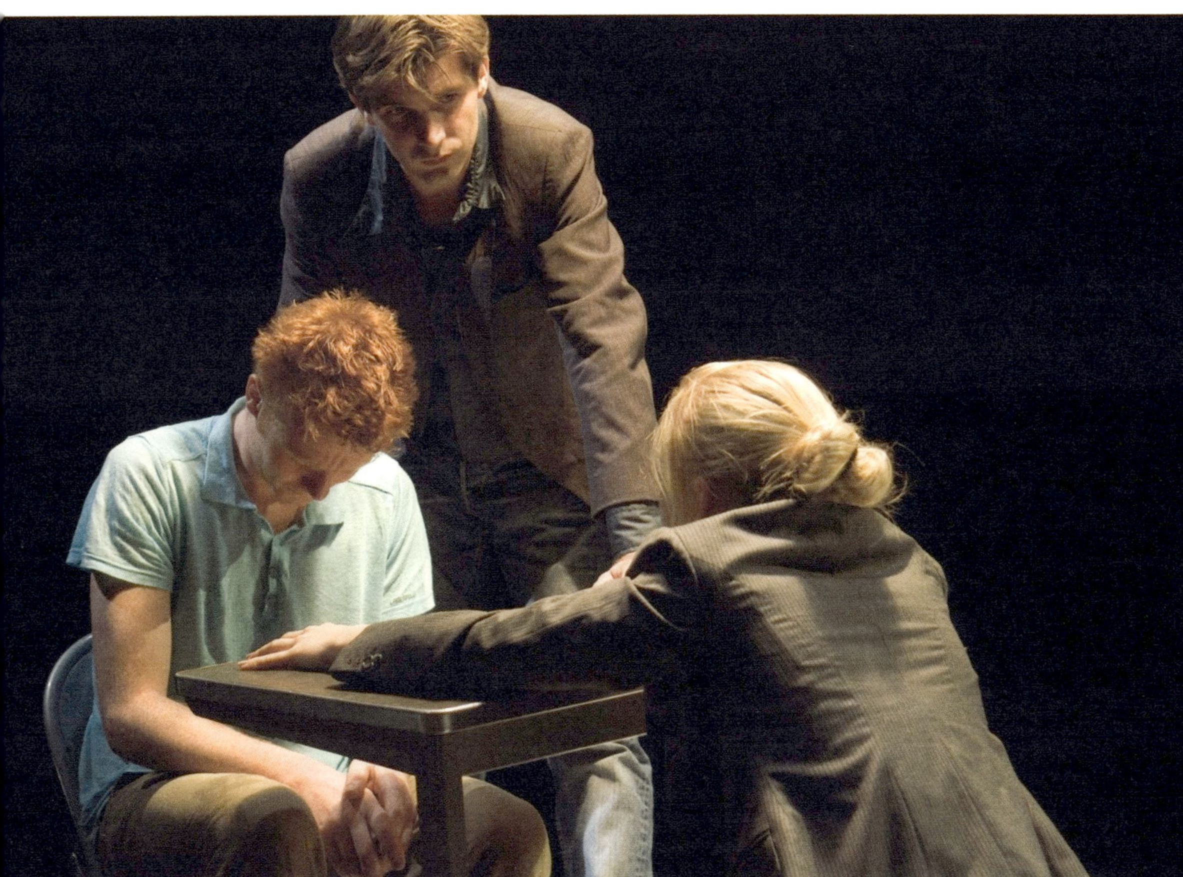

In your essay you describe the interrogation as a "ritual in a post-democratic society". What do you mean by this?
"With the term 'post-democratic society' I am referring to what I see as the extreme emphasis on security in our society. The government is gaining more and more possibilities to trace our private lives at the cost of our personal freedom. The suspect in my piece is summoned for an interrogation without there being any real evidence of his guilt. Although I did not want to make it a visionary piece, I do fear that in the future we will find it self evident to have to report for arbitrary questioning and to have to account for all our movements, just as we now regard it as self evident to report the birth of a child. This is what I was concerned with when I wrote the piece and although I did not want to mention it explicitly, I do hope that the audience can recognise it as an undertone."

How does *Snelcursus Onschuld* relate to your earlier work? *"Before starting at the MFA Scenography course I studied graphic design at the Willem de Kooning Academy in Rotterdam. After graduation I felt that I was not completely finished. I wanted to investigate other media and see whether I could use these to tell 'my story', and so I ended up at the Frank Mohr Institute. Initially I was involved in writing texts. My project* **Ruimte,** *(Space) was an attempt at making a theatrical exhibition. I completely filled the space with yellow Post-Its, for which I asked people I met in the street to write down five things that they should have done, but had not. This resulted in a big pile of scribbled notes that together formed a space full of the little structures of daily life; a poetry of the everyday. I was interested in lifting something out of everyday life, giving it a twist and putting it back again. In the same framework I made 'Instant Theatre', where I was concerned with singling out the everyday pieces of theatre that I saw everywhere all around me. I had two girls hold a banner and set it down at all sorts of places as a portable frame. Everything and everyone walking past it became part of the 'instant theatre-performance' for a moment.*

I also made a video about my self-image, using fragments of interviews with six of my age group talking about themselves, which I then edited under the image of myself. This way the viewer wonders who I actually am. For me this was about the 'Pirandello-effect'. Pirandello wrote a book in which he proposes that in different situations one assumes a different personality. He asked himself questions like these: How can we determine whether someone is actually the same person at different moments? To what extent is our identity determined by the social context in which we live? Does the 'self' end at the boundaries of the body?"

Both your essay and your traineeship were connected with the theme of 'topicality in the theatre'. Could you say more about this?*"In 'topical theatre' there are references to certain processes within society. It is not a direct reflection of reality, but it does have a clear connection with it. Research for 'topical theatre' is done in today's society, rather than in (theatre) history. Although it might well deal with political issues, 'topical theatre' is not political theatre. It does not have to bring up new arguments for political debate, nor does it have to be analytical, or to represent an opinion. It is meant to reveal the drama behind current events and provide a different view of the topical, placing it in a new, theatrical framework.*

For my traineeship in 2004 I went to the United States where I helped the dramatist John Malpede with his Eastern Kentucky performance project: **RFKinEKY** *which involved a series of public debates and art activities around a theatre performance. It was based on the two-day tour that Robert Kennedy made in February 1968 through the east of Kentucky in order to investigate the poverty in that region. People living in the region who had experienced the event, and for whom the subjects dealt with were still relevant, were appointed as actors while the text of the piece was based on government transcripts. This is an example of 'topical theatre', since Malpede focussed on a historical event and gave voice to new ideas about the social politics of the 1960s and today. I did research and helped looking for the costumes. It was this traineeship that made me realise that I also wanted* *to make 'topical theatre', dealing with things that might or might not be topical, but which I feel deeply about, and which do not necessarily be 'theatre-genic'. People are full of ideas and images concerning the past and the present, and as a theatre maker I can frame these, translate them into theatre and thus give them new meanings."*

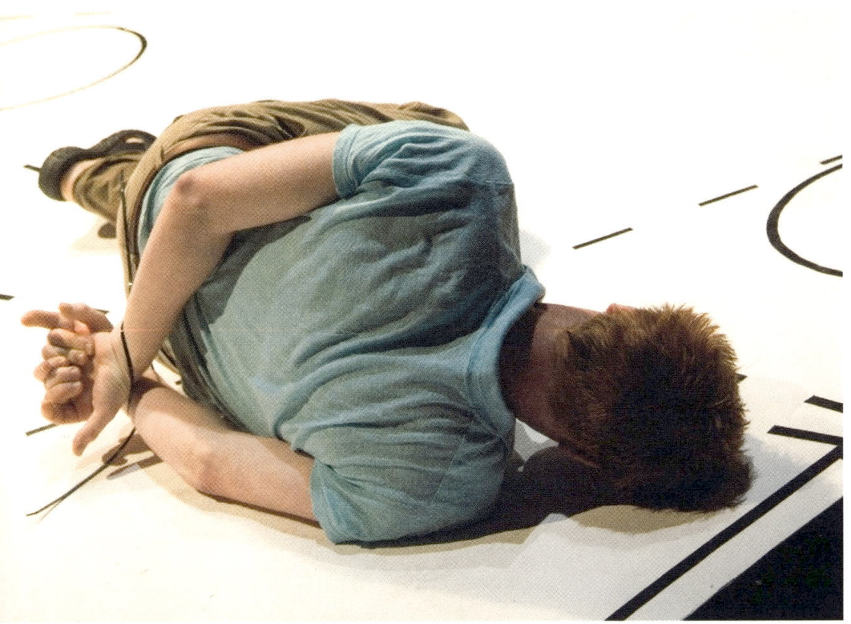

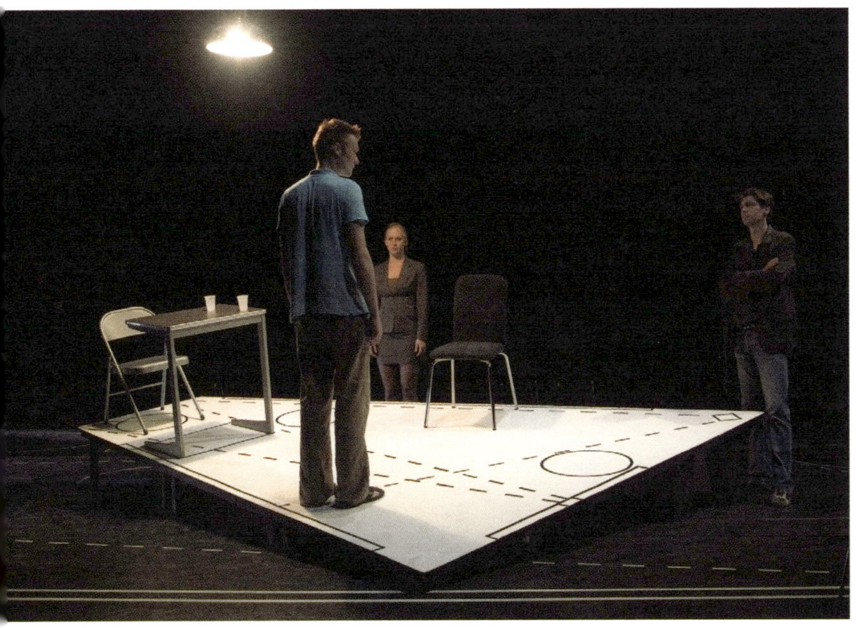

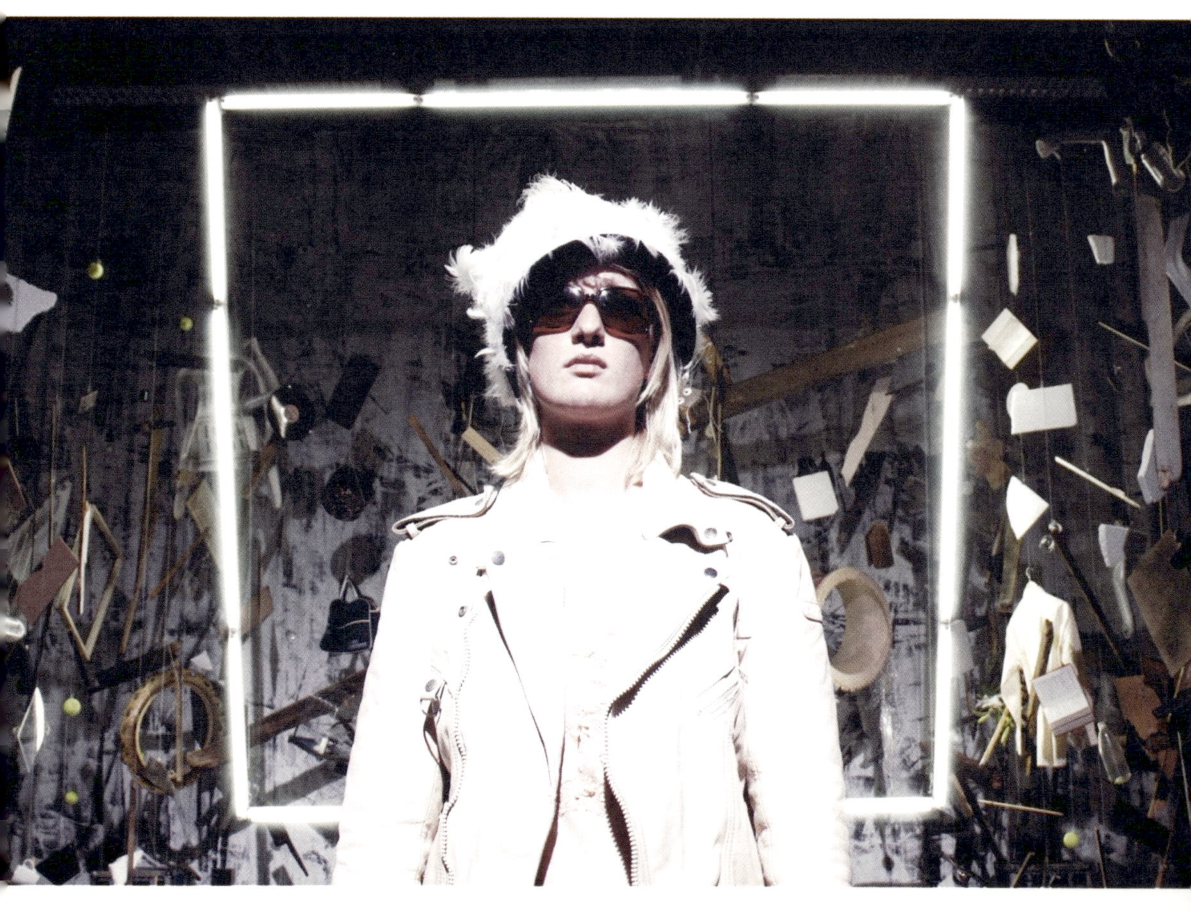

Wikke van Houwelingen

The art of lying

An interview with Wikke van Houwelingen
by Gitta Snijders

Wikke van Houwelingen characterises theatre as 'the art of lying'. Nevertheless, it is this 'lying' art form which is his biotope, precisely because it exposes these lies. He is fascinated by the game played in the theatre with truth and lies, with what is real and what is not real, and with reality and the dream world. A non-existent world is created and the public has a choice to enter into it or not. As a theatre designer, Wikke van Houwelingen gives the unreal theatrical world a real form. In his designs, the question of how the public relates to the image which is presented to them is crucial. Because of the questions which his designs evoke, he raises his sets above the boundaries of theatre. At the same time, the sets are also about our society flooded with images.

For Wikke van Howelingen theatre is the perfect art form for examining the relationship between man and images. We are overwhelmed by images all around us in our everyday reality. At the point that images come from other images, which in turn come from other images, the distinction between what we should or should not believe becomes very vague. Walter Benjamin wrote about this in his work **Het kunstwerk in het tijdperk van zijn technische reproduceerbaarheid,** (The work of art in the age of its technical reproducibility, first published in German in 1936). Jean Baudrillard also examined the dimensions of our image culture. In the wake of their work, Wikke van Houwelingen investigates in his sets how one should look at a manufactured space which creates an illusion of reality; this is the paradox of the theatre. With his sets he tries to make the public aware of this paradox and tempt them into a game of deconstruction.

What do you want to show your audience with your designs? *"Our society forces us to be suspicious. The image culture is all around us. Surrounded by all these illusions and realities, people become perplexed and are lost. The facts change every day, and as human beings we are always looking for our own place in this chaos. Paradoxically, theatre is the genre in which you can see this contrast very directly: there is a person of flesh and blood, an icon of reality, in the middle of a constructed image. With my designs I want to entice the viewer to think about the relationship between the physical presence of a person and the manipulated space around him. In our culture, we do not have enough time to think about this connection, but in the theatre there is still room for the slowness which is necessary for deconstruction."*

You wrote an essay entitled 'De zoveelste leugen: een onderzoek naar video in het theater', (Yet Another Lie: an investigation of video in theatre) in which you show your fascination with the new theatrical space, created by the use of video. What is the added value of video in the theatre for you? *"In the theatre, video has a special effect on space in different ways. It turns the theatre into a sensory experience. Video creates the possibility to divide images, sound and content in the theatre. It is as though video becomes an extra actor. The audience no longer sees a total picture which is like a ready-made that you can interpret in only one way, but they have to use their own imagination. In addition, video can also add a suggestion of depth, particularly when there are several screens. You can play around with the mobility of the space and with the experience of time. Video makes the theatre and the stage more flexible: you can use live projections which stretch the space, or pre-recorded images which show a completely different location. It also changes the scale of the acting space: small details can be blown up to become life-size. The relationship with the actors becomes more intense, for example, when close-ups can show every drop of sweat. Contact with the actors takes than place through different channels, through the physical presence of the* *actors and the projections of them. All these applications of video in the theatre add an extra dimension to the theatre space.*

For me, actually the most characteristic aspect of video in the theatre is that its use adds a certain dynamic to the set. It transforms it, it makes sure that the total image is not the same at any moment. This is exactly what I want to achieve with my designs. The audience should become confused because when they enter the theater, they do not realise how the image exactly works. I want to make the audience unsure."

The confusing décor is a recurrent theme in many of your designs. In this respect you use two stylistic means: dynamics and an abundance bordering on the baroque. Despite the similarities in the themes, your designs are executed in very different ways. We will take two by way of example: a presentation Race/Milieu/Moment, and your virtual reality project The Cave. But let us look first at an earlier installation. In your first year, you transformed a room at the Frank Mohr Institute into a dump of thoughts and pictures related to your own experiences with image culture. What is the place of this 'organised chaos' in the line of your work? *"I was trying to grasp the image culture around me. At that time I was working on the tension between the original and the reproduction which Walter Benjamin wrote about. I thought it would be an interesting experiment if I would lock myself up, as it were, for a month, and stuff everything I found and thought about our image culture into one room. So that is what I started doing. I dragged all sorts of things in the room, even my desk and my music system. I put up large canvasses, spread newspapers on the floor, covered them with plastic and then with white tape, and then I started writing on them. I had televisions there and hung fishing line in the space with transparent sheets of words hanging from them. Gradually there was an explosion of texts which related to the image culture. I created a sort of collage effect by making photographs of photographs and then drawing from these photographs. The images became more and more abstract. My aim was that when you*

entered that room, you would experience a sort of supranormal stimulus, as in everyday life. In the end, you are so overwhelmed by all the texts, bombastic expressions and colours that you shut yourself away."

There appears to be a direct link between this experiment and your design for the presentation Race/Milieu/Moment. For that you also created a décor which was an organised chaos. The general picture was of a meaningless surfeit, in which the actors have lost their way. This presentation went one step further than your installation because it was a design which also included acting. Can you explain what this extra theatrical dimension added to the design for your set? *"Although the design for Race/Milieu/ Moment was commissioned, and I was not able to choose the theme of the work myself, what really fascinated me once again entered into it. It is striking that there was no video at all in my design, though there was a concept of dynamics, which I see as closely related to video. For me, the good thing about the design was that the décor moved with the actors. Because the stage was so full of things, and there were all sorts of things hanging in the air as well, the actors touched something with almost every move they made. This then moved with them, softly when they were moving around quietly, and swinging wildly when they ran through the set. The set was constantly in movement and also made sounds, in other words it was alive. It became an extra actor on the stage, one which interacted with the other actors. As is the case with video, the décor suddenly became an autonomous element in the production because it was literally playing together with the human actors. Another thing which worked very well was a large white square which dropped down between all the hanging, rotating and squeaking things during the performance. It was the only change. It worked as a contrast with the hanging objects which had their own life, and which attracted splinters and dust, which were used - a sort of multiplicity of chaos. The square was a rigid, stylised form which introduced a sense of calm, serving as a focal point. I have the sense that I must offer this*

Both images right:

Wikke van Houwelingen, Race/Milieu/ Moment 2006, Scenography, Photo: Thijme Breukers

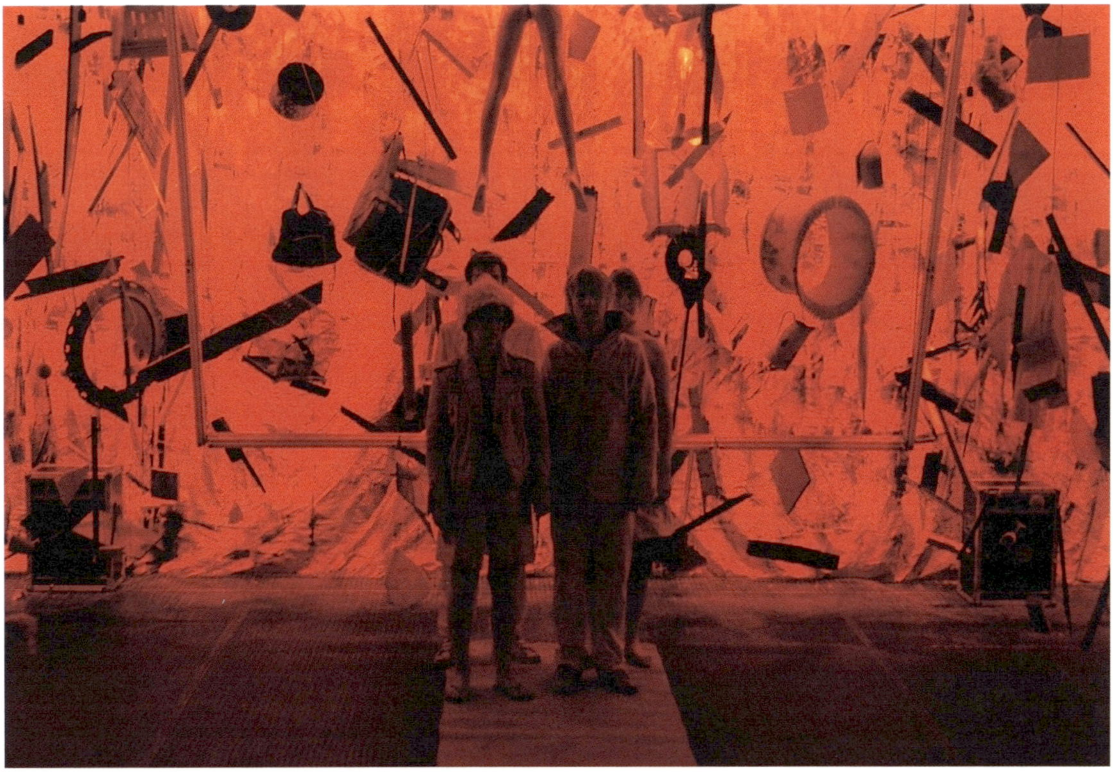

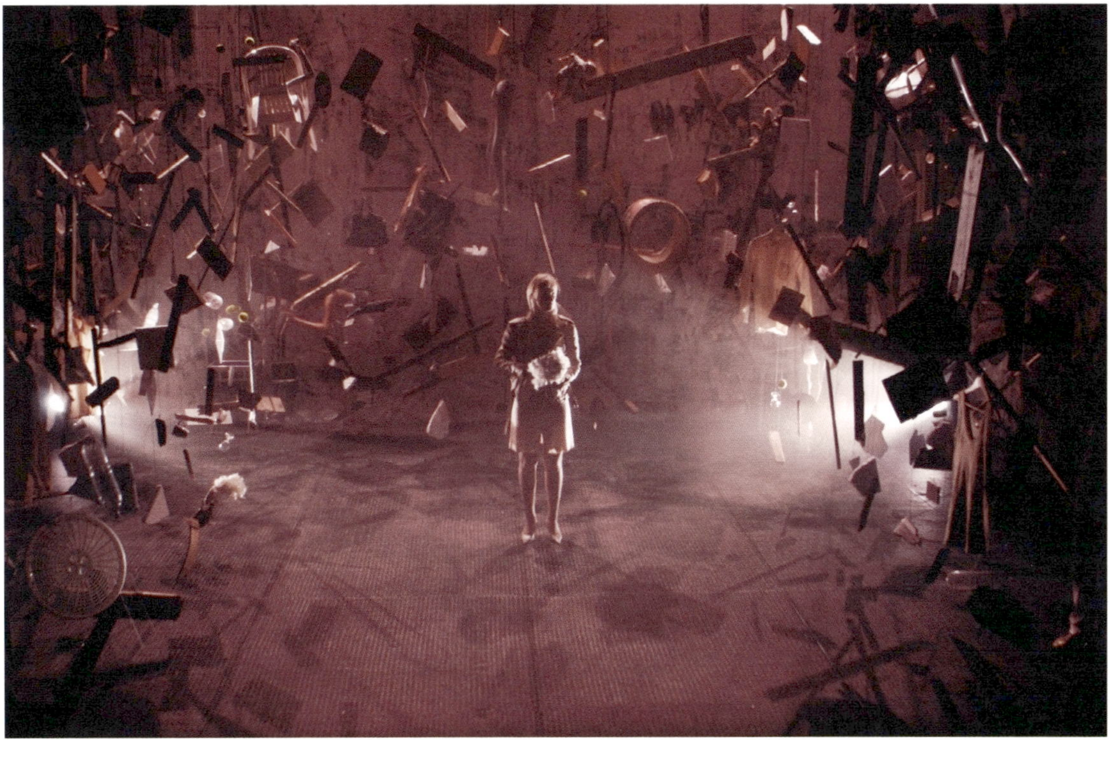

dynamic movement to the public, whether the dynamics are created by video, by a constantly changing set, or by a living set. If the set has its own story, this adds a constant awareness of the space. I want people to experience the mobility of the space. Theatre only really comes into its own when all the elements play a role. It is only then that you can experience the totality. You enter a room and you cannot see immediately how it works. Then you think about it, but you may not understand it completely, so you feel un-certainty. There is a sense of threat in a mov-ing space, as though you are on a ship which is constantly moving and where you have to watch where you put your foot with every step. I think there is something very special *about seeing a space which moves with the person. When you perform a scene and the stage moves with the people, this creates a sort of magical world, a kind of dream."*

The constant thread which runs through your work is the question of how man relates to the space around him. In your virtual reality project *The Cave* you link this question to your fascination with the image culture. How were these two themes expressed in your design? *"For The Cave, I worked to-gether with the computing department of the University of Groningen in a room which they call C.A.V.E.[1] There is a theatre in which they are able to project three-dimensional images. When you sit there wearing 3D glasses, it is*

[1] Computer Assisted Virtual Environment

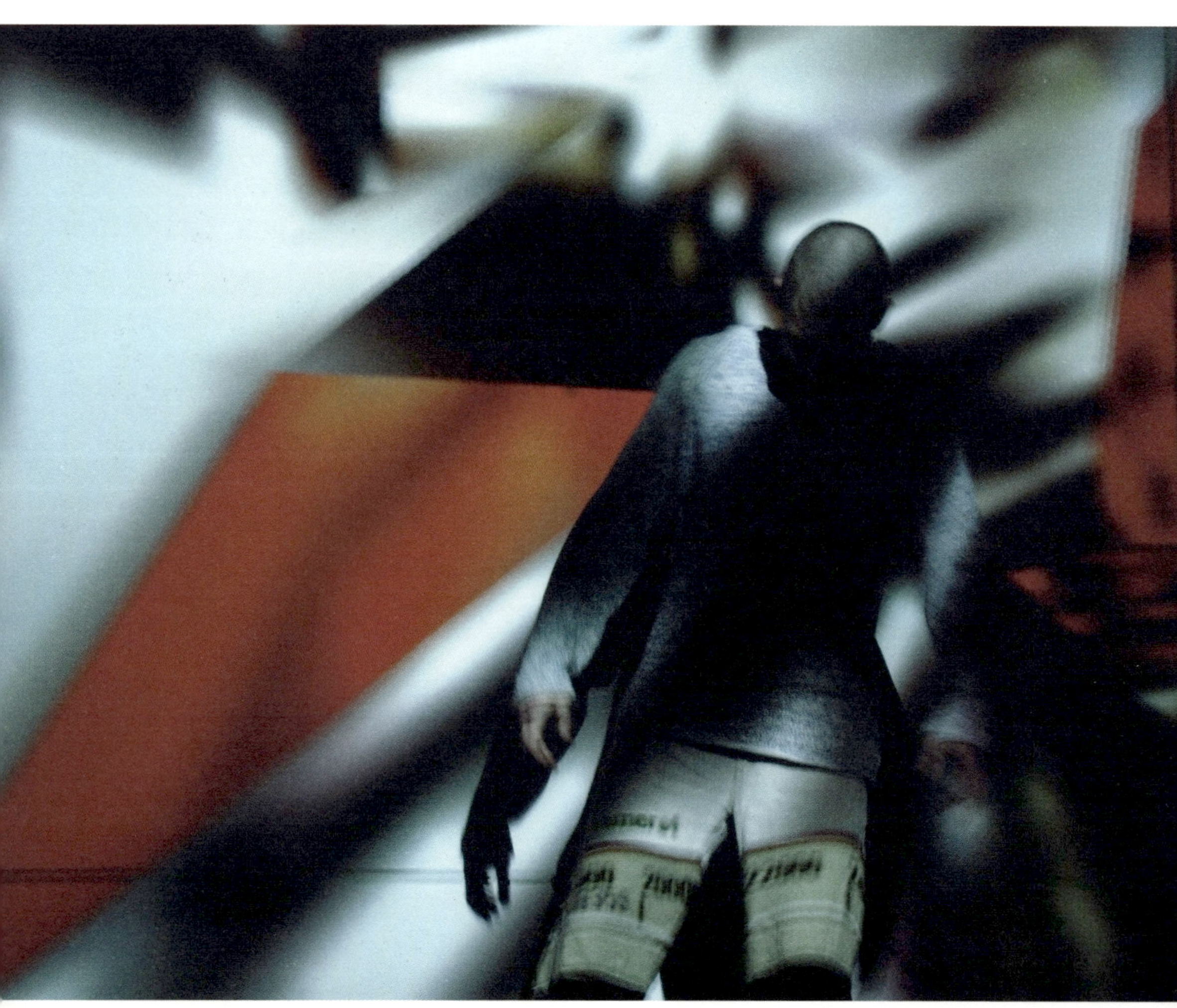

as though you can take hold of the projections. I was fascinated by the questions this evoked in relation to our technological image society. I thought about Plato's cave theory, in which he states that what we experience as reality is merely a representation of a representation. This is exactly what is happening in our society: we are also flooded with images of objects, but no longer see those objects themselves. I wanted to confront the audience with this and used the nature of virtual reality as a starting point. Is a world which is created with projections and glasses three-dimensional, or is it really flat? Is it real or is it fake? In a certain way, the virtually real is more present than a video which remains flat, but it is by no means as tangible as a static set. It is fluid and ephemeral, but at the same time compulsive. The 'appearance' of virtual reality is somewhere between being and not being.

It interested me what would happen with vitual reality, when a human being of flesh and blood moved around in it. Therefore I created a work in which the set really consisted only of a computer generated film, projected onto three walls with a plane of polystyrene on the floor consisting of uneven blocks. The actor walked over this plane for short distances and because the floor was uneven, his movements were remarkably clumsy. But when you looked at the whole thing through 3D glasses, the actor suddenly seemed to be wandering through a strange nightmare-like

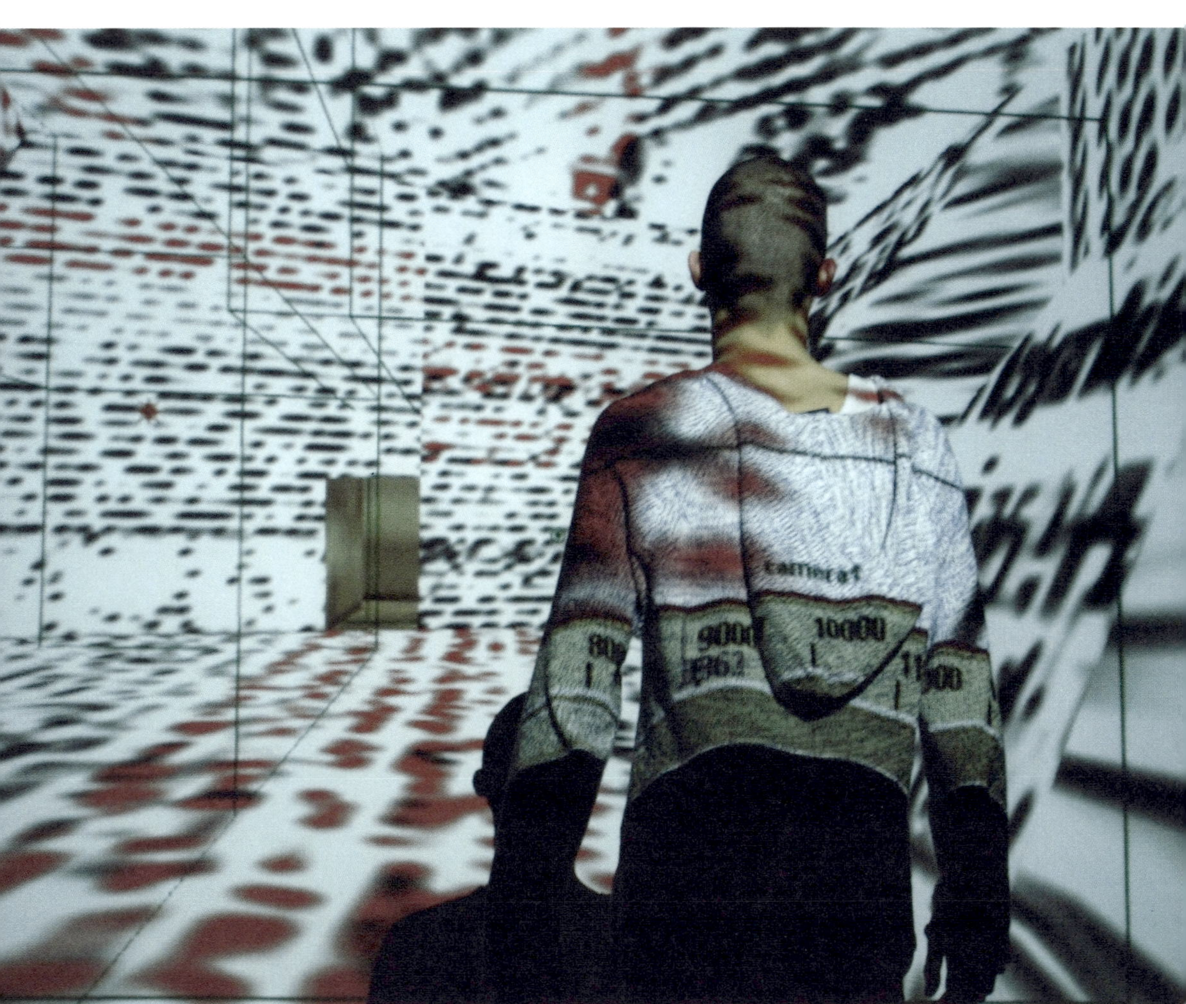

*world of rooms and cubes. It was fascinating
to see how the actor, who was really there,
merged with the 'lie' of the background.
It was even stranger that the public was
aware of this fusion, but was still led into the
projected world by the actor. In this way, I ex-
posed the tension between the different ways
in which objects appear in our reality.
Working with vitual reality sounds very
spectacular and in making the set, I really
wanted to provide the audience with a 'wow'
factor. I believe that you go to the theatre for
an experience, so the décor can certainly be
spectacular. But theatre is a multidisciplinary
art form which is best when all the separate
elements come together. Then the performance is balanced."*

Image below:
*Marieke
Küttschreutter,
Still-perfor-
mance. Blaak
Rotterdam, 01-
05-2006, Dag
van de Arbeid,
17:00-17:09
uur. 2006,
Photo: Inge
Rosekrans.*

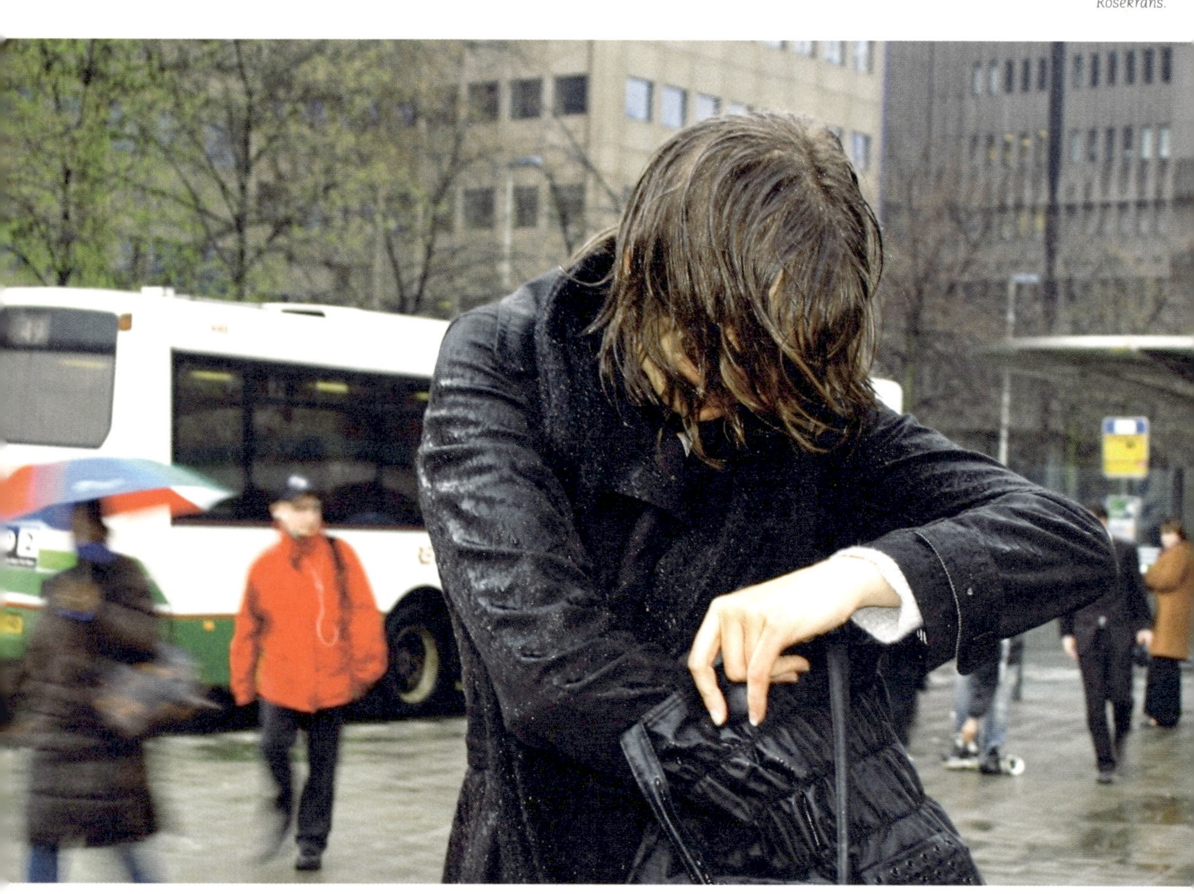

Marieke Küttschreutter

spring 2004
Rotterdam

get up from behind my desk
walk to the kitchen
open the fridge
bend forward
look in the fridge
stand up again
shut the fridge door
walk to the corridor
get my coat
look for my bag
lift up my bag
feel in my coat pocket
put on my coat
zip it up
run down the stairs
undo my lock
hang my bag on the handlebar
get on my bike

bike

buy files
look around me on my bike

autumn 2007
Rotterdam

get up from behind my desk
walk to the bedroom
jump on the bed
put my arms around a body
get up
walk to the kitchen
bend forward
look in the fridge
stand up again
shut the fridge door
walk to the bread bin
stretch my toes
take a slice of bread
open a kitchen cupboard

spread

chew the sandwich

every day

get up
get dressed
eat
go
come back
eat
undress
go to bed

The visualisation of everyday acts and movements *An Interview with Marieke Küttschreutter by Josien Beltman*

Marieke Küttschreutter's work is positioned, as she herself says, in the hybrid area between theatre and visual art. Her actions and interventions in the public space are perhaps best described as performances, in which details from everyday life are isolated or habitual structures and conventions are challenged and laid bare. The work has an expressive character. Small, personal actions or details contain a beauty that the artist hopes will also be noticed by the viewers. Some everyday movements, like bending over, result in an intimate, theatrical live-sculpture when immobilised. The spectator is invited to really look at and discover, for example, the rhythm of breathing or a birthmark.

Before you started at the MFA Scenography course, you already had a training as a drama teacher and a director, and you were already active as theatre maker for some time. Why did you choose to do the course? *"When I began at the MFA Scenography course in 2004, I had already been making theatre productions with Komma 4 for a number of years. This was a collective consisting of myself, two dancers and another person with a background in theatre. We primarily made movement-theatre. Though our company was going well, at some point I thought: this does not correspond with what I am or what I feel I should be doing; not at this moment and not with these people. Because we were a collective, all four of us would work on one idea. After three years I felt I was starting to make compromises, so I looked for a place where I could develop my work further.*

The teachers at the Frank Mohr Institute encouraged me to think more about my own ideas and to elaborate one idea at a time, without being busy with other things the whole time. I found out that I am fascinated by small, everyday gestures, such as bending over. This I developed by making a piece consisting just of people bending over. All these bent bodies pretended to be organising a space by lifting up objects, which meant they had to stand up. Then putting the objects down, they had to bend over again. So at the time I was already more interested in 'actions' than in 'acting'."

Is the action in itself more important than the story in your work? *"Yes and no, because the actions themselves are actually the stories. Every person has his own way of moving or talking. Worlds lie behind the details of how someone places his hand on a table; each detail contains a big story. Someone may well try to present himself in a certain manner, but the individuality of people emerges from small unconscious gestures, like the way you brush your hand through your hair."*

In the second year of the course you started doing interventions in the public space; the so-called 'still performances'. You made 'actors' in the street stand motionless in a certain position. Was it a concious decision to shift your work from the theatre to the street? *"Yes. I made my first street projects as a reaction against the theatre. Not because I think that theatre should get out of the theatre building, but because I find the idea of making the street a stage an exciting and interesting idea. I break into the public space by placing there a specific image of motionless bodies. That image is devised for the public space and not for the theatre because I place the body in a different way than it would normally function in the theatre. The street also does not become a 'theatre space'. What characterises a theatre or stage is that the viewers sit on chairs, they look at a story, and they know how they are supposed to behave. These codes are virtually paramount in the 'game', but they all disappear in the public space: people do not know they are supposed to look at something. The street provides the best training for a theater maker because you immediately sense whether people are reacting or not.*

It is also exciting that everybody can see or notice the performance or the 'intervention'. There are no restrictions to being present, in contrast to the theatre. So there is also a social idea behind this: you can question why one should have to pay ten Euros to be able to see a performance. It is still only the upper classes who go to the theatre, while on the street there are people of many more social layers to whom you can appeal.

*Actions on the street also show what the fixed patterns of certain situations are; how people act in those specific situations. In the restaurant at the central station in Groningen - a place where you find people from different social strata - I did the happening **A smile from a stranger** (2004). In that happening the waiter, after taking a customer's order, asked if he would also like a free smile from a stranger. If the customer answered 'yes' he would receive from me, dressed as a waiter, a smile. Such an action also reveals how people communicate or react, particularly non-verbally: What are the gestures and the culturally determined codes? What are the rules that structure the social network?"*

Is breaking these codes also an aim in your work? *"A while ago I was cycling through the city and thinking: what is going on here? There were a lot of people on the street. Then I realised it was five o'clock in the afternoon and they all were going home from their work. So there are these structures that we are part of, whether we want it or not. I do not want my work to say things like: this is impossible or this is ridiculous. I react with my work through showing that there exists an array of possibilities. Why do we all have to walk on the right side of the street? Why do we all have to sit together on the bench around that tree? Maybe it would be nice to lie down under the tree instead."*

On Monday the 1st of May 2006, Labour Day, you carried out a 'still performance' in the office area around the Blaak in Rotterdam. You got sixteen peopel, working in the area, to stand still at five o'clock in the afternoon for nine minutes. How did you arrive at

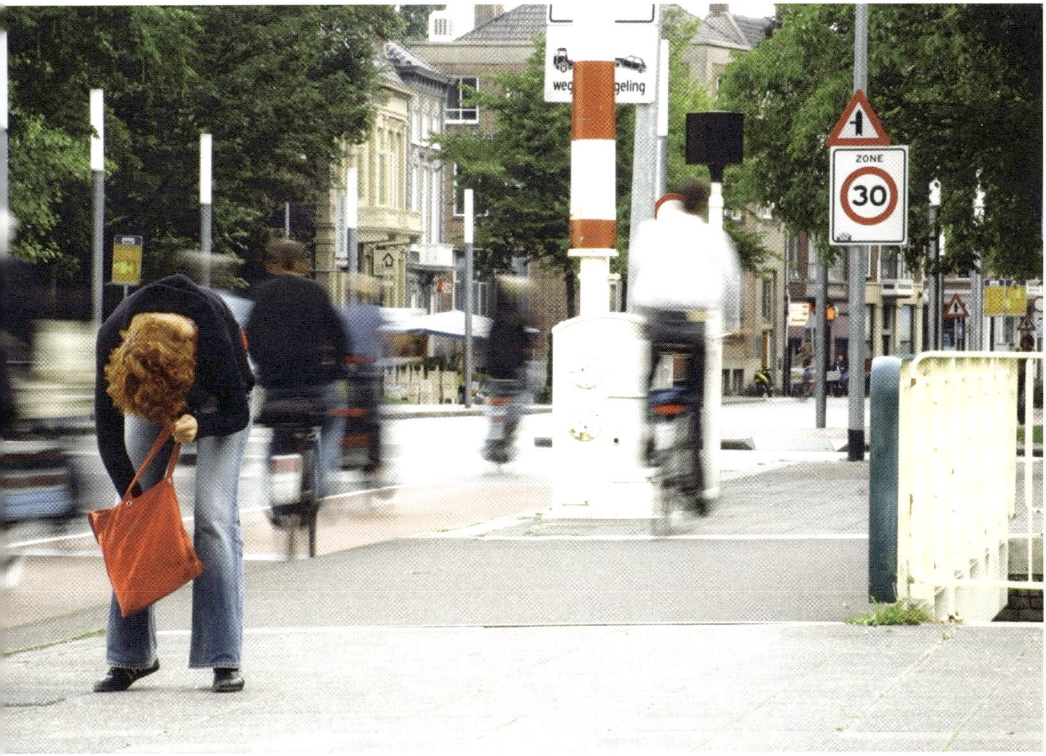

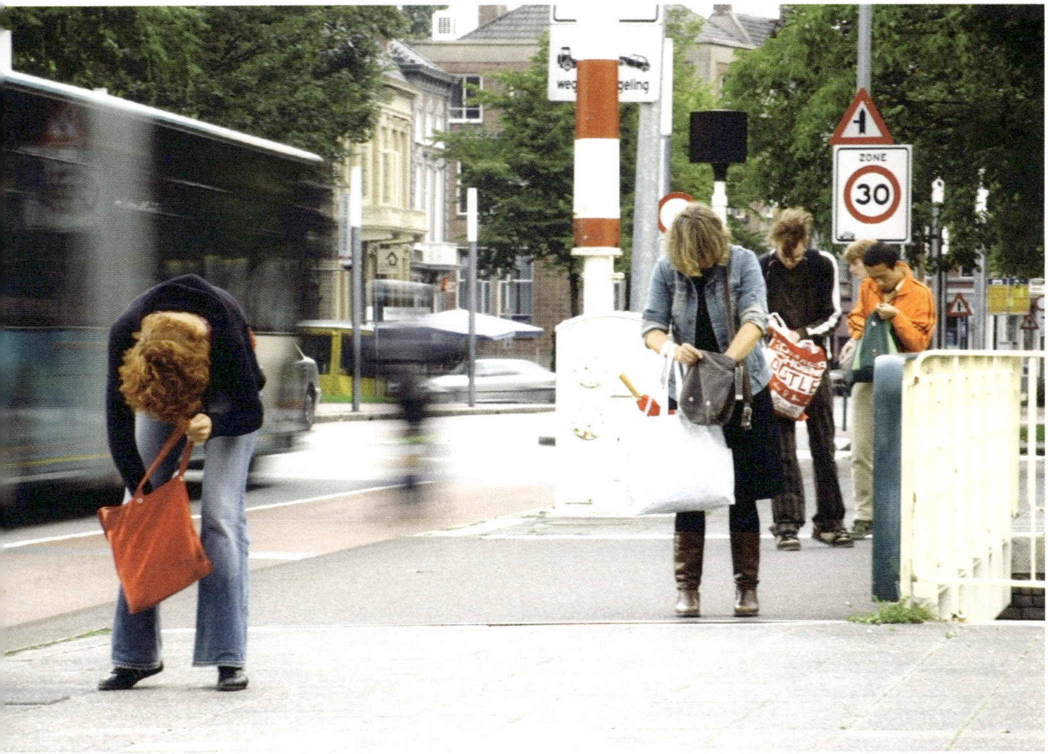

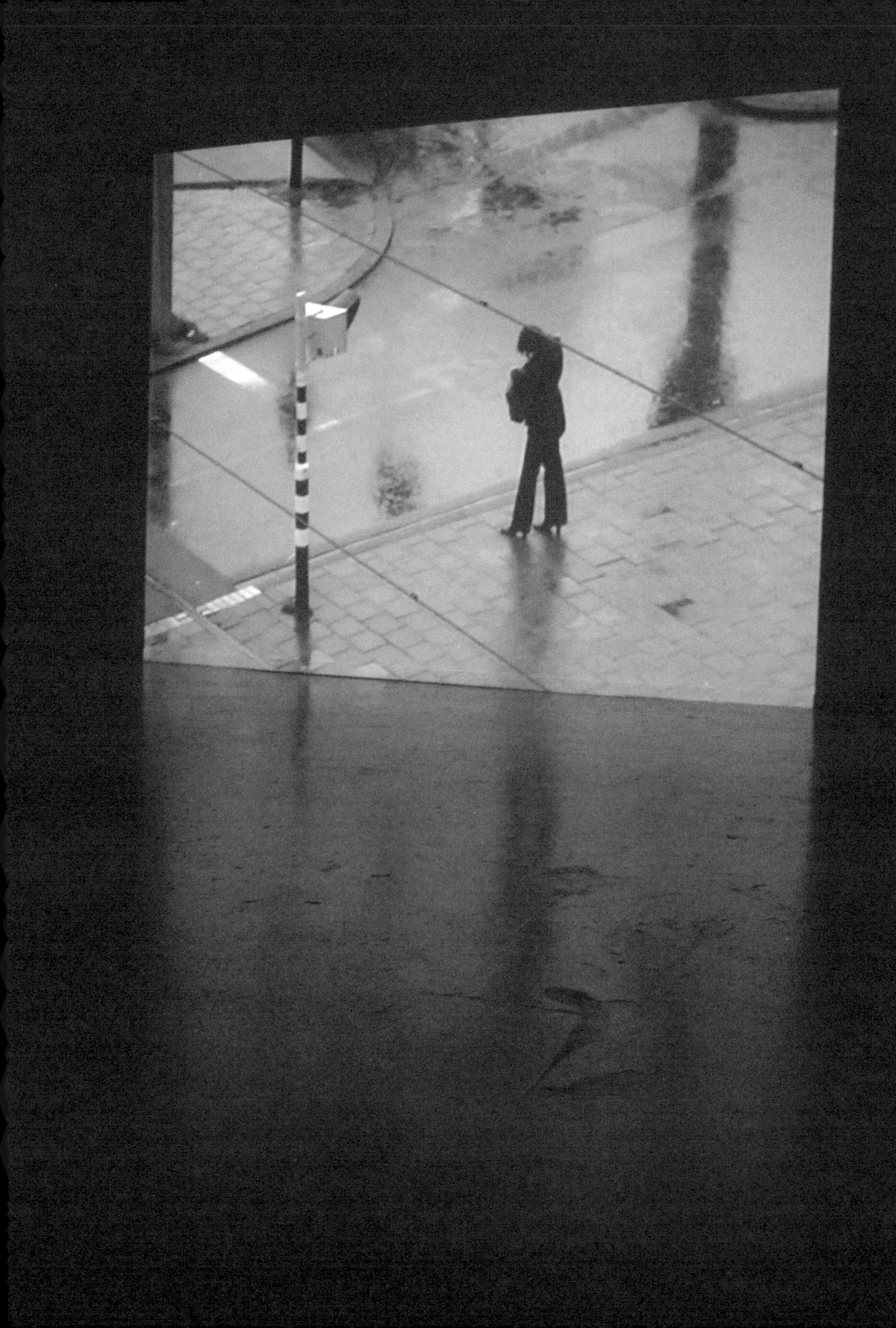

this idea?” *“I wanted to intervene in the character, the structure and the meaning of the situation at the Blaak by the image of motionless office workers, surrounded by the everyday hecticness. I went to observe the place in advance, which I did according to the working method of Lino Hellings (theatre maker and co-founder of Dogtroep), whereby you map out a place by looking: what is happening, what kind of place it is, what exchanges do people make, what are the primary movements or the main flows of people? The Blaak is a place of transition, where people are merely passing through. I often look for places which are passageways because in such spaces different movements and rhythms are manifest: cars, trams, pedestrians. Through the dynamics of the surroundings the motionless figures come more clearly to the fore. The situation at the Blaak also has its own codes: everyone looks to the left and right when crossing a busy cycle path. People walk on the pavement, but there are also people who sidestep or walk right across it. I then redefined the space by making my own story, by giving the flow of people another cadence. I determined very precisely where my ‘actors’ should stand still in order to get the right image or the right choreography; close to a lamp-post or further away from it.*

Prior to the performance, I paid a number of visits to the office buildings around the Blaak in order to find people to take part in the action. This process, which took a month, is for me just as important as the actual execution of the performance, as is the fact that the ‘actors’ actually work in the area of the Blaak. For me, the work starts the moment I enter, for example the Fortis building, and tell the receptionist what I am going to do. Already at that moment I set people in motion as they react to me and my idea. Something arises - you briefly make them imagine something other than what they would usually think of during a typical working day.”

Left image:

Marieke Küttschreutter, Still-performance. Blaak Rotterdam, 01-05-2006, Dag van de Arbeid, 17:00-17:09 uur. Video. Photo: Arend Groenewegen.

You observe people and their daily, often involuntary, actions. You make these action visible by isolating them, for example by having a girl in the Blaak performance stand still, while she has her hand tucked into her handbag. What do you find fascinating in this? *“My work is full of these details of actions. What I like about it is that it is so personal, and that it always emanates an individual strength. Many of these details of actions, or unguarded moments, are not normally registered. I call them ‘in between’ moments. In these moments there is a beauty which I want to make visible. The posture of the girl who is bending over looking for something in her handbag is a fraction of a movement you normally do not notice. For me such a bent posture is exciting to look at because it emanates vulnerability. There is also a tension in such a sight because, as a spectator, you do not know if she is taking something out of her bag or putting something into it; the image is motionless. Yet as a viewer you do sense a movement in a certain direction; you are just before the moment of release.”*

Repeating the action is also a recurrent aspect of your work. Does this have to do with transitoriness? *“I wrote in my thesis about a woman I once saw. She had her back bent and was shuffling along in a repetitive rhythm; ssh, ssh, ssh, ssh, ssh, ssh. I thought: ‘she is wearing out her rhythm’. What I mean by this is that her rhythm is getting slower and slower, and that her life and body are wearing out. For me this has to do with ‘going’, with doing the same necessary actions again and again each day: getting up, dressing, eating, going away, coming back, eating, going to bed, and so on. I made a performance: **Day** (2006), with two actors who are constantly repeating these actions. There is no getting away, you have to keep on with it; otherwise it means ‘not going’. ‘Going’ is what everybody all over the world is doing. Does this have to do with transitoriness? Maybe.”*

When is a performance or an ‘intervention in a situation’ succesful for you? *“I believe I have the responsibility to create in one work a number of layers, so that more* *people can be addressed through it. This is also connected with the choice of the public space as a stage because there I am faced with a very diverse public. When I place motionless people on the street, I often get reactions from young people or tramps who approach me saying: "Look, there is a living sculpture". They understand perhaps only the first layer. They think: 'what is this?', and associate the happening with something that is familiar to them. If it goes no further, then the performance is not successful. My aim is to make the other layers also visible. I hope that people think further and perhaps ask themselves things like: When do we address people and when not? When do we stay in our own world? How do we communicate?*

Do we go our own way, and do we keep to this or not?"

Do you have ideas about where you want to go with your work in the future? *"In doing the 'still performance' Blaak Rotterdam. 01-05-2006, I discovered the medium of video. The intervention at the Blaak was not only a performance. The event was also filmed, so it is just as much a video piece. What I generally try to do with my work is to make small details visible and video can enhance that. Video is all about movement and image, and that is what I am now busy with as well.*

I recently made in Groningen the performance **Still for a moment** *(2006), where a row of motionless people are all executing the same*

Image below: Marieke Küttschreutter, Glimlach van een vreemde 2004, Photo: Menno Vinke.

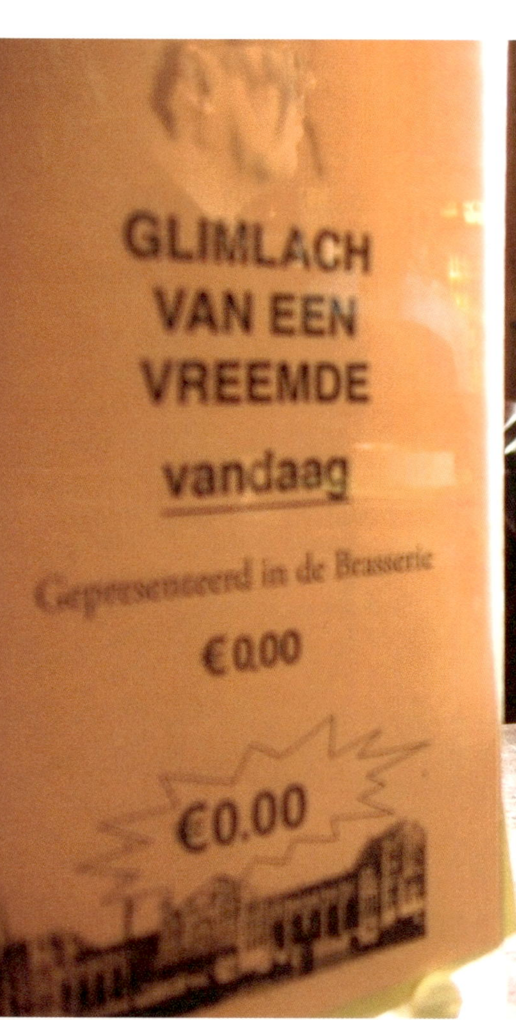

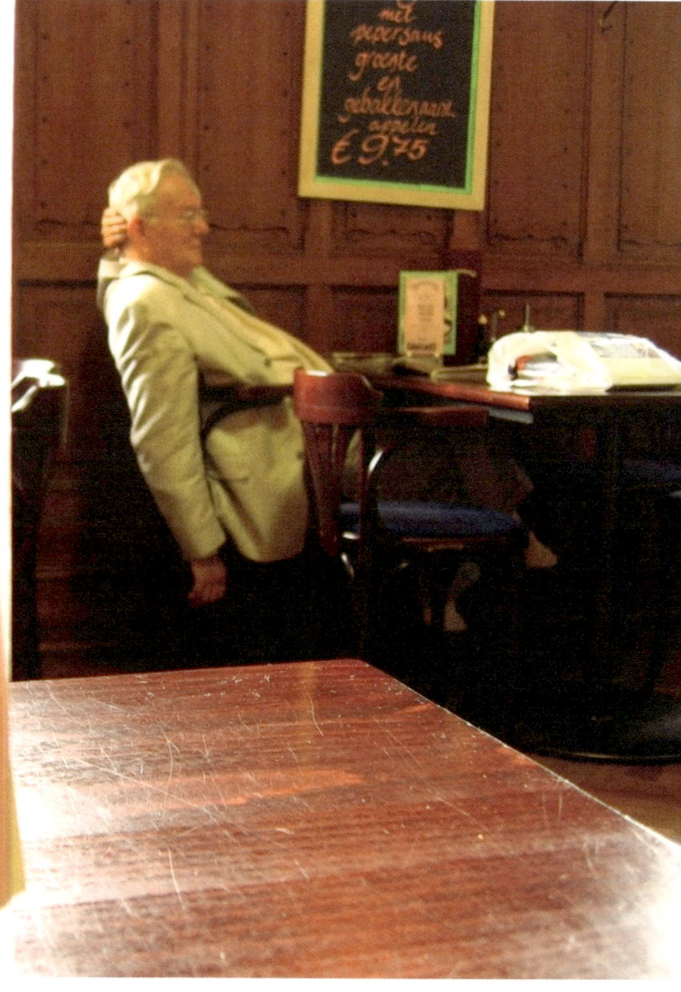

action [they are looking for something in a bag], forming one sequence of movement. Photographs were taken, and I am now turning these into a video. I am trying to capture in film the idea of a live performance, where it is about the movement of the surroundings as opposed to the non-movement of the still bodies, on the basis of twenty photographs. So the still image in the photos can be used to create movement again."

Curriculum Vitae:

Rachel M. van Balen (1980)

Education
2004-2006
MFA Painting, Frank Mohr Instituut,
Hanzehogeschool Groningen, Groningen
1999 – 2004
Academie Minerva, Faculty of Arts,
Hanzehogeschool Groningen, Groningen

Exhibitions
2007
Grand Theatre, solo exhibition,
Groningen
2006
Universitair Medisch Centrum Gronin-
gen, solo exhibition, Groningen
Graduation Show, MFA Painting, Frank
Mohr Instituut, Groningen
MFA DEFKA, DeFKa, Assen
2005
Licht, Galerie Vonkel, Den Haag
2004
Galerie Kunst in de Kop, Groningen
Jonge Verf II, Informatie Beheer Groep,
Groningen
M/V, Graduation Show, Academie Mi-
nerva, Groningen
Decoratie & Ornament, UMC, Leeuwarden,
(permanent exhibition)
2003
Galerie Theater Romein, solo exhibition,
Leeuwarden
Young Composers Meeting, De Gigant,
Apeldoorn & Kröller-Müller Museum,
Otterloo
Met open ogen, Kunsthuis De Perma-
nente, Groningen

Siebe de Boer (1982)

Education
2004-2006
MFA Interactive Media and Environments, Frank Mohr Instituut, Hanzehogeschool Groningen, Groningen
2000-2004
Academie Minerva, Faculty of Arts, Hanzehogeschool Groningen, Groningen

Exhibitions
2006
De Animatie Top Tien, CBK Groningen,
'25 Jaar RKZ' Filmfestival, RKZ Bioscoop,
Groningen
Humble Origin, De ïs Ka, Amsterdam
State of the Image Festival, in: *Square Eyes
Festival,* Arnhem
Signs of Graduation, Graduation Show,
Frank Mohr Instituut 2006, Galerie Sign,
Groningen
2005
Informatie Beheer Groep (IBG), solo
exhibition, Groningen
De Intermediale Zone, Museum Boijmans
van Beuningen, Rotterdam
*Inside the Magic Bubble, a New Media Expe-
rience,* U-Theater, Utrecht
Animatie Programma, Vera, Groningen
Reconstructie, Galerie Sign, Groningen
2004
Noordelijk Filmfestival DAD, Filmhuis
Leeuwarden, Leeuwarden
Lab 10 Filmklup, Noorderzon Festival,
Groningen
M/V, Graduation Show, Academie Mi-
nerva, Groningen

Publications
Isabella Werkhoven, 'Groninger kun-
stenaars exposeren in Amsterdam',
Dagblad van het Noorden, 9,13,2006
Wytske Visser, 'Het Nachtpodiumverhaal
Deel VIII: Siebe de Boer over technologie
en ambacht', *8 Weekly,* 10,22,2005
Wytske Visser, 'Nachtpodium: Vorm en
Inhoud, item: *8 Weekly* (Siebe de Boer)',
VPRO, 10,24,2005

Sibylle Eimermacher (1979)

Education
2004-2006
MFA Painting Frank Mohr Instituut,
Hanzehogeschool Groningen, Groningen
2000-2004
AKI, Academie voor beeldende kunst en
vormgeving, ArtEZ Hogeschool voor de
Kunsten, Enschede
2003
KiT, Kunstakademiet i Trondheim,
(Fakultet for arkitektur og billedkunst),
Norges teknisk-naturvitenskaplige uni-
versitet, (NTNU)), Norway

Exhibitions
2007
One; & the Other Painting, Sandberg Insti-
tuut, project W139/ BASEMENT, Amster-
dam
Anonymous Drawings 5, blütenweiss-Raum
für Kunst, Berlin, Germany
2006
House_in_space, Galerie Ayacs, solo exhibi-
tion, Amsterdam
Koninklijke Prijs voor Vrije Schilderkunst,
Gemeentemuseum Den Haag, Den Haag
Nieuwe Uitleenschatten 2006, Aa-Kerk,
Groningen
Graduation Show, MFA Painting, Frank
Mohr Instituut, Groningen
Air galerie, Lochem
Beeldstof, Kunstcentrum Hengelo, Hengelo
MFA DEFKA, DefKa, Assen
2005
Presentatie Frank Mohr Instituut, Ministerie
OW & C, Den Haag
Zomertentoonstelling Grote Kerk, Lochem
PPF, MFA Painting Frank Mohr Instituut,
Groningen
Galerie Ungrund, Neuenkirchen, Ger-
many
Poem-Express, Boekhandel Donner, Rot-
terdam
2004
Graduation Show, AKI, Academie voor
beeldende kunst en vormgeving, En-
schede
Poem-Express, Boekhandel Donner, Rot-
terdam

2003
Semesterutstilling #2, Galleri KiT, Trondheim, Norway

Publications
2007
Blütenweiss (ed.), *Anonyme Zeichner 5*, Raum für Kunst, Berlin
Roos Stamet-Geurs, Kunst van de dag/galeries.nl
Arno Kramer, Kunst van de dag/galeries.nl
2006
Wim van der Beek, 'Vertellers van vreemde verhalen', *De Stentor*
Lennard Dost, 'DeFKa presenteert werk eindexamenkandidaten Frank Mohr Instituut', *Tubelight 42*
Daniel Gould, 'Daniel Gould's 3 D art report', *Art.net*, Amsterdam
2004
Peter Sonderen and Wouter Hooijmans (eds), *AKI 2004, Graduation Catalogue*, Enschede

Marloes van der Hoek (1980)

Education
2003-2006
MFA Scenography, Frank Mohr Instituut, Hanzehogeschool Groningen, Groningen
1998-2002
Willem de Kooning Academie, Graphic Design, Rotterdam

Traineeships and Projects
2004
Robert F. Kennedy in Eastern Kentucky of John Malpede, Community Art, Whitesburg Kentucky, USA, (trainee production)
2002
Proforma Design, strategics and management, Rotterdam (traineeship graphic design)
2001
Calarts Academy, Los Angeles, USA, (exchange graphic design)

Theater Projects
2007
Assistent to the director and dramaturgy, *Mighty Society 4*, (Director: Erik de Vroedt)
2006
Programming theater, Pleintheater, Amsterdam
Snelcursus Onschuld, Graduation Show, Grand Theatre, Groningen
2005
Assistent to the director and research for *Groeikoorts*, Theatergroep PeerGrouP, Veenhuizen
2004
Stage design for *Trias+*, Dance Unlimited, Dansacademie Arnhem en orkest De Ereprijs, Arnhem
2003
Tutor theater, Ojobi and Acropong, Ghana, Africa
2000
Actor in: *Heartbreak Hotel*, Onafhankelijk Toneel, Rotterdam

Design

2007
Colour design for Theater De Vrijburcht, IJburg, Amsterdam
2005
Video for exhibition, *De Noorderlingen,* Kasteel Groeneveld, Baarn
2005
Ruimte, Installation, Frank Mohr Instituut, Groningen
2005
Curation for *Real Life,* two lectures and a film about community based theater, Academie Minerva, Groningen
2004
Sound walkingtour, *Man in de straat,* Frank Mohr Instituut, Groningen
2004
Video, Het *Pirandello-effect / Zelfbeeld,* Frank Mohr Instituut, Groningen

Wikke L.C. van Houwelingen (1979)

Education
2004-2006
MFA Scenography, Frank Mohr Instituut, Hanzehogeschool Groningen, Groningen
2003
Audiovisual Design, Willem de Koning Academie, Rotterdam
2001-2003
Theater Design, Hogeschool voor de Kunsten Utrecht, Utrecht

Work Experience and Design
2007
Design of scenery for *Zoek,* het Gasthuis, Amsterdam, (Director: Anne van Dorp)
Second assistent scenography to *Romeinse Tragedies,* Toneelgroep Amsterdam, (Director: Ivo van Hove, Design: Jan Versweyveld)
Assistent scenery to *Caravan,* Toneelgroep Beumer & Drost, (Director: Rene van 't Hof, Design: Gerrit Timmers)
2006
Design of scenery and sound for *Race/Milieu/Moment,* Graduation Show, (Director: Jeroen De Man)
Direction of *The Cave,* a virtual reality theatershow, Rekencentrum Zernikeborg, Rijksuniversiteit Groningen, Groningen
2005
Short film, *Ballade van de veerman,* for the Over het IJ festival, Amsterdam
Short film, *AmsterdHamm* for La fête festival, Hamm, Germany
2003
Traineeship with Marc Warning in which assistance to:
-*Proust 1,* Ro-theater, (Director: Guy Cassiers)
-*Beroerd,* Toneelgroep de Appel, (Director: Gerardjan Rijnders)
2002
Design of scenery for and realisation of *Huid en Haar,* a performance of Daan Hofman, at the It's festival 2002, Hochschule in Essen, Germany
Design of scenery for and realisation of *Slaapschuld,* at the HKU festival 2002, (Director: Daan Hofman)

Karl Klomp (1979)

Education
2004-2006
MFA Interactive Media and Environments, Frank Mohr Instituut, Hanzehogeschool Groningen, Groningen.
1996-1999
MBO Social Cultureel Werk, Regionaal Opleiding Centrum, Nijmegen

Live Audio Visual Performances
17-03-2007 *New Dutch Electronix*, Het Paard, Den Haag, 'vj mnk'
10-03-2007, Sign, Groningen, 'E.A.B.'
27-01-2007, *Dead Media Party*, Worm, 'gieskes'
10-11-2006, *Hardware*, Moira, Utrecht, 'E.A.B'
20-10-2006, *ReSort Off*, Extrapool, Nijmegen, 'mnk_toonk'
07-10-2006, *The Overload*, Atak, Enschede, 'mnk_toktek'
06-10-2006, *Afx*, Ketelhuis, Amsterdam, 'mnk_toktek'
02-10-2006, *Afregelsalon*, Dnk, Amsterdam, 'mnk_toonk'
08-09-2006, *Square Eyes Festival*, Arnhem, 'mnk_toonk'
18-08-2006, *Up2date*, Electron, Breda, 'mnk_toktek'
24-02-2006, *Sonic Acts XI*, Paradiso, Amsterdam, 'mnk_toktek'
16-12-2005, *State-x Festval*, Lomechanik, Den Haag, 'mnk_toktek'
25-11-2005, *Cynetart Festival*, Dresden, Germany, 'mnk_toktek'
12-11-2005, *Noisivision*, Electron, Breda, 'mnk_toktek'
18-10-2005, DeFKa, Assen, 'mnk_toktek'
12-10-2005, *Rawpikzl Dvd*, Merlijn, Nijmegen, 'vj mnk'
09-09-2005, *Gogbot*, Planetart, Enschede, 'mnk_toktek'
04-06-2005, *Lo Mechanik*, Goes, 'mnk_toktek'
02-05-2005, *ReSort Off*, Worm, Rotterdam, 'mnk_toktek'
12-01-2005, >50% *Beeld*, Montevideo, Amsterdam, 'mnk_toktek'
14-12-2004, *Cinematiek06*, 't Hoogt, Utrecht, 'mnk_toktek'

Screenings, Presentions, Workshops
25-03-2007, 5 day workshop, Video Circuit Bending, Teks, Norway
15-10-2006, Stedelijk Museum, presentation, 'gieskes', Den Bosch
22-09-2006, *Todaysart*, screening "elst", 7 Projectors, Den Haag
15-07-2006, Live clip edit for *Apzolut*, 'stench', Lomechanik
30-05-2006, *Synchronator* 3 day workshop, Impakt, instructor, Utrecht,
07-05-2006, *Flipped Chips*, screening "rex", New York
06-05-2006, *Floss-Sound*, presentation, Leeuwarden
02-04-2006, *Speech Uncaged*, Heiner S. Behrends, Groningen
09-09-2005, *Gogbot*, 3 day open workshop and toktek, Enschede
18-04-2005, Hunter College, The City University of New York, presentation, New York,
18-07-2004, *Teek Festival*, screening "elst", The Mezz, Breda

Saskia Koops (1969)

Education
2004-2006
MFA Painting, Frank Mohr Instituut,
Hanzehogeschool Groningen, Groningen
2005
Hunter College, The City University of
New York, New York, USA, (exchange)
1997-1999
Environmental Design, Koninklijke
Academie van Beeldende Kunsten, Den
Haag
1987-1993
Academie Minerva, Faculty of Arts, Han-
zehogeschool Groningen, Groningen

Exhibitions (a selection)
2006
*BSTR*CT, Kunstruimte 09, Groningen
Graduation Show, MFA Painting, Frank
Mohr Instituut, Groningen
Presentatie Boteringesingel, Groningen,
(Curator: Maxine Kopsa)
MFA DEFKA, DeFKa Assen
2005
PPF, Groningen, (Curator: Roos Gortzak)
2002
Spiegel Mij, with Barthold Boksem, Gal-
erie Sign, Groningen
2000
Meervoudige middelen, Noorderlicht foto-
galerie, Groningen

Publications (a selection)
2006
Lennard Dost, 'DeFKa presenteert werk
eindexamenkandidaten Frank Mohr
Instituut', *Tubelight 42*
Het Lokale Brein, radio-interview, radio
Assen
2005
Roos Gortzak, *PPF,* A publication of post-
ers
2002
Illand Pietersma,'Nabeelden van hon-
derd oude exposities in galerie Sign',
Dagblad van het Noorden, 6,5,2002

Grant
2002
Grant PABK for *Spiegel Mij*

Marieke Kütt-schreutter (1975)

Education
2004-2006
MFA Scenography, Frank Mohr Instituut,
Hanzehogeschool Groningen, Groningen
1994-1998
Hogeschool voor de Kunsten Arnhem,
Faculty of Theatre, Arnhem

Exhibitions
2006
*Still-performance. Blaak Rotterdam. 01-05-
2006. Dag van de Arbeid.* 17:00-17:09 uur
(video), workshop Acting Out Technology, Monty, Antwerp
*Still-performance. Blaak Rotterdam. 01-05-
2006. Dag van de Arbeid.* 17:00-17:09 uur
(video), Galerie Sign, Groningen

Projects
2007
Artist-in-Caravan, Stichting Sanders Ge-
luk, Kip Vis, Zonnemaire buitengewoon,
Schouwen Duiveland
2006
Weggegooide dromen, performance in
assignment of the Province of Drenthe,
Veenhuizen
Even Still, bodysculpture-performance,
(one action by eight performers),
Festival Noorderzon, Groningen
Kijkgat, intervention in two bus shel-
ters in the city of Groningen, Festival
Noorderzon, Groningen
Weggegooide dromen, performance,
Festival Kleur van de nacht, Stichting
Interart, Arnhem
*Still-performance.Blaak Rotterdam. 01-05-
2006. Dag van de Arbeid,* (Performance
by sixteen workers in the office buil-
dings at the Blaak Rotterdam)
Dag, performance, (two performers),
Frank Mohr Instituut, Groningen
NWU Weltrusten, Onafhankelijk Toneel,
Rotterdam, (Coaching: Bea deVisser)
Powergame, interdisciplinary theatre,
Stichting Interart, Arnhem
2005
Berichtje van een vreemde, happening,

Theaterfestival Boulevard, 's Hertogen-
bosch
Een zakje geluk, happening, Buitenkunst
Drenthe, Elp
2004
Berichtje van een vreemde, happening, Festi-
val Circus Colourful City, Nijmegen
Glimlach van een vreemde, happening,
restaurant at the central station of Gron-
ingen
Gewoon even heel even zitten, happening,
Grote Markt, Groningen
Robert F. Kennedy in Eastern Kentucky, train-
eeship, Community Art,
Whitesburg Kentucky, U.S.A., (Director:
John Malpede)
2003
Fietsen, 16 mm film, with Boris Joeri Brink,
Stichting Sanders Geluk, Rotterdam
Bar, happening, with Kuin Heuff and
Jasper le Clerq, Stichting Sanders Geluk,
Rotterdam
2002
16:00 uur, Project Tijdbedrijf, Stichting
Sanders Geluk, Rotterdam
2001
Assistant to the director with *De Drie-
stuiversopera,* Het Noord Nederlands
Toneel, Groningen, (Director: Matthijs
Rümke)
2001-2004
Co-founder, maker and performer with
interdisciplinary theatre group *Komma 4,*
Arnhem

Performer/actor
2005
Geluksfabriek, Maasdijk, Stichting Sanders
Geluk, Rotterdam, (Director: Fransje Kraaij)
2003
Studioproject, Onafhankelijk Toneel, Rot-
terdam, (Director: Mirjam Koen)
2002
The sense of organs, performance with
MAPA, Berlin (Director: Frans Poelstra)
1999-2000
De Nederlandse Humorstichting, BOS BROS,
Net 5, Dutch Television
1998-1999
Hildegard van Bingen, Theatergroep De
Kern, on tour in Holland (Director: Dirk
Laroy)

Workshops
2006
Noordelijke Hogeschool Leeuwarden,
Interfaculteit der Kunsten, Leeuwarden
2006-2005-2004
ArtEZ Hogeschool voor de Kunsten,
Arnhem

Xinjian Lu (1977)

Education
2005-2006
MFA Interactive Media and Environments, Frank Mohr Instituut, Hanzehogeschool Groningen, Groningen
2004-2005
Design Academy Eindhoven (interior, industrial and identity design)
1998-2000
Nanjing Arts Institute, China

Projects
2006
Poster for the new identity of KPN
Special issue design for NOORDER-BREEDTE magazine
2005
Interior design of Canadian Exhibits International / Kubik
Identity design of Amsterdam Central Station

Exhibitions
2006
Galerie Pictura, Groningen
Galerie Sign, Groningen
2005:
7 posters exhibited in the Second Graphic Design Moscow 2005, Moscow, Russia
Poster exhibition, Galerie Linka, Amsterdam
'Nature, Fuck for Peace, Bottled', Graphic Arts Festival, Chaumont, France
2004
'Nature, Fuck for Peace, Bottled', Lahti Poster Biennale, Lahti, Finland

Work Experience
2006-2007
Studio Dumbar Shanghai, China
2005-2006
Studio Dumbar, the Netherlands
2005-2006
KUBIK / Exhibits International, the Netherlands
2003-2004
Beijing Jiuge Design Company, China
2001-2003
Shenzheng Zhang Dali Design Company, China

Award
Chaumont Prize at the 17th Chaumont International Poster Competition

Alex Winters (1977)

Education
2004–2006
MFA Painting, Frank Mohr Instituut, Hanzehogeschool Groningen, Groningen
2006
Hunter College, The City University of New York, New York, USA (exchange)
1998 – 2002
Academie Minerva, Faculty of Arts, Hanzehogeschool Groningen, Groningen

Projects
2005–today
PaseenpoP, collective of artists
2003–2005
Multiplx, collective of artists
2002–2004
Okn, association of artists
1999–2004
Buxus, performance duo with Jan Bokma

Exhibitions (a selection)
2007
Room 60, Art Rotterdam, Booth 60, Galerie Fons Welters, solo exhibition, Rotterdam
Room 11, Buro Leeuwarden, solo exhibition, Leeuwarden
Room 25, Galleria Klerkx, Milan, Italy
2006
140°, Galerie Fons Welters, solo exhibition, Amsterdam
Brief tableau, Kunsthuis Syb, Beetsterzwaag
Stop Motion, Medium Gallery, Groningen
Graduation show, MFA Painting, Frank Mohr Instituut, Groningen
CineView, De Fabriek, Eindhoven
MFA DEFKA, DeFKa, Assen
2005
Leegte, De Leegte, Nieuwolda
Zomer Tentoonstelling, Stichting Dag Lochem, Lochem
2004
Part II, Galeria Plastifikatory, Lubon, Poland
2003
#pres. Oktober, De Fabriek, Eindhoven, (Buxus)
Eenzaam zonder God, Lokaal 01, Antwerpen, Belgium
Sacred Spaces, Sacred Spaces Festival, La Bisbal, Spain, (Buxus)
Streetwise, Streetwise Festival, 's Hertogenbosch, (Buxus)
2002
High Caliber, High Caliber Festival, Berlin, Germany, (Buxus)
Graduation Show, Academie Minerva, Groningen, (Buxus)
2001
Ontmoeting met de meeter, Koetshuis Mensinge, Roden
Uitgenodigd, Academie Voor Schone Kunsten, Antwerp, Belgium
2000
Zuigen aan lucht, Centrum Beeldende Kunst, Groningen, (Buxus)
1999
Insignific, Galerie Sign, Groningen, (Buxus)

Grant
2006
George Verbergstipendium

The institute

The Frank Mohr Institute (FMI) is the Institute for Graduate Studies and Research in the Arts and the Emerging Media. It is situated in the School of Fine Arts and Design of the Minerva Academy which is part of the Hanzehogeschool Groningen. In co-operation with the University of Groningen, the FMI accommodates three Master of Fine Arts courses: MFA Interactive Media and Environments (IME), MFA Painting and MFA Scenography.

The institute is named after Frank Mohr (1931-1998), cultural advisor to the city and the province of Groningen and chairman of the advisory boards of the Minerva Academy and the Prins Claus Conservatory. Frank Mohr was a fervent advocate of innovation within the art education of the Northern Netherlands. He especially promoted the deepening of knowledge through collaboration between art and scientific education. Since 1996 the FMI works together with the Institute of Art and Architecture History (K&A) within the Faculty of Arts of the University of Groningen. This collaboration has been gradually extended to include other university departments. In February 2005 a covenant standardised the collaboration between the Hanzehogeschool and the University of Groningen. Right from the start this relation resulted in an interaction between art and theory, artistic and scientific research that is unique in art and scientific education in the Netherlands. Within a co-operative Platform for Art and Media (part of the covenant of 2005), the FMI now works together with the University of Groningen (Faculty of Arts), the Centre for High Performance Computing and Visualisation and the Groninger Museum. This platform will provide integrated education and research at graduate and doctoral levels.

Image below:

Main building
Frank Mohr
Instituut

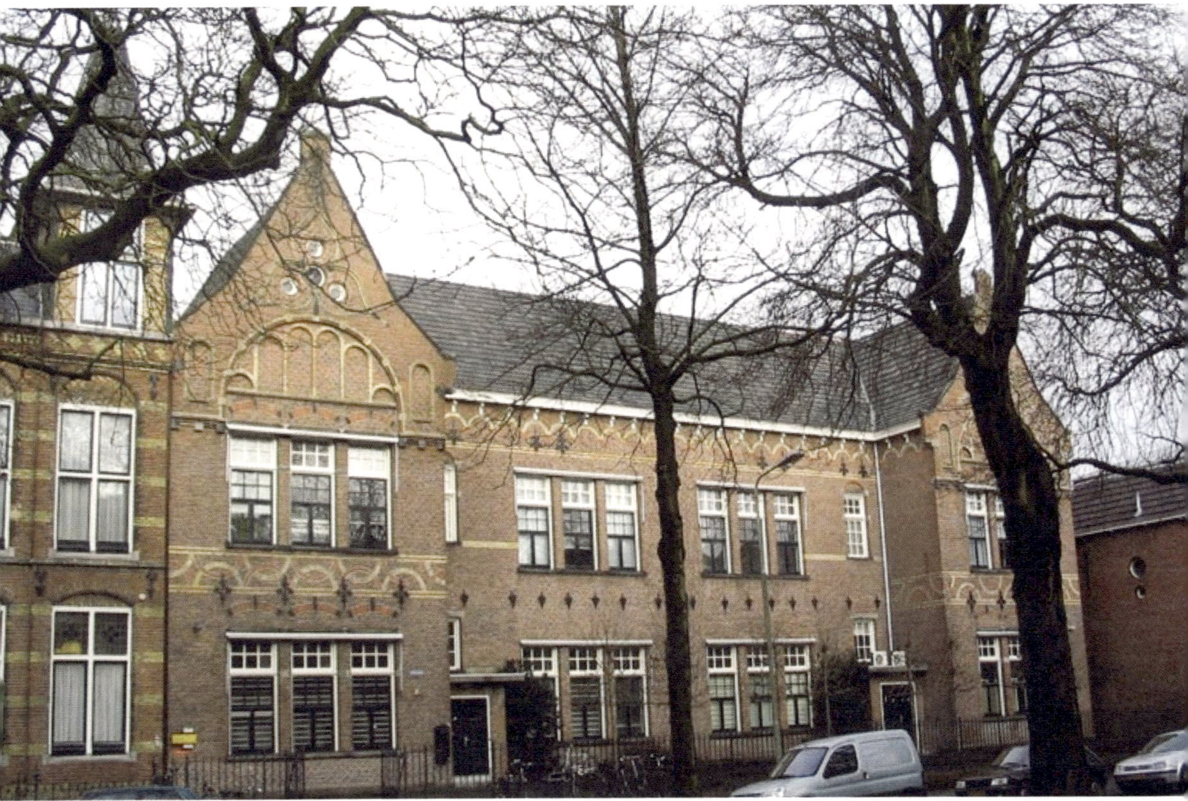

Lectureship in Computer Visualisation

In 2003 Rob de Bruin was appointed as Lecturer in Computer Visualisation. Computerability and visualisation will increasingly fulfil an important role in future knowledge and communication processes, in design, art, interactive environments, theatre, scientific projects and in everyday communication. Together with specialists from art and scientific education, Rob de Bruin is developing an educational and research programme exploring the crossovers between art and science in the field of visualisation. He will co-operate with a still to be appointed lecturer in Art and Media and will direct the activities of the Platform for Art and Media while he is helping to develop the MFA courses of the institute, as well as taking on teaching commitments.

Platform for Art and Media

The renewed covenant on the arts between the Hanzehogeschool Groningen and the University of Groningen was signed in the Senate Room of the University of Groningen on February 2 2005. This covenant provides for further collaboration and joint educational programmes, as well as the possibility for the participation of the Groninger Museum. Joint education and research in the area of contemporary art and new media will take place on this platform. This co-operation at postgraduate level in which scientific education and research are combined with art education will lead to an even more fruitful climate for art practice and scientific development.

Joint class *The Genealogy of Art and New Media*

Following the covenant between the Hanzehogeschool and the University of Groningen, a joint series of lectures on art and new media were designed by K&A, the Arts, Culture and Media programme (KCM) of the University of Groningen, the Lectureship and the Frank Mohr Institute. The lectures commenced in September 2005 in the Singelzaal of the FMI and consisted of lectures and seminars by Arie Altena, Eric de Bruyn and Kurt Vanhoutte. They were supplemented with lectures by the media artists and the theoreticians Lev Manovich, Igor Strohmajer and Bojana Kunst, Eric Joris and Thomas Levin. The seminars consisted of presentations of various issues and were prepared by small groups involving the participation of students from FMI and the university. The presentations showed crossovers between existing disciplines and viewpoints which were enriching and clarifying for the understanding and interpretation of the issues dealt with. The relationship between art and new media was discussed in the lectures on the basis of the history and theory of modern art (Eric de Bruyn), philosophy, theatre (Kurt Vanhoutte) and media theory (Arie Altena).

Hunter College and New York

The collaboration between the Minerva Academy and the Art Department of Hunter College (CUNY, City University of New York) has existed since 1994. In 1996 it was concentrated on the (post)graduate level of the two institutes' MFA programmes. Each year students from MFA Painting work in New York in one of the studios in the MFA building of Hunter College, and students from Hunter College come to the FMI in Groningen. The FMI students also follow seminars and theory classes at Hunter College, have critical discussions about their work with the tutors (such as Sanford Wurmfeld, Andrea Blum, Roy DeCarava, Constance DeJong, Robert Morris, Stephen Davis, Jeff Mongrain and Thomas Weaver) and visit the many museums and galleries of the city. Students of Hunter College come to the FMI in order to intensify their artistic research in an atmosphere of peace and concentration.

Image right:
Studio visit
MFA Building
Hunter College,
New York

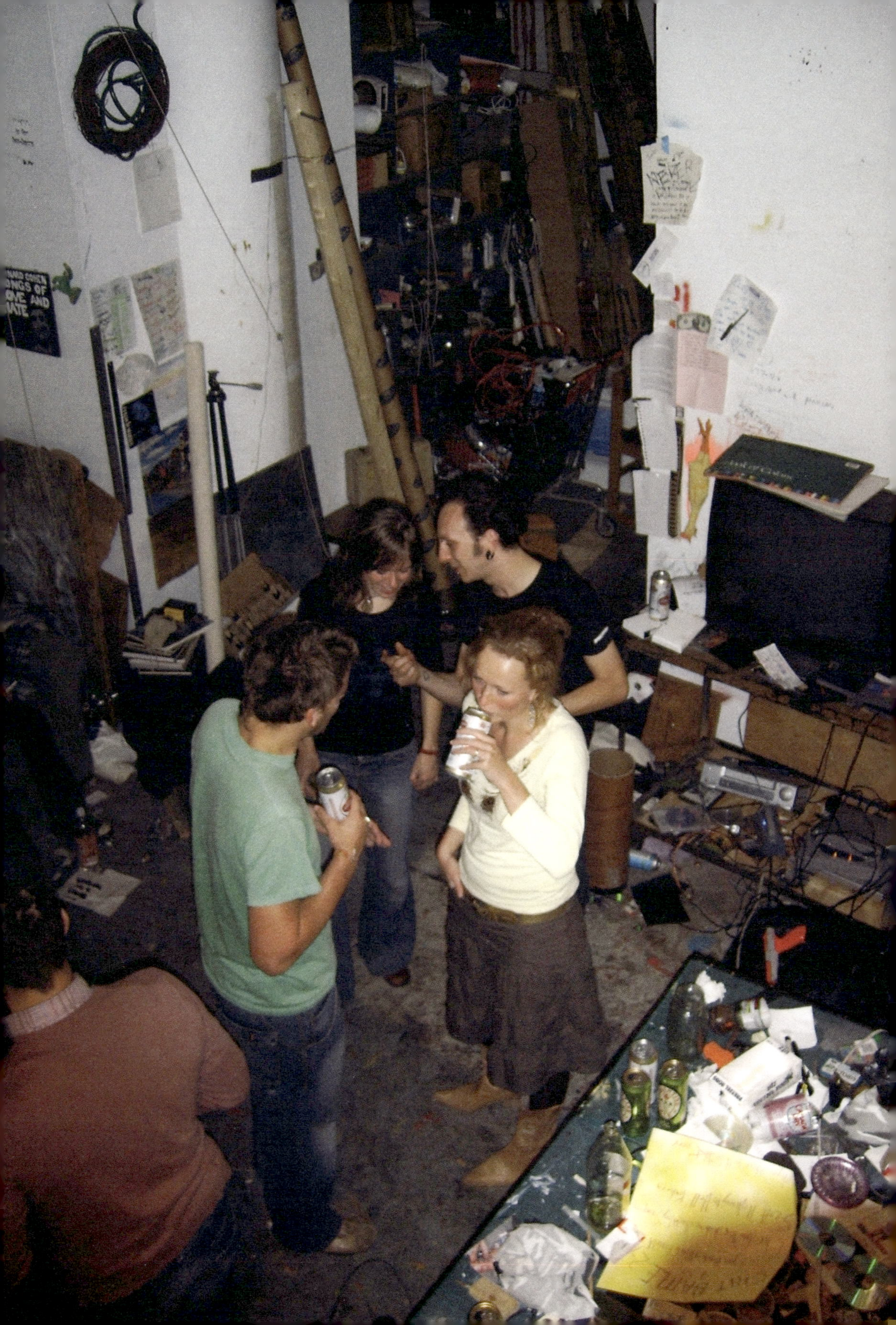

Annual excursion to New York

Each year the FMI undertakes a group excursion to New York and to Hunter College. The group initially consisted only of students from MFA Painting, but the covenant stipulates that the excursion should be an obligatory part of the master programme of the University of Groningen's K&A. MFA IME and MFA Scenography students have also been given the option of taking part in the excursion. The excursion involves attending seminars in the MFA Programme of Hunter College, visiting galleries and museums, discussing exhibitions, visiting artists' studios and exchanging presentations of work with MFA students at Hunter College.

Lecture and Masterclass by Dan Graham

On Monday 9,20,2004 the American artist Dan Graham gave a lecture about his work after a screening of his film *Rock my Religion* in the Auditorium of the Groninger Museum. Dan Graham, born in 1942, and resident in New York, received a prize from the International Association of Art Critics (AICA) for his touring retrospective which was shown in 2001 in the Kröller-Müller Museum. Graham's work is closely connected with that of other (post-) minimalistic artists such as Sol LeWitt, Dan Flavin and Robert Smithson. He is a versatile artist and works in various media, including conceptual publications, films, video installations, performances and architectural structures such as *Two Adjacent Pavilions* (1978-1982), permanently on show in Otterlo. Dan Graham is also a productive writer; his essays deal with varied subjects like art and architecture, pop music and drug culture. It is sometimes difficult to separate his role as art critic from that of artist.

After the lecture, Marianne Brouwer, art critic and tutor at the Frank Mohr Institute, and Eric de Bruyn, assistant professor at the University of Groningen (K&A), talked with Graham about his work.

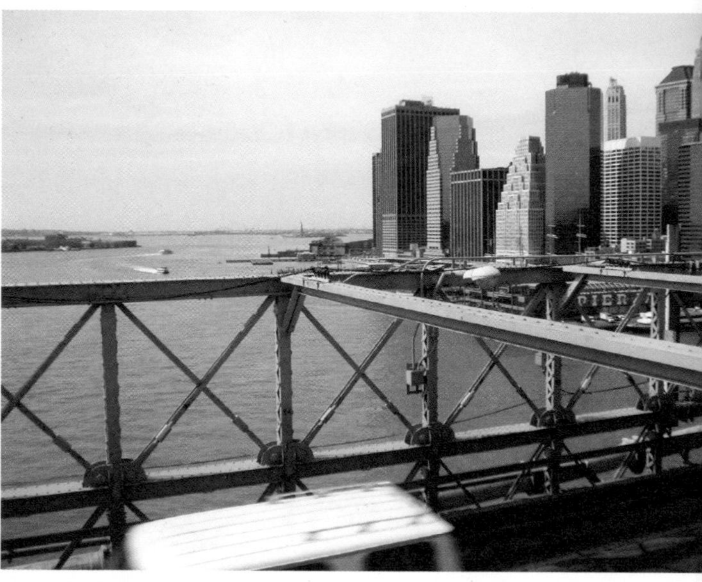

Excursion New York

A day later, Dan Graham held a masterclass in the Studiobuilding of the MFA Painting, discussing the work of the students who were present along with students from the University of Groningen. The lecture and the masterclass were organised by the FMI together with the University of Groningen (K&A).

International Exchange Exhibition

The International Exchange Exhibition opened on Thursday 10,7,2004 in the spacious Times Square Gallery in the MFA building of Hunter College. It was preceded by a symposium about MFA studies in Europe and the USA. The exhibition was organised by the Art Department of Hunter College and included work by (former) graduate students from three other renowned European art schools with master programs: the Ecole Nationale Superieure des Beaux-Arts in Paris, the Slade School of Fine Art in London, and the Glasgow School of Art. Hunter College itself, working closely together with all these programmes since 1990, was also part of the show they initiated.

Under the title *Expanded Painting, Expanded Viewing*, Petri Leijdekkers and Ton Mars conducted a careful process of discussions and studio visits and se-lected work by the following twelve ex-students: Edwin Adema (drawings and objects), Cor Groenenberg (paintings), Leslie Kamps (computer animations), Michiel Koelink (computer installation), Sanja Medic (photos), Rune Peitersen (computer animations), Libia Perez and Olafur Olafson (photos), Anne Jaap de Rapper (three-dimensional objects and photos), Ellemiek Schoenmaker (paintings), Martijn Schuppers (paint-ings), Anneke Wilbrink, (paintings) and Barbara Wijnveld (paintings). The FMI contribution was highly regarded. The works from Groningen stood out among the work of the other schools because of their sharp balance between concep-tuality and material manifestation. A catalogue was published to accompany the exhibition and there was a separate flyer about the FMI's contribution.

Presentations in the hall of the Minerva Academy

From 2,22,2005 till 3,4,2005 the FMI made a presentation in the Minerva Academy comprising an exhibition of work by students of MFA Painting, intro-ductions by tutors and students about the programme, research and the sig-nificance of postgraduate courses. Mar-loes van der Hoek, a MFA Scenography student, invited Robin van 't Haar and Igor Dobricic to bring the significance of socially engaged art into the limelight. Treva Wurmfeld, a guest student from Hunter College, gave an introduction on art education at masters level in the United States.

Kijkwijdte

Under the title *Kijkwijdte* (Breadth of View), the Centre of Visual Art (CBK) in Groningen showed the FMI's contribu-tion to the New York exhibition from 2,2,2005 until 5,29,2005. The exhibition was well attended and opened by Henk Pijlman, president of the Hanzehoge-school, and Sanford Wurmfeld, chair-person of the department of art and art history at Hunter College.

On the occasion of *Kijkwijdte*, the Frank Mohr Institute, together with the CBK and the Minerva Academy, organised a number of activities and lectures about painting spread over the semester. On 3,16,2005 in the hall of the Minerva Academy, a workshop took place under the title *Young Paint* with lectures, discussions of work and a forum debate in connection with the book *Verf* (Paint) in which art critic and writer Hans den Hartog Jager interviews well-known Dutch painters about the meaning of their use of form and material. Two evenings were organised in the CBK on 3,24,2005 and 4,21,2005 with discussions between Hans den Hartog Jager and the artists (former FMI students), Barbara Wijnveld, Anne Jaap de Rapper, Michiel Koelink and Cor Groenenberg.

Image below:
Alumni Exhibition New York

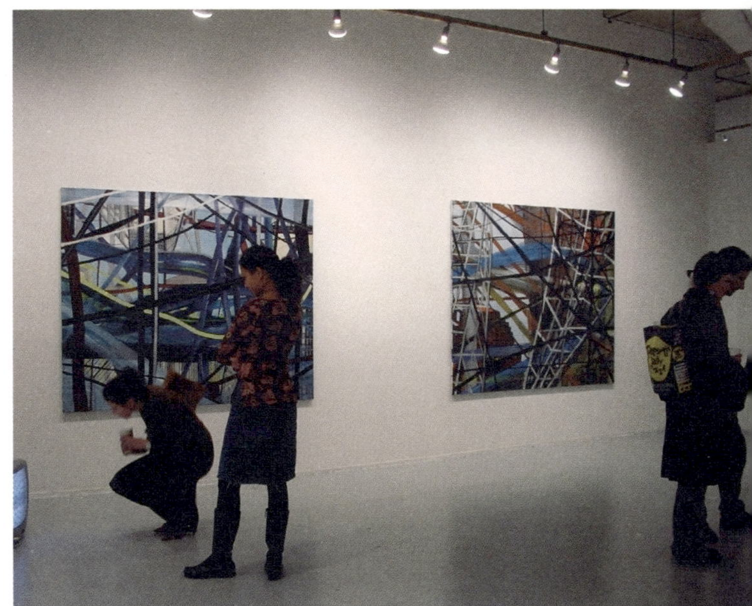

Lectures at the FMI

-4,7,2005 Jan Verwoert, German art critic, editor of *Frieze Magazine* and guest tutor at the art academy of Umea, Sweden. Under the title *Life continues to be free and easy, painting after conceptualism,* he dealt with the liberation of conceptual self-critique and the contemporary longing for beautiful, uncomplicated painting. -5,12,2005 Maxine Kopsa, art critic, gave a lecture titled *Wish you were here* on contemporary depictions of paradise in painting and the uncomplicated form of representation whereby traditional boundaries of beauty and taste are transgressed, sometimes provocatively. -5,26,2005 Elly Stegeman, curator of modern art at Museum De Beyerd in Breda, under the title *The Sacrifice/An Intimate*. Taking as her theme Andrej Tarkovski's film *The Sacrifice*, she talked about paintings from the collection of the Dutch collector Swagemakers. Her lecture was followed by one by Sybrandt van Keulen, titled *The Deconstruction of Painting*, about the significance of artists' statements in reference to Hans den Hartog Jager's book.

Presentation of Show me the Moves

A special book, *Show me the Moves*, published by the FMI and the Institute for Art and Architecture History, was presented in the auditorium of the Groninger Museum on 7,8,2005. The book contains seven essays on the principles of art, and on art education by Katalin Herzog who worked for the MFA Painting course from within the University of Groningen from 1996 until 2005. The presentation took place in the auditorium of the Groningen Museum with reflections on the essays by Sybrandt van Keulen, philosopher and lecturer at the Amsterdam University and the Frank Mohr Institute, professor Johan Swinnen, art historian and lecturer in Art and Culture at the University of Brussels, Albert van der Schoot, lecturer in Art and Reflection at the Artez School of Art, Albert van der Weide, dean of the School of Fine Arts and Design of the Minerva Academy, and Anne Jaap de Rapper, former student of the FMI and faculty member of Academy Minerva. Katalin Herzog then commented on the reflections. Petri Leijdekkers, director of the FMI, was moderator of the presentation.

Symposium on digital art at the Tsinghua University in Beijing, China

From 4,11,2006 till 4,17,2006 Petri Leijdekkers, art historian and director of the Frank Mohr Institute and Xinjian Lu (student MFA IME) were invited to take part in a symposium on art and media in the Department of Art and Media of the Tsinghua University in Beijing. Other participants of the symposium were Kurt Vanhoutte, assistant professor on theatre and media at the University of Antwerp and Groningen, Philip Bekaert, professor in computer technology at the University of Hasselt (Belgium) and Eric Joris, artistic director of *CREW*, a theatre company in Antwerp that works with new special constructed media. The symposium opened in the attendance of the ambassadors of Belgium and Holland. The program of

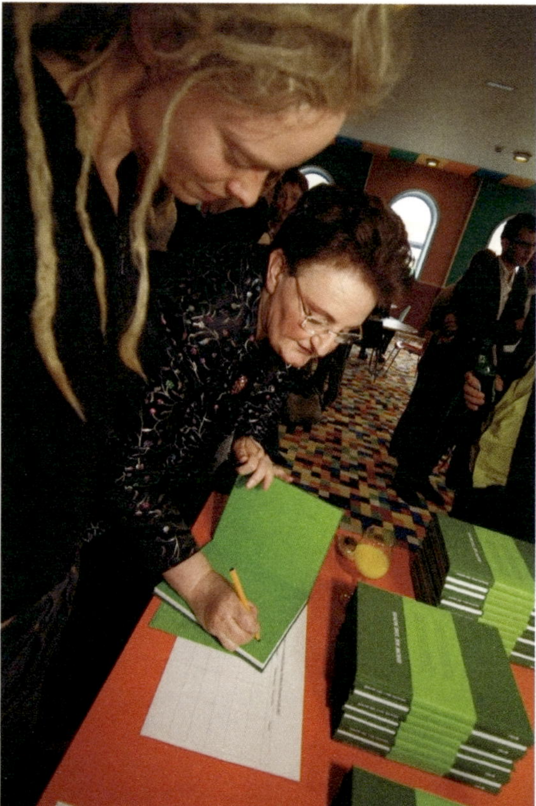

Image left:

Katalin Herzog signing her book "Show me the moves"

the symposium consisted of lectures on art and media, workshops and discussions. The symposium had a very good attendance of students and faculty members.

Art & Brain, seven lectures about the working of the brain in relation to the arts

The fascination with the working of the brain in art is an old one. This interest, however, has gained new impetus since the sciences of cognition (neurosciences, evolutionary psychology) have become important. A confrontation with other disciplines like philosophy, semiotics, art history, psychology and sociology, are unavoidable. What do the neurosciences learn us about art? And do these new findings match with insights from philosophy, art history and semiotics?

The series of lectures on *Art & Brain*, organized by the Platform for Art and Media, staged this confrontation. It brought the various perspectives together and asked the following questions: What has been achieved until now? In what directions should we proceed? How can we increase our understanding of the artistic, as well as the art-contemplating brain? Should we not strive for collaborative projects, in which artists, scientists and scholars co-operate? Lecturers: Douwe Draaisma, professor of the history of psychology at the University of Groningen, who wrote the prize-winning study 'Waarom het leven sneller gaat als je ouder wordt; over het autobiografisch geheugen' ('Why life runs faster when growing up; about the autobiographical memory'); Frans Cornelissen, a neurophysiologist and assistant professor at the the Laboratory of Experimental Ophthalmology of the University Medical Centre Groningen; Barend van Heusden, assistant professor to the Department of Arts, Culture and Media Studies of the University of Groningen. His research focuses on the evolution of culture, with specific reference to the changing of the arts in culture; Bernhard Ridderbos, assistant professor to the Department of Art History of the University of Groningen focusing on the art of the early Italian and early Netherlands painting; Jan de Roder, assistant professor to the Department of Literature and Art of the Maastricht University; Frans Ellenbroek, biologist and director of the Natuurmuseum Brabant in Tilburg who published recently a book on the biological evolution of the arts; Rob de Bruin, lector computer visualisation of the Hanzehogeschool who's main research is on size and shape of 'population of objects' and the visual perception.

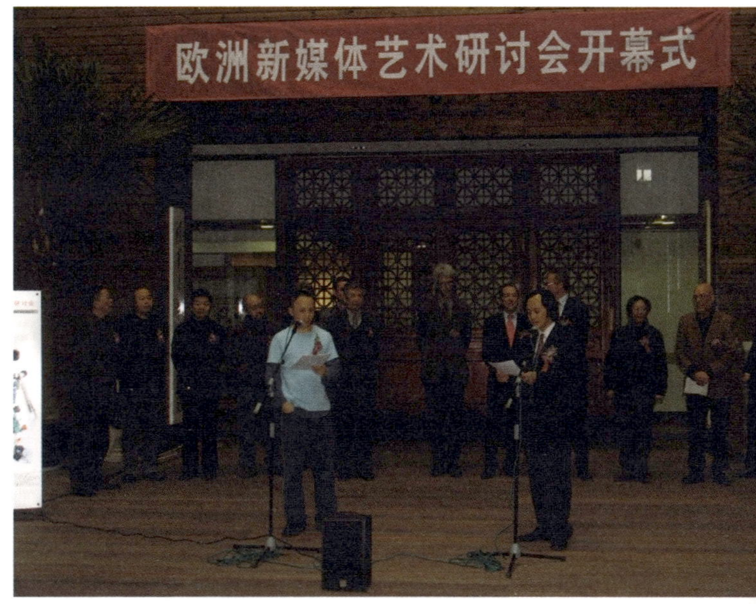

Image above:

Opening New Media Arts Conference, Tsinghua University, Beijing

=MORE,
the FMI at the Kunstvlaai

 On Saturday 6,6,2006 the *Kunstvlaai 6* in Amsterdam opened her doors under great public attention. Part of this bi-annual exhibition of young fine art was =MORE, a show and book of the Frank Mohr Institute. In this show and book the FMI exhibited twelve alumni who graduated since May 2005 Jan Bokma, Jeroen Brouwer, Mariëlle Buitendijk, Chrysante Dimbitsara, Benjamin Gaulon, Jeroen Glas, Annegret Kellner, Lucienne Pereira, Berndnaut Smilde, Heiner Behrends, Renske Vera de Kam and Menno Vinke. Petri Leijdekkers, director of the institute, presented the first copy of the book to Jos Houweling, director of the Sandberg Institute and Kunstvlaai, during a happening wherein Hyun-Bae Lee, first year student of the MFA Painting, drew a huge portrait of Jos Houweling. Below you will find a survey of the activities of each department of the FMI during the academic years 2004-2005 and 2005-2006. A complete list of FMI activities (both past and present) can be consulted on the website: www.mohr-i.nl

Image below:

Preperation FMI presentation, Kunstvlaai Amsterdam, 2006

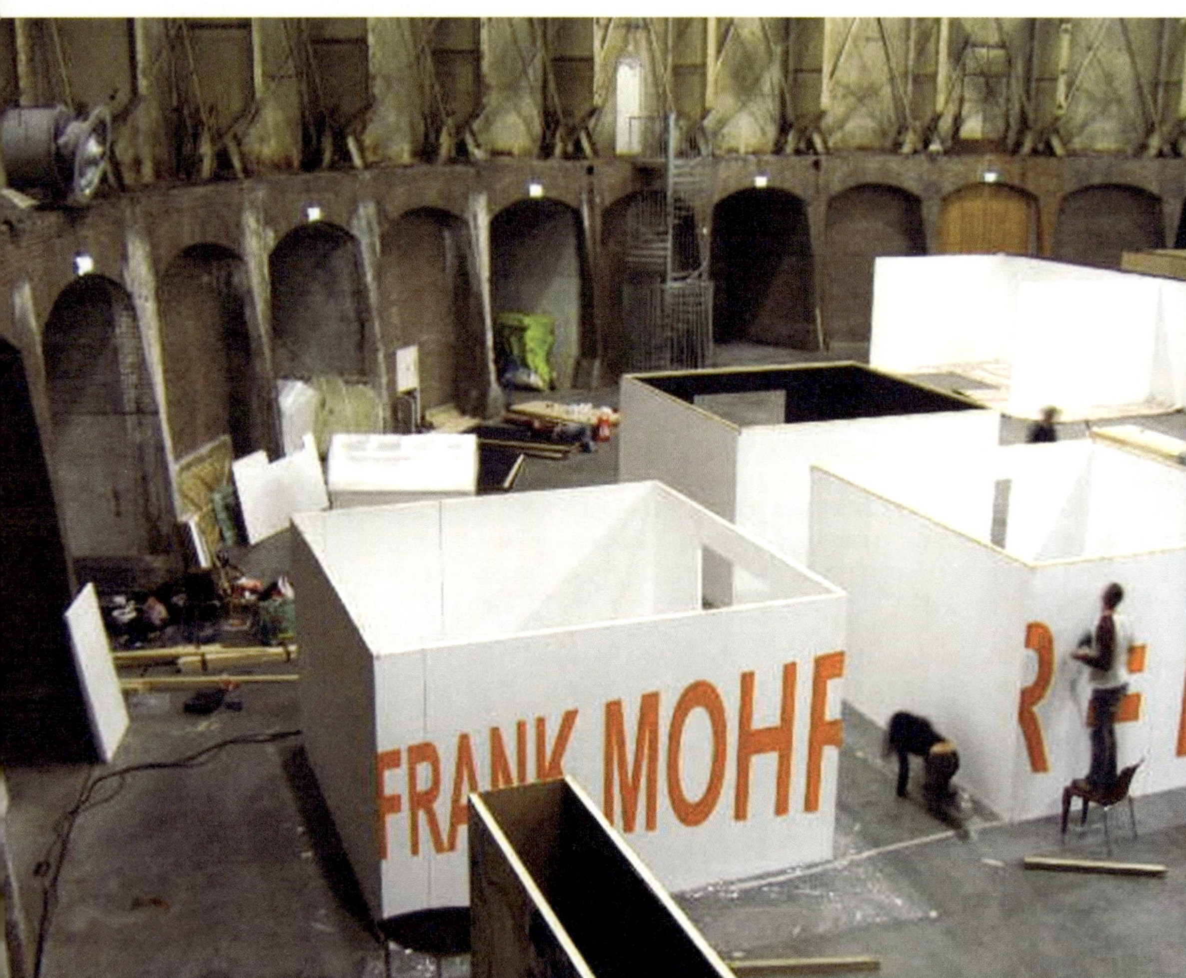

MFA INTERACTIVE MEDIA AND ENVIRONMENTS

Interactive Media and Environments (IME) is an inter-disciplinary studio program for experimental art research, through media and computer generated art.

Art

The program includes development of digital art in performances, sculptures, installations, interactive events, moving images and sound. This is realized through, for example, web based works, artistic software development, video, (3D) computer animations and digital imaging.

All these forms can lead towards specific programming and electronics, as well as to exploring perception in relation to daily used applications such a video, blog, Ipod and mobile phone.

Participants are stimulated as visionary story-tellers to explore new technologies in the context of a hybrid and changing environment.

Art & Science

The program includes knowledge and reflection on (computer-mediated) art and media theory, and also theoretical, technological and scientific developments. Media art is now being created in relation to digital communication, artificial life, algorithmic art, nano-technology, artificial intelligence, and as yet unknown technologies. Participants are challenged to investigate the intersections of art, technology and science, and thus become acquainted with contents and contexts creating a changing relation to the traditional definition of art.

About the program

The works of the participating professionals are backed up by reflection and art theory. The complexity of the practice of (interactive) media requires clear structures in which skills, knowledge and vision come together. Participants choose their combination of disciplines, deepen their skills and collaborations in which they direct others, and in which the institute can facilitate. Theoretical skills will be developed through both written text as well as debate. The program includes visits and participation in (international) art shows and conferences.

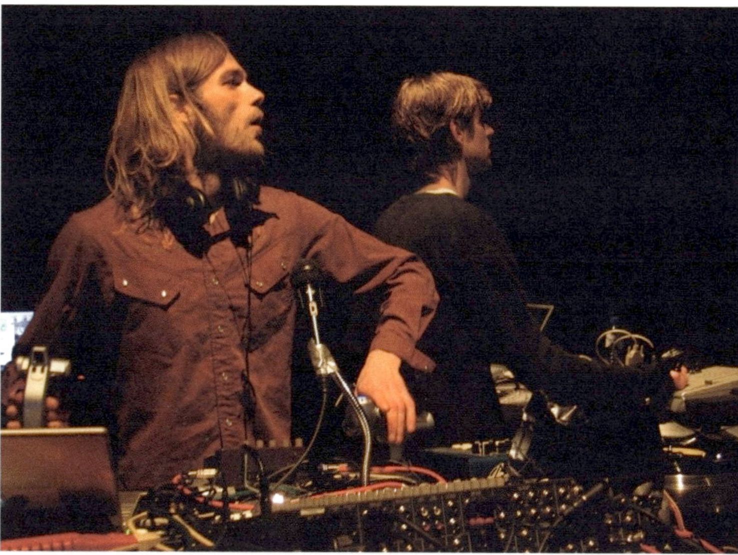

Image above:

*Performance
Karl Klomp,
MFA Interactive
Media & Envi-
ronments*

A short history

The current MFA IME programme is the result of fourteen years of media art education in Groningen. In the second half of the 1980's, the Minerva Academy worked together with staff of the University of Groningen on setting up SCAN (Stichting Computer Animatie Nederland). This center started in 1988 with a subsidy from the Ministry of Economic Affairs and developed the first, still experimental, MFA course in computer animation. In the early 1990's the name SCAN was changed to 'Media GN, Centrum voor Emergent Media'. Shortly after, the Ministry of Education, Culture and Welfare officially allowed Media GN to initiate an advanced course in Computer Graphics. This course, together with the MFA courses in Painting and Scenography, developed in the meantime, was accommodated in 2000 in the Frank Mohr Institute, which was specially established for this purpose, and acquired its present name of MFA Interactive Media and Environments.

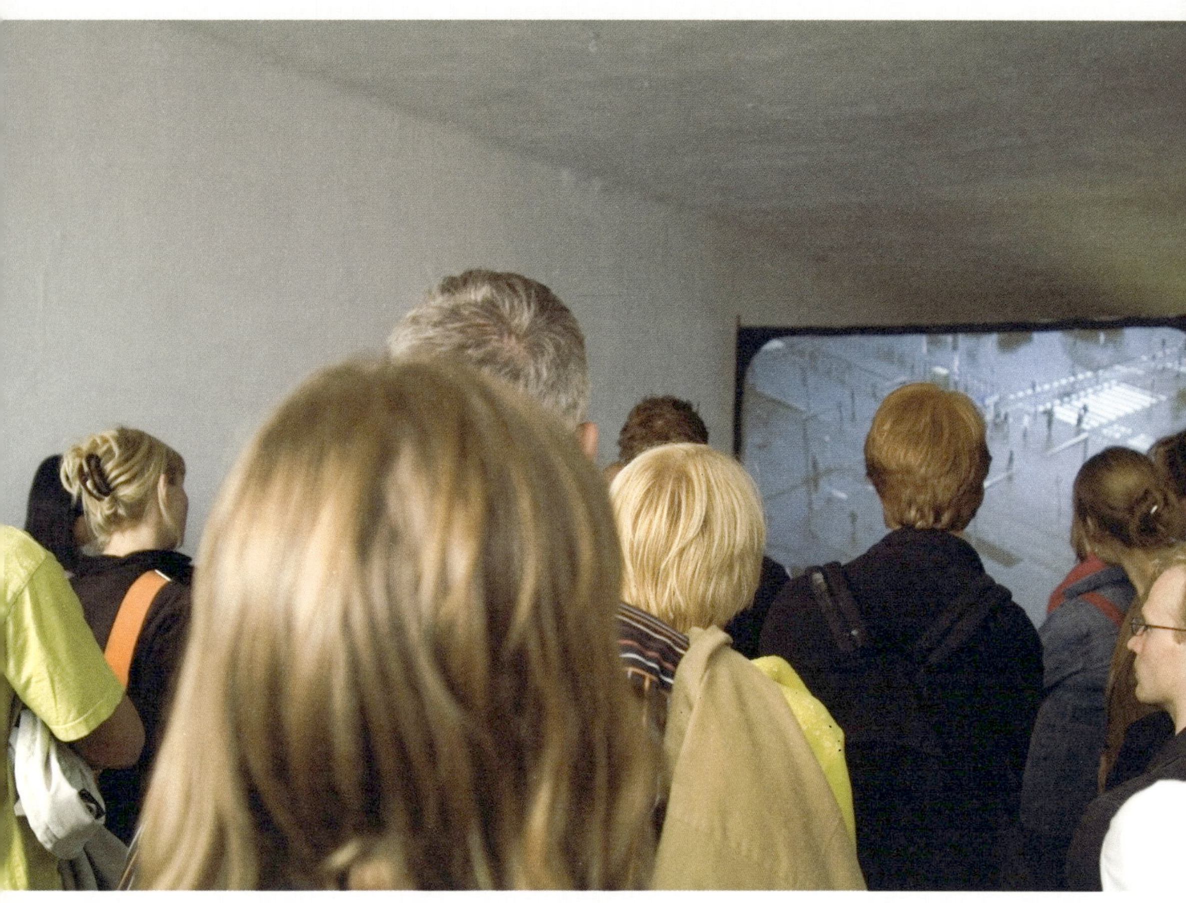

Faculty and activities, September 2004- June 2006

The teaching staff consists of a principal tutor, a theory tutor, one term tutor per semester or block coming from the professional and/or academic field. They are supplemented by visiting lecturers and renowned workshop directors with a wide knowledge and experience in their field of activity.

Core tutors

Karen Lancel, core tutor
Arie Altena, theory tutor
Rob de Bruin, Lecturer Computer Visualisation
Daan Tweehuizen, tutor 3-D programming
Tatiana Goryucheva, mediatheorist and curator media-art

Term tutors

Peter Luining, media artist
Graham Smith, media artist
Giny Vos, media artist

Technical instructors and support

Arjan Westerdiep (Flash, processing)
Jan Klug (MAX/MSP Jitter)
Marcel Vermeulen (system manager)

Technical lab

2005-2006 Roger Muskee

Guest tutors, Workshops, Projects, Lectures

Martijn van Boven, Paul Groot, Heide Hagebölling, Derek Holzer & Sara Kolster, Anja Hertenberger, Felix Hess, Michiel Koelink, Bert Otten, Noortje Marres, Telcosystems, Lucas van der

Opening in Sign, June 2006 Groningen.

Velden, Arjan Westerdiep, Telcosystems (Lucas van der Velden & Gideon Kiers), DePonk (Benjamin Gaulon, Lourens Rozema, Karl Klomp), Driessens & Verstappen, Eric Kluitenberg, Marianne Brouwer, Arno Coenen, Paul DeMarinis, Karl Heinz Essl, Georg Hajdu, Jan Klug, Anne La Berge, Mechtild Prins, Lourens Rozema, Peter Sinclair and Cyrille de Laleu, Arjan Westerdiep, Giny Vos, Sonia Cillari, Felix Hess, Eric Joris, Thomas Levin, Lev Manovich, Igor Strohmajer & Bojana Kunst, Hans Rijpkema, Remko Scha, Ellen Zweig

Workshops
-*Welcome to the Hybrid World!*, Eric Kluitenberg
-*Metacreation: Art and Artificial Life*, Driessens and Verstappen
-*Real Time/False Time and Relocalized Space*, Peter Sinclair and Cyrille de Laleu
-*Selling (non) material works of art*, Marianne Brouwer
-*Metacreation*, Driessens and Verstappen
-*MAX/MSP Telcosystems*, Lucas van der Velden and Gideon Kiers
-*Locative art, GPS and Hybrid Space*, Eric Kluitenberg
-*E-Waste*, DePonk
-*History of New Media Art*, Tanya Goruchyeva
-*Art by Numbers, Processing*, Arjan Westerdiep
-*Writing & Publishing*, Arie Altena

Graduation Exams 2006
Siebe de Boer, Xinjian Lu, Karl Klomp. Board of examiners, Rob de Bruin, Graham Smith, Daan Tweehuysen, Karen Lancel, Petri Leijdekkers (chair). External examiners: Martijn Veldhoen, Hermen Maat

Graduation Exams 2005
Benjamin Gaulon, Dezzie Dimbitsara. Board of examiners: Arie Altena, Marianne Brouwer, Jeroen Meijer, Rob de Bruin, Gideon Kiers, Lucas van der Velden, Petri Leijdekkers (chair). External examiner: Martijn van Boven

Activities and exhibitions (a selection)
-Symposium, *Is the Medium Still the Message?*
Esther Polak, Arie Altena, Petran Kockelkoren, Henk Slager, Annette W. Balkema
-Symposium *user_mode: Emotion & Intuition in Art & Design*
A collaboration between Central Saint Martins College of Art and Design and Tate Modern, London.
-Lecture Series *Future's Past*
-2005, Kurt Vanhoutte, Eric Joris, Igor Strohmajer, Bojana Kunst, Lev Manovich
-2006, Geert Lovink, Thomas Levin, Arie Altena, Karen Lancel

Visits
-Ars Electronica Symposium and Exhibition, Linz, Austria
-Transmediale Symposium and Exhibition, Berlin, Germany
-DEAF festival of V2_Institute for Unstable Media, Rotterdam
-Hunter College, New York, USA

Exhibitions students/alumni
- *FMI in Sign, Signs of Graduation*, Graduation Show, Galerie Sign, Groningen, Siebe de Boer, Xinjian Lu, Karl Klomp, 6,24 – 7,9,2006
- *Project for the Martinitower*, Institute for High Performance Computing & Environments University Groningen, Xinjian Lu, July 2006
- *Dia-Exit*, Tschumi Pavillion, Steven Jouwersma, 8,19 – 9,25,2006
- *Sonic Acts XI*, Paradiso, Amsterdam, Benjamin Gaulon, 2006
- *ISEA2006, Thirteenth International Symposium of Electronic Art*, Benjamin Goulon, 2006
- *Gogbot, New Media Art Festival*, Enschede, Karl Klomp, 2006
- *Kunstvlaai 2006*, Amsterdam, Daniel Valentim, Steven Jouwersma, Jobbe Holtes, 6,6 – 6,14,2006
- *Met Stip*, Gemeente Museum Den Haag, Den Haag, Josien Niebuur, 2006
- *Graduation Show*, Galerie Sign, Groningen, Benjamin Gaulon and Dezzie Dimbitsara, June-July 2005

- *Kijkwijdte*, New York, USA, Michiel Koelink, 2,2 – 5,29,2005
- *The International Exchange Exhibition*,
New York, USA, Michiel Koelink,
10,8 – 11,20,2004

MFA PAINTING

At the present time, when artists can make use of all media, genres and types of art, a distinct artistic mentality and an individual artistic system (a recognisable, associative and poetic cohesion of all the work) are of prime importance. These should be strong enough to guarantee a lengthy career as an artist. The MFA Painting course is therefore mainly aimed at developing such an individually-based artistic system, a clear artistic mentality and a strong professional discipline. To this end the visual work of the young artists, who have already graduated from art school, is carefully and critically supervised, while their work itself is backed up by reflection and theory. One requirement is the making of qualitatively good visual work, but this can only come about through good thinking and a clear view of the kind of artist that the student wants to be. Practice and theory within the program thus go together in order to achieve these aims.

The students have a studio of their own on the Noorderplantsoen, close to the centre of Groningen. The tutors (core and term tutors for practice and theory) regularly visit the students in their studios in order to conduct critical discussions about their work and ideas. In consultation with the tutor theory, students follow a program of lectures geared to their interests at the University of Groningen. Concepts and subjects connected with art practice

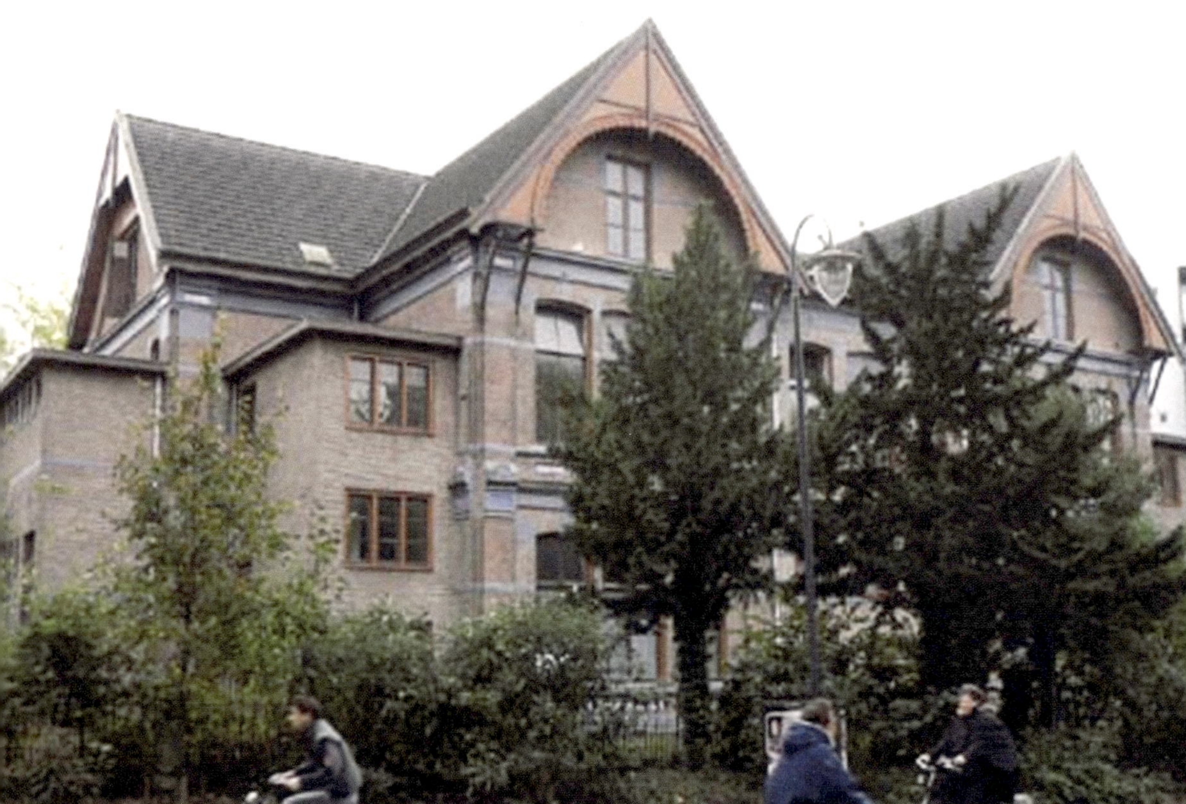

Image below:

Studio building

MFA Painting

and art theory are discussed in monthly round-table discussions as a means of clarifying ideas. Seminars are also regularly held, in which work is presented and discussed in the group. Students are trained in speaking about their work and they organize exhibitions in order to learn how to present their work. A request can be submitted to study for a few months at Hunter College in New York. An excursion to New York is organized towards the end of the course. Well-known professionals from the art world (artists, critics, curators, gallery owners) function as guest tutors. They supervise presentation projects and visit the studios regularly to provide critical commentary on the students' work and ideas.

The Faculty, September 2004- August 2006

The teaching staff consists of a principal tutor, a theory tutor, one or more term tutors per semester or block coming from the professional and/or academic field. They are supplemented by visiting lecturers with a wide knowledge and experience in their field of activity.

Core tutors

Ton Mars, visual artist, principal tutor
Katalin Herzog, art historian
Sybrandt van Keulen, philosopher
Margo Slomp, art historian
Martin van Vreden, visual artist

Term tutors

Martin van Vreden, visual artist
Esther Tielemans, visual artist

Guest tutors

Madeleine Hatz, Liet Heringa and Maarten van Kalsbeek, Rudi Hodel, Maxine Kopsa, Javier Marchán, Sanja Medic, Libia Pérez de Siles de Castro and Ólafur Árni Ólafsson, Martijn Schuppers, Joëlle Tuerlinckx, Thomas Weaver, Sanford Wurmfeld, Barbara Wijnveld, Akiko Yanagimoto, Sue-an van der Zijpp

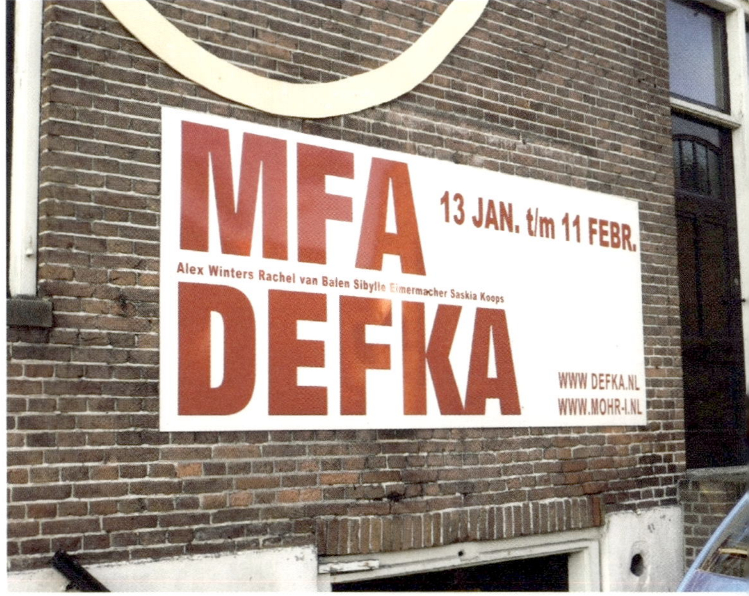

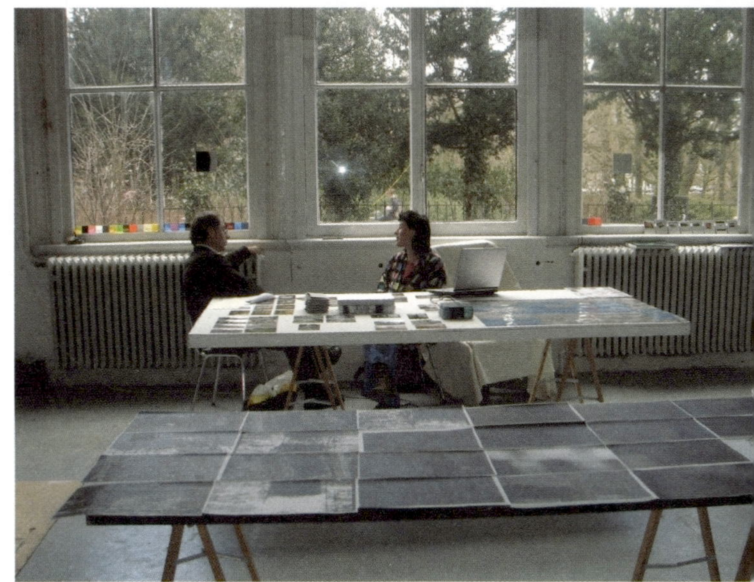

Projects and workshops

Roos Gortzak, Dan Graham, Madeleine Hatz, Maria Hljavajova, Gerard Polhuis

Lectures

Dan Graham, Liet Heringa and Maarten van Kalsbeek, Sybrandt van Keulen, Maxine Kopsa, Javier Marchán, Martijn Schuppers, Elly Stegeman, Joëlle Tuerlinckx, Jan Verwoert, Sanford Wurmfeld

Image above:
Exibition MFA Painting at DefKa Assen, 2006

Image below:
MFA Painting, studiovisit guestteacher

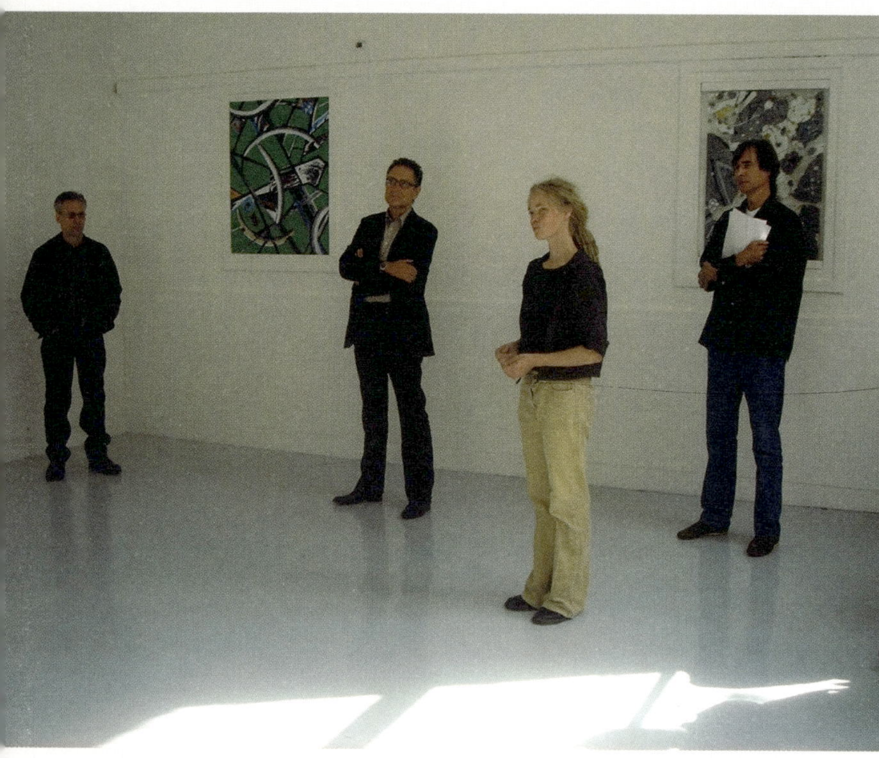

Graduation Exams

-6. 23,2006, Rachel van Balen, Sibylle Ei-
mermacher, Saskia Koops, Alex Winters.
Board of examiners: Ton Mars, Margo
Slomp, Esther Tielemans, Martin van
Vreden, Petri Leijdekkers (chair).
External examiners: Thomas Meijer,
Peter Schuyff, Thomas Weaver (Hunter
College)

Activities and exhibitions
(a selection)

-*Thesis Show MFA Painting 2006*,
6,24,2006-7,14,2006, at the Studiobuild-
ing of the MFA Painting, Groningen,.
Graduating artists: Rachel van Balen,
Sibylle Eimermacher, Saskia Koops and
Alex Winters
-=MORE, *The FMI at the Kunstvlaai*,
6,6,2006-6,14,2006. Exhibition of the
work of twelve alumni of FMI who grad-
uated since May 2005: Jan Bokma, Jeroen
Brouwer, Mariëlle Buitendijk, Chrysante
Dimbitsara, Benjamin Gaulon, Jeroen
Glas, Annegret Kellner, Lucienne Pereira,
Berndnaut Smilde, Heiner Behrends,

Renske Vera de Kam and Menno Vinke
-Presentation of student's work at the
Studiobuilding of the MFA Painting,
3,11,2006, Guestcurator Roos Gortzak
(workshop 3,6,2006-3,10,2006)
-MFA *DeFKa*, 1,14,2006-2,12,2006, DeFKa,
Assen. Rachel van Balen, Sibylle Eimermacher, Saskia Koops, Alex Winters
-*FMI in OCW*, 7,25,2005-10,16,2005.
Presentation of the work of four alumni
and one student of MFA Painting, Anne-
gret Kellner, Mariëlle Buitendijk, Jeroen
Glas, Berndnaut Smilde and Sibylle
Eimermacher, in the Department of Edu-
cation, Science and Culture, The Hague
-*Final Presentation MFA Painting 2005*, June
2005, Studiobuilding of the MFA Paint-
ing, Groningen
-*Kijkwijdte*, 1,29,2005-5,29,2005. Thirteen
alumni who took part at *Expanded Paint-
ing, Expanded Viewing, Youg artists of the
Frank Mohr Institute* in the Times Square
Gallery in New York, CBK, Groningen
-*.PPF (Past, Presence, Future)*, 3,12,2005,
Presentation of work and ideas about
the ideal exhibition in the Studiobuild-

ing of the MFA Painting. Guestcurator Roos Gortzak (workshop 3,7,2005-3,11,2005)

MFA SCENOGRAPHY

MFA Scenography is the youngest of the three studies at the Frank Mohr Institute. The course contains the dramaturgy of the theatre space in the broadest sense. Especially in the era where the image culture reigns and where people look but do not see, scenography captures the content of the sight. MFA Scenography reaches for the concize knowledge of interpretation. During the course students are considered to set up their own research paths, guided by a core tutor, theory tutor, term tutor and by the inspiration of guest tutors and lecturers. Also software knowledge is given by special tutors.

For their own research projects the students are expected to study different angles of the theatrical space, giving content to first intuitions and layer them in designing, practical, theoretical and productional sense. In the end the students have learned to recognize their own sources of inspiration, to use these sources and to share the outcomes generously with everybody.

One of the important aspects of the MFA Scenography course of the Frank Mohr Institute is the scientific approach. This stems form in the collaboration with the University of Groningen. Here students follow courses in theatre history and art history. This connection was realised in order to give students the best theoretical tools to be able to analyse and reflect theatre in general and their (future) the-

Image below:

MFA Scenography, project 'Speech', John Cage, 2005

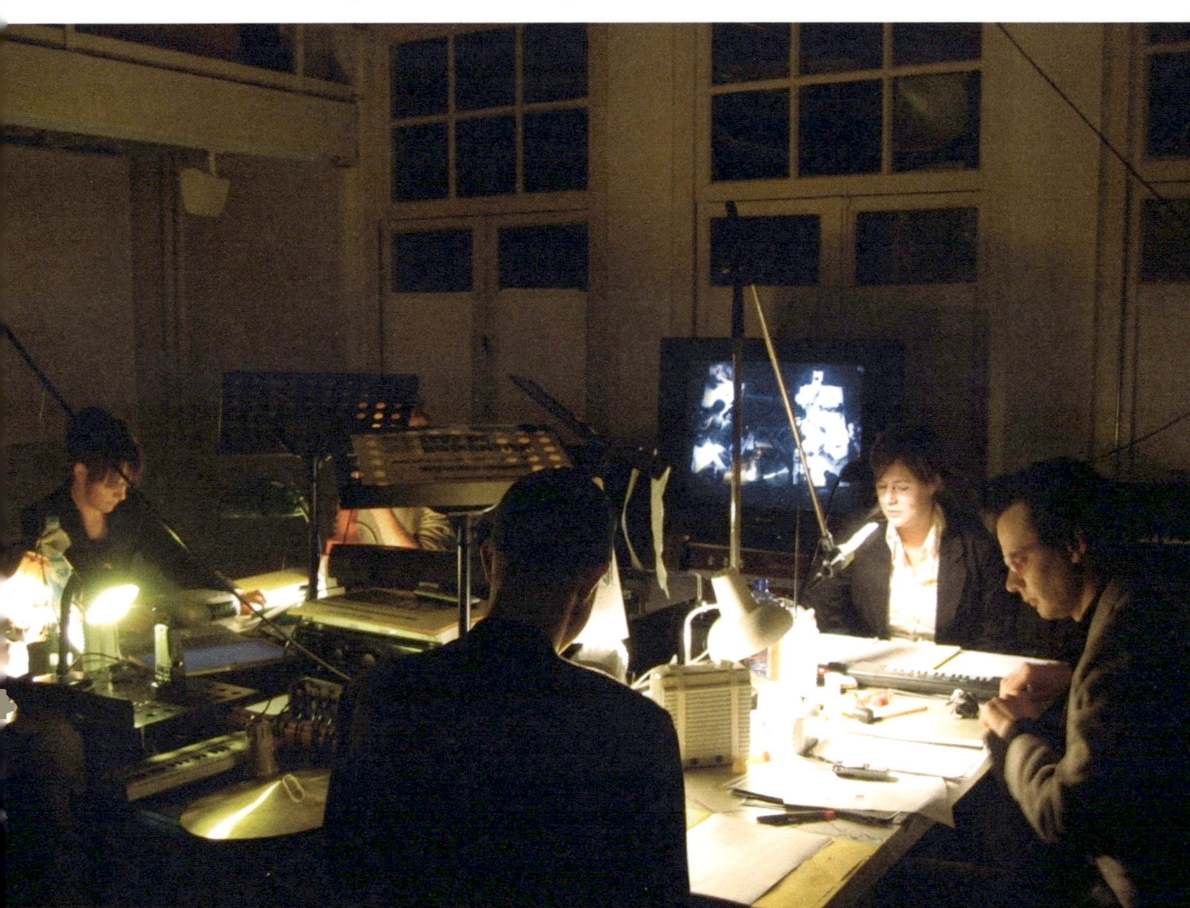

atre work in particular, and to develop the capacity of reflection on theatrical performances and their work.
Next to this university programme, the theory tutor coaches the students in the dramaturgy of the moving theatre image and the content of this. He organises moments in the course in which the students attend theatre productions of all kind and reflects on them at round table discussions in which temporary theatre in given a larger context.
During the four semesters, students develop their own vision of theatre and the field they want to be involved with by assignments and research projects. They are guided in their search for clarity, challenged to stretch the borders, framing and outframing the input.

Faculty, September 2004- August 2006

The teaching staff consists of a principal tutor, a theory tutor, one term tutor per semester or block coming from the professional and/or academic field. They are supplemented by visiting lecturers and renowned workshop directors with a wide knowledge and experience in their field of activity.

Core tutors

Sjoerd Wagenaar, theatre-maker, principal tutor
Judith Wendel, dramaturgist
Mirjam Grote Gansey, scenographer, principal tutor
Linda Nijenhof, art theorist
Nathalie Wevers, theatre-scientist

Term tutors

Fenneke Wekker, theatre maker, director
Soheila Najand, director Interart
Mirjam Grote Gansey, scenographer
Bea de Visser, performing and cine-graphical artist
Jos Thie, director

Guest tutors

Cilia Eerens, Mirjam Grote Gansey, Heide Hagebölling, Lino Hellings, Chiel Kattenbelt, Marianne van Kerkhoven, Jan

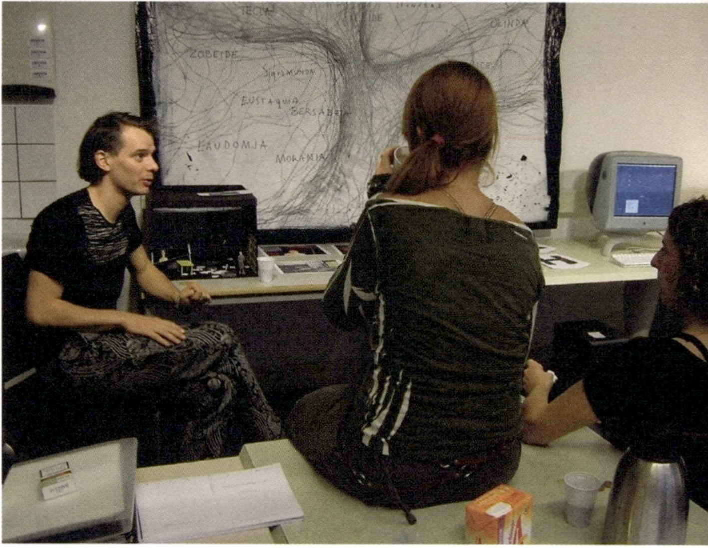

Klug, Elwin Koster, Javier Lopez Pinon, The Lunatics, John Malpede, Joop Mulder, Soheila Najand, Peter Sinclair, Rieks Swarte, Raoul Teulings, Kurt Vanhoutte

Projects and workshops

Henry Alles, Henk van der Geest, Mirjam Grote Gansey, Lino Hellings, Henk Kraayenzank, Soheila Najand, Mechtild Prins, Wim T. Schippers, Rieks Swarte, Raoul Teulings, Anna Tilroe, Gerrit Timmers, Fenneke Wekker, Willem de Wolf, Renee Zonnevylle

Lectures

Marianne van Kerkhoven, Raoul Teulings, Jelle van Toorn Vrijthof, Heide Hagebölling

Graduation Exams

- *Race/Milieu/Moment*, Wikke van Houwelingen. Graduation production, 6,11,2006. Board of examiners: Miriam Grote Gansey, Petri Leijdekkers (chair), Fenneke Wekkers, Nathalie Wevers. External examiner: Peter de Kimpe
- *Snelcursus Onschuld*, Marloes van der Hoek. Graduation production, 6,29,2006. Board of examiners: Miriam Grote Gansey, Petri Leijdekkers (chair), Nathalie Wevers. External examiner: Willibrord Keesen
- *Even Still*, Marieke Küttschreuter. Graduation production. 8,23,2006. Board of

Image above:
*Assesments,
MFA Scenography*

examiners: Miriam Grote Gansey, Renee Kool, Petri Leijdekkers (chair), Linda Nijenhof. External examiner: Karin Arink -*Gott ist Rund*, Heiner Sönke Behrends, Renske Vera de Kam. Graduation production, 6,30,2005. Board of examiners: Sjoerd Wagenaar, Miriam Grote Gansey, Judith Wendel, Petri Leijdekkers (chair). External examiner: Peter te Nuyl - *Brassica Nova*, Menno Vinke. Graduation production, 11,24,2005. Board of examiners: Miriam Grote Gansey, Bea de Visser, Linda Nijenhof, Petri Leijdekkers (chair). External examiner: Marcel Bogers

Activities (a selection)

-*Weltrusten, Sleep well*. On 3, 4 and 5 February 2006 NWU (Not Wearing Uniforms), an occasional compagny of MFA Scenography performed 'Weltrusten, Sleep well' in the new theatre house of the Onafhankelijk Toneel (OT) in Rotterdam. 'Weltrusten' was a theater performance about time and based on the fairy-tale of Doornroosje (Sleeping Beauty). The project was conducted by Bea de Visser, Dutch artist and filmmaker and term teacher of the programme of MFA Scenography.
-*The Cave*, 6,9,2006. 3D-theatreproject of Wikke van Houwelingen in the Zernikeborg, Groningen
-=MORE, *The FMI at the Kunstvlaai*, 6,6,2006-6,14,2006. Exhibition of the work of twelve alumni of the FMI who graduated since May 2005: Jan Bokma, Jeroen Brouwer, Mariëlle Buitendijk, Chrysante Dimbitsara, Benjamin Gaulon, Jeroen Glas, Annegret Kellner, Lucienne Pereira, Berndnaut Smilde, Heiner Behrends, Renske Vera de Kam and Menno Vinke
-*Brassica Nova*, 11,27,2005. Graduation project of Menno Vinke, SYB, Podium voor Hedendaagse Kunst, Beetster zwaag, (supported by the Mondriaan Stichting)
-Performance project by Kurt Vanhoutte with students of Theatre Science of the University of Groningen and the FMI, 5,9,2005-5,25,2005
-*Almost Real*, An international working conference exploring innovative ideas on artistic strategies, in a rapidly changing Europe, Utrecht
-*RFK in EKY*, August- September 2004. Three students of MFA Scenography (Marloes van der Hoek, Menno Vinke and Marieke Küttschreuter), participated in a social based location project by John Malpede in Kentucky, a remake of two days *Poverty tour* of Robert Kennedy in 1968, just before he died
- *Speech*, October 2004. Radioplay for six transistors and one newsreader, by John Cage. Workshop of Henry Alles. Public presentation at the Frank Mohr Institute, Groningen

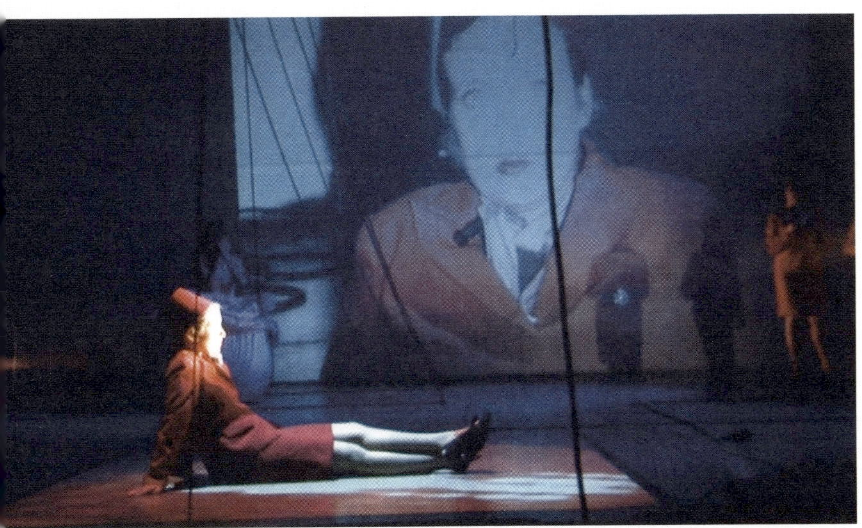

Left image:
Weltrusten. Sleep Well, MFA Scenography, 2006

Colophon

General Editors Ton Mars, Linda Nijenhof, Margo Slomp

Editors of Texts Katalin Herzog, Art Historian, (editor-in-chief)
Peter de Ruiter, Assistant Professor Modern and
Contemporary Art, Faculty of Arts, University of
Groningen (editor of Dutch interviews)

Authors Marian van Os, Vice Chairman of the Executive
Board, Hanzehogeschool
Groningen
Ton Mars, Head of the Frank Mohr Institute, and
Core Tutor of the MFA Painting course
Arie Altena, Publicist fine arts and new media,
and Tutor Theory of the Interactive Media and
Environments course, Frank Mohr Institute
Linda Nijenhof, Lecturer at the Faculty of Arts,
University of Groningen, and Core Tutor Theory
of the MFA Scenography course, Frank Mohr
Institute
Margo Slomp, Free lance author, editor and ad-
visor for the fine arts, and Core Tutor Theory of
the MFA Painting course, Frank Mohr Institute
Josien Beltman, Art Historian
Natalja Oosterbaan, Art Historian
Gitta Snijders, Student of Arts, Culture and Me-
dia, University of Groningen
Jacob van Stolk, Art Historian

Artists Rachel van Balen, Siebe de Boer, Sibylle
Eimermacher, Marloes van der Hoek, Wikke
van Houwelingen, Karl Klomp, Saskia Koops,
Marieke Küttschreutter, Xinjian Lu, Alex Winters

Translation Michael Gibbs, Amsterdam

Photography Thijme Breukers, Arend Groenewegen, Harold
Koopmans, Inge Rosekrans and artists

Graphic Design Marieke Tempelman,
marieke@marieketempelman.nl, amp/R*
Academie Minerva Producties

Printing Veenman Drukkers, Rotterdam

Publication Frank Mohr Instituut, Hanzehogeschool
Groningen

Impression 500 copies

ISBN 978-90-77962-02-2

Frank Mohr Instituut
Institute for Graduate Studies and Research in the Arts and Emergent
Media, part of the School of Fine Arts and Design, Academie Minerva,
Hanzehogeschool Groningen
Radesingel 6, 9711 EJ Groningen, The Netherlands
Telephone: 00 31 (0)50 595 11 50
Fax: 00 31 (0)50 595 11 99
E-Mail: info@mohr-i.nl
Internet: www.mohr-i.nl

Visiting addresses
Studio Building MFA Interactive Media and Environments and MFA
Scenography: Radesingel 6, 9711 EJ Groningen, The Netherlands
Studio Building MFA Painting: Boteringesingel 14 (entrance Noorder-
binnensingel), 9712 XR Groningen, The Netherlands

The Frank Mohr Institute is subsidized by the Department of Education, Culture and Science